Transactional Analysis

Transactional Analysis (TA) is a versatile and comprehensive system of psychotherapy. *Transactional Analysis: 100 Key Points* synthesizes developments in the field, making complex material accessible and offering practical guidance on how to apply the theory and refine TA psychotherapy skills in practice.

Divided into seven manageable sections, the 100 key points cover:

- the philosophy, theory, methods and critique of the main approaches to TA
- TA perspectives on the therapeutic relationship
- diagnosis, contracting and treatment planning using TA
- a trouble-shooting guide to avoiding common pitfalls
- refining therapeutic skills

As such this book is essential reading for trainee TA therapists, those preparing for examinations as well as experienced practitioners who will find much practical guidance on the skilful and mindful application of this cohesive system of psychotherapy.

Mark Widdowson is a Teaching and Supervising Transactional Analyst and a UKCP Registered Psychotherapist. He is Director of Training at CPTI Edinburgh, Associate Director at The Berne Institute, Kegworth and Senior Lecturer at The Athens Synthesis Centre, Greece. He lives in Glasgow where he has a private practice, offering supervision and psychotherapy for individuals and couples.

'Widdowson has not only produced a book which is essential reading for anyone interested in contemporary TA, but also offers a critical reading of TA in the context of the wider and changing fields of psychotherapy and psychology.' – **Keith Tudor, Teaching and Supervising Transactional Analyst; Senior Lecturer, Department of Psychotherapy, Auckland University of Technology, Aotearoa New Zealand**

'Consistently stimulating and informative, this book is essential reading for anyone interested in learning about current developments in Transactional Analysis theory and practice. The structure of the book makes it easy to identify ways in which TA addresses fundamental practice issues, and is highly accessible both to TA specialists and those trained in other orientations who are seeking to integrate TA perspectives into their work with clients.' – **John McLeod, Professor of Counselling, University of Abertay Dundee**

'Mark Widdowson provides us with a wise and engaging presentation of contemporary Transactional Analysis in theory and practice. Throughout this text are the constant reminders of the importance, clinically and ethically, of the therapist's necessity to engage in self-examination. While written in the voice of a psychotherapist, this book has much to offer fellow professionals engaged in other aspects of human relations work.' – **William F. Cornell, Independent Private Practice, Pittsburgh, USA**

Transactional Analysis

100 Key Points and Techniques

Mark Widdowson

Routledge
Taylor & Francis Group

LONDON AND NEW YORK

First published 2010 by Routledge
27 Church Road, Hove, East Sussex BN3 2FA

Simultaneously published in the USA and Canada
by Routledge
270 Madison Avenue, New York NY 10016

Reprinted 2010 (twice)

Routledge is an imprint of the Taylor & Francis Group, an Informa
business

© 2010 Mark Widdowson

Typeset in Times by Garfield Morgan, Swansea, West Glamorgan
Printed and bound in Great Britain by TJ International Ltd, Padstow,
Cornwall
Paperback cover design by Andy Ward

This publication has been produced with paper manufactured to
strict environmental standards and with pulp derived from
sustainable forests.

British Library Cataloguing in Publication Data
A catalogue record for this book is available from the British Library

Library of Congress Cataloging-in-Publication Data
Widdowson, Mark, 1973–
   Transactional analysis : 100 key points and techniques / Mark
Widdowson.
      p. ; cm.
   Includes bibliographical references.
   ISBN 978-0-415-47386-6 (hardback) – ISBN 978-0-415-47387-3 (pbk)
1. Transactional analysis. I. Title.
   [DNLM: 1. Transactional Analysis. WM 460.6 W638t 2010]
   RC489.T7W53 2010
   616.89'145–dc22

                                                              2009014438

ISBN: 978-0-415-47386-6 (hbk)
ISBN: 978-0-415-47387-3 (pbk)

Contents

Introduction

Transactional Analysis (TA) has a thriving international community made up of a dynamic body of practitioners who are developing their theory and innovating in practice. TA has developed into a therapy that is now proudly psychodynamic, and yet also fiercely humanistic. TA therapists consider many of their methods to be similar to those of cognitive-behavioural therapy. TA is also viewed as being an existential psychotherapy. I introduce some concepts from existential psychotherapy in this book, and invite the reader to explore how they can inform our use of transactional analysis and how we think about various TA concepts, and more importantly, how we relate to our clients. The history of TA reveals the origin of this range of approaches – Berne developed TA from his knowledge as a psychoanalyst. His development of the theory of the Adult ego state, and concepts such as contamination also enabled him to develop a cognitive approach to therapy which did not exist at the time of Berne's innovations (Schlegel, 1998).

There is the most incredible diversity among TA psychotherapists, and in how we use TA. We share a common body of theory that has shown in this diversity its wonderful versatility. To me, what defines a transactional analyst is not what they do (which may be indistinguishable from other types of psychotherapy), but rather why they do what they do and how they think. Transactional analysts of all types use the concepts of ego states and scripts as their most basic thinking structures.

Following the work of Tudor and Hobbes (2007) I discuss cognitive-behavioural and psychodynamic applications of TA in practice and also include the modern TA approaches of integrative TA and relational TA. This book attempts to develop the readers' skills and knowledge in effective use of all approaches to TA. A word about the level of this text: this is not an introductory book, and I assume that the reader has a familiarity with TA concepts and methods. For those readers who do not have that knowledge, I would advise reading the following books first:

Lister-Ford, C. (2002) *Skills in Transactional Analysis Counselling and Psychotherapy*. London: Sage.

Stewart, I. (2007) *Transactional Analysis Counselling in Action*. London: Sage.

Stewart, I. and Joines, V. (1987) *TA Today*. Nottingham: Lifespace.

Expecting the reader to have such background knowledge enables me to move directly into an intermediate level of discussion without need to explain the basics, which are adequately covered in other books. This book is calibrated at an intermediate level, to bridge the gap between introductory texts and advanced texts and will be particularly useful to TA students who have completed their foundation year. I hope that more experienced practitioners will also find the book to be interesting and stimulating.

Part 1 covers the philosophy, theory, methods and some critique of the main approaches and schools of TA in practice. Readers who are not so interested in this theoretical background can go directly to Part 2. Part 2 deals with the therapeutic relationship. Psychotherapy research has consistently shown that the therapeutic relationship is critical to the outcome of the therapy, and is a precondition for effective therapy work (Norcross, 2002). In line with this research, this section includes material on the effective 'ingredients' of the therapeutic relationship including empathy, transference and countertransference and also alliance rupture and repair. It has been my intention to make some of these complex concepts more accessible to newcomers. Parts 3, 4 and 5 take the reader through the process of diagnosis, contracting and treatment planning from a TA perspective. Part 6 deals with common pitfalls in TA practice, suggesting ways of avoiding them. The book concludes with Part 7, the longest part, which is on refining therapeutic skills. Each part contains new and original material that I hope will be of immediate practical use to the reader. Many of the points in this book are firmly grounded in evidence-based practice, and are supported by psychotherapy research as being 'effective ingredients' in psychotherapy. Psychotherapy research demonstrates the effectiveness of empathy, attention to alliance rupture and repair, skilful transference interpretation, accounting for the client's cultural context, wider relationships and strengths, developing a personally tailored treatment approach for each client, goal consensus and collaboration, appropriate self-disclosure, and all are empirically supported. The discussion of such research is beyond the scope of this book, and the interested reader is recommended to read *Psychotherapy Relationships That Work*, edited by John Norcross (2002).

It has been my intention throughout to write a book that is practical and promotes the development of thinking, rigorous clinicians. Rather than present a whole book of techniques, I have been more interested in writing a book that stimulates and engages the reader's thinking.

> When one is well versed in the theory . . . it is not even necessary to know a lot of techniques, as ideas for interventions will arise from understanding and applying theory to a particular client, at a particular moment . . . when a therapist is well versed in theory, it becomes possible to adapt the therapy to the needs of the client rather than requiring the client to adapt to the demands of a particular technique.
>
> (Rothschild, 2000: 96)

In many ways this book is similar to a Greek *meze*, or Spanish *tapas* meal. Readers may find some of the 'appetizers' particularly 'tasty' and want more. I invite those readers to pursue the references given in the points they particularly like where they can find more material to digest at their leisure.

The material in this volume is gathered from my experience My experience is collected from my client work, but also from my work as a trainer and supervisor of psychotherapists where I can see common mistakes or misconceptions 'second hand'. One of the advantages that a trainer and supervisor has is a degree of distance from the direct interpersonal encounter. This distance gives us the space to make our observations and frame our comments. Some of the insights or ways of working I present here I have had to learn the hard way. While there is a place for learning the hard way in life, I think it has a limited place in learning psychotherapy, where clients can be given a disservice on the basis of a therapist 'needing' to learn the hard way. This is especially so when experience is available for them to learn from in a more comfortable, and all-round desirable fashion. I hope that this book both helps you learn the easy way and reminds you that the work of a psychotherapist is not easy. It requires deep and complex thought, a robustness, flexibility and openness of emotion. It requires a curiosity and receptivity to experience, immense patience and a willingness to sit and hear of profound distress and of the many horrors that humans can inflict upon each other and yet not lose faith in humanity or the tenacity of the human spirit.

A word on terminology

For ease of reading, I use both 'he' and 'she' interchangeably throughout this book, and trust the reader will make the necessary changes to suit their own particular situation. I often refer to 'you' throughout the text. When I do so, I am referring to you, the reader. I am using this conversational writing style in order to invite you, the reader, into thinking and reflection.

Acknowledgements

I would like to particularly thank Alison Ayres for her thoughtful comments on many of the early drafts of the points in this book. I would also like to thank Helena Hargaden, Ray Little, Claude Steiner, Ian Stewart, Gudrun Stummer, Keith Tudor and Jane Walford who also provided invaluable feedback on various drafts of this book. Special thanks go to Glenn, for his patience, understanding and unwavering support while I have been writing this book. I would also like to thank my supervisees and trainees, many of whose comments or questions triggered me to write the points in the first place and who also have commented on drafts. I would finally like to thank my clients who have patiently over the years taught me how to do psychotherapy.

Part 1

APPROACHES IN TRANSACTIONAL ANALYSIS (TA) PRACTICE

1

Three modes of therapeutic action

To begin this brief summary of the schools of TA, and approaches to TA, I present here Martha Stark's (2000) model for understanding the nature of therapeutic action, and the focus of the therapeutic work. Stark's work is based on an analysis of streams within psychoanalysis. However, her model provides a useful framework to think about the differences within the schools and approaches to TA and where each approach focuses the attention of the therapist and how they consider the process of change, and the important ingredients in facilitating change. Stark's position is that effective therapists need to be fluent in all three approaches, and tailor their therapy to suit the individual client, using a combination of approaches as appropriate.

One-person psychology

This model emphasizes the 'importance of knowledge or insight . . . it is a one-person psychology, because its focus is on the patient and the internal workings of her mind' (Stark, 2000: 3). From a TA perspective, a client generating greater knowledge or insight into their own process would develop the Adult ego state. The greater degree of executive control the Adult has over the personality, the less anxiety a person feels, and the greater the range of options the individual has in experiencing and relating. In this approach the stance of the therapist is as a neutral, objective observer. 'Her focus is on the patient's internal dynamics . . . The therapist formulates interpretations with an eye to advancing the patient's knowledge of her internal dynamics. The ultimate goal is resolution of the patient's structural conflicts' (Stark, 2000: 4).

One-and-a-half-person psychology

This model emphasizes the 'importance of experience, a corrective experience; it has been described by some as a one-and-a-half-person psychology because its focus is on the patient and her relationship with a therapist . . . (for) whom it is not she that matters but rather what she provides' (Stark, 2000: 3). 'The therapist offers some form of corrective provision with an eye either to validating the patient's experience, or more generally to providing the patient with a corrective experience. The ultimate goal is filling in the patient's structural deficits and consolidating the patient's self' (Stark, 2000: 4). The stance of the therapist in this model is empathic, focusing on the client's subjective reality and affective experience. From a TA perspective, the empathic validation of a client's subjective experience may reduce felt levels of tension in different ego states (particularly Child ego states). The resultant reduction in tension may enable greater movement between ego states. The validation aspect may also strengthen Adult functioning. Perhaps most importantly, in this model the experience of sustained empathic understanding provides the client with an experience that may have been missing for them in their history, and which they have been seeking ever since in order to address, repair or make good the developmental deficit(s).

Two-person psychology

This model emphasizes the 'importance of relationship, the real relationship; it is a two-person psychology because its focus is on patients and therapists who relate to each other as "real" people' (Stark, 2000: 3).

The therapist pays keen attention to their emotional and countertransference reactions throughout the work, and uses their emotional reactions to deepen their understanding of the client and the client's way of relating to others including the client's protocol. From a TA perspective this equates to social diagnosis and the analysis of transactions and games. Ego states manifest in the therapy room and transference is noted and tracked as part of the client's unique history and also in relation to how it colours the client's here-and-now experience of the therapist. The therapist seeks to promote the client's capacity for intimacy through this vibrant here-and-now engagement.

Effective, versatile therapists need to be able to move fluently between all three models according to the individual needs and presenting issues of each client.

> ... the most therapeutically effective stance is one in which the therapist is able to achieve an optimal balance between (1) positioning herself outside the therapeutic field (in order to formulate interpretations about the patient and her internal process so as to resolve the patient's structural conflict), (2) decentering from her own experience (in order to offer the patient some form of corrective provision so as to fill the patient's structural deficit), and (3) remaining very much centered within her own experience (in order to engage authentically with the patient in a real relationship so as to resolve the patient's relational difficulties).
>
> (Stark, 2000: 147)

2

The classical school: foundations

Background

The classical school of transactional analysis is the original version of TA, as developed by Berne and the members of the San Francisco seminars. Almost all the core of TA theory springs from this group of people, which includes Claude Steiner, Steve Karpman, Jack Dusay, Muriel James, Fanita English and Franklin Ernst. This pioneering group of trans-actional analysts were particularly keen on developing concepts that were simple to grasp, and yet described complex human behaviours and internal processes. Emphasis was also placed on being able to diagram concepts. The purpose of this was to 'facilitate Adult analysis of whatever problem the client brings, while stimulating the intuitive powers of the Child to aid in solving that problem' (Stewart, 1992: 132).

Philosophy and approach

The classical approach to TA stresses the importance of observation in psychotherapy. Berne repeatedly emphasized the importance of direct observation of the client as the basis for any theoretical and therapeutic formulations. The classical TA therapist also uses their intuition in making diagnoses, and in ascertaining the psychological level message in ulterior transactions. Observation and intuition were to be combined with theory and clear therapeutic rationale. To Berne, diagnosis and much of therapy was 'a matter of acuteness and observation plus intuitive sensitivity' (Berne, 1972: 69). Berne was also interested in the therapeutic and appropriate use of humour, particularly as a means of inviting the Adult ego state of the client to reappraise a situation, belief or so on.

The therapy approach proceeds in sequence from structural analysis, transactional analysis, game analysis and finally to script analysis. Nowadays, most transactional analysts move between these different stages of analysis with a degree of fluidity. The initial aims of therapy are to decontaminate the Adult ego state, and identify the structural origin of the client's different thoughts, feelings and beliefs. Similar to the gestalt approach to therapy, the classical school of TA places emphasis on how the client's ego states, scripts and so on are manifesting in the here-and-now (Barnes, 1977). Clients are discouraged from endlessly going over the past as this was seen to be game of 'archaeology' (Berne, 1964).

The 'three Ps' of *protection, permission* (Crossman, 1966) and *potency* (Steiner, 1968) are a key feature of the approach of classical TA, and indeed all TA therapy (see Points 83 and 84). The therapist is expected to monitor their work to ensure that there is sufficient protection, permission and potency for the client to engage in the therapeutic work necessary to achieve script cure. Once the 'three Ps' are in place, therapy proceeds with establishing behavioural contracts which are seen as a central aspect of therapeutic change in classical TA (Stewart, 1992).

The classical school of TA is a one-person approach (Stark, 2000), as the emphasis is on resolution of structural conflict and generating increased Adult options. The conflict model (Lapworth *et al.*, 1993) is the primary model of psychopathology in classical TA, which views psychopathology as being the result of conflict between and within different ego states and conflict between the individual's drive towards autonomy (physis) and the individual's script (Berne, 1972).

Key theoretical concepts

Much of the core TA theory forms the classical school of TA as developed by Berne. This includes: ego states, structural analysis, contamination, exclusion, functional analysis, transactional analysis, games and game analysis, scripts and script analysis. Other classical concepts developed by other TA authors include: script matrix (Steiner, 1966), contracting (Berne, 1966; Steiner, 1974), OK corrall (Ernst, 1971), options (Karpman, 1971), stroke economy (Steiner, 1971) and egograms (Dusay, 1972). In some respects it is impossible to practise transactional analysis, and not use classical TA concepts.

3

The classical school: methods

Methods

The eight therapeutic operations (Berne, 1966)

The eight categories of interventions (interrogation, specification, confrontation, explanation, illustration, confirmation, interpretation and crystallization) form the nucleus of the method of TA therapy (see Müller and Tudor, 2001).

Decontamination (Berne, 1961, 1966)

This is a procedure designed to strengthen the Adult ego state and involves the challenging of distorted thinking and sometimes the provision of accurate information to facilitate reality testing.

Contractual method (Berne, 1966; James and Jongeward, 1971; Steiner, 1974)

Contracting is a central method used in all types of TA therapy, which was initially developed by classical TA writers.

Permission transaction (Berne, 1966, 1972)

The therapist ascertains what key permission the client needs to promote their growth, and then seeks to give the client the key permission (directly and indirectly) throughout therapy.

Script antithesis

The script antithesis is a decisive and focused intervention (Berne, 1972). The antithesis is like the 'spell breaker' in a fairy tale. It is a bullseye transaction (Woollams and Brown, 1978) that aims to block the trajectory of the individual's script and challenge the major script theme of the individual.

Group therapy (Berne, 1966)

Classical TA was developed extensively in group therapy settings, and it is believed by some TA therapists that by virtue of these origins, TA is best done in group settings.

Critique

Although recognizing the admirable intention behind the use of colloquial language, some critics of this approach feel that TA has suffered from being considered superficial by people who see the names of concepts and dismiss them outright. Also, the use of colloquialisms has meant that some of the language is unfamiliar to modern, non-American audiences.

The power of the therapist is emphasized in classical TA, in a way that can be considered incongruous with TA philosophy. The therapist is seen as a 'permission giver', and interpreter of the client's experience; analysing the client's life patterns using TA theory. This quasi-parental therapist stance of 'permission giver' is incongruous with a therapeutic approach that emphasizes the client's autonomy.

A classical TA approach can suggest that either knowledge about one's patterns (by gaining insight using TA theory) or direct behavioural change is sufficient for transformation and healing. Classical TA concepts can be used to gain understanding into one's process, patterns and ways of interacting with others, but as Berne cautioned, insight alone is insufficient to generate change (Berne, 1971). Similarly, behavioural change will not necessarily result in deep structural change.

4

The redecision school: foundations

Background

The redecision school of TA was created by Bob and Mary Goulding. The Gouldings were original members of Berne's San Francisco seminars, who also trained with Fritz Perls, the originator of gestalt therapy. The Gouldings were interested in developing ways of working that were active and promoted rapid change. They integrated techniques from gestalt therapy such as two-chair work into a TA theoretical approach as they saw that these methods could be used to work directly with ego state conflicts. The Gouldings specialized in the therapy marathon format, and would hold extended group therapy marathons, sometimes for up to a month at a time.

Berne originally used the term redecision to mean making a new (life) decision in an Adult ego state. In contrast, the Gouldings defined redecisions as involving the changing of a particular script decision within the Child ego state. Their view was that the original script decisions were made in the Child ego states, and therefore it is in these Child ego states that the change or redecision needs to occur. They developed their methods to work with a contractual regression and increased the affective intensity of the work to facilitate the redecision in the client's Child ego state(s). The process involved accessing this Child ego state and using the client's Adult ego state to provide support for the Child.

Philosophy and approach

The Gouldings, firmly in the humanistic and existential tradition and influenced by gestalt therapy, emphasized the client's personal responsibility, and in their work invited a shift away from Berne's medical model, whereby the therapist *cures* their patients, to one whereby the therapist *facilitates* the process of the client curing themselves ('the power is in the patient' was the Gouldings' slogan) (Goulding and Goulding, 1978). The Gouldings developed a crisp and confrontational style in their work, for example challenging the use of language which discounts personal power (such as inviting clients to change *can't* to *won't* etc). Redecision therapists seek to create a nurturing and compassionate environment that supports and provides protection for the Child, and enables the client to access their Child ego state in order to make the necessary redecision.

In their work, the Gouldings often noticed the client holding on to magical or self-defeating thinking, for example holding a position in Child that they wouldn't change until someone else changes (usually one of their parents). Such magical thinking was actively challenged. Vengeful Child beliefs, such as 'I'll stay sick until you're sorry', were also challenged and the client was invited to let go of these beliefs that were seen to be major blocks to the client's therapy.

The Gouldings would actively avoid, or 'side step', the transference. If the therapist becomes aware of the client transferring from their past onto the therapist, the therapist would invite the client into a two-chair dialogue. In this dialogue the client projects the transferential figure onto a chair, and engages the projection in a dialogue. The Gouldings believed that this approach was more effective than inviting transference onto the therapist and the owning of projections is congruent with the redecision philosophy of taking personal responsibility and owning one's feelings and projections (Goulding and Goulding, 1979).

With its emphasis on structural conflict and the therapist's role as facilitator, with an active confrontational approach and the avoidance of working with transference, the redecision school is a one-person approach (Stark, 2000) and is based on a conflict model of psychopathology (Lapworth *et al.*, 1993). Impasse theory is perhaps one of the most obvious examples of a conflict model within TA psychotherapy.

Key theoretical concepts

Injunctions (Goulding and Goulding, 1979) (see Points 80 and 81).

Decisions (Goulding and Goulding, 1979).
Redecision (Goulding and Goulding, 1979).
Impasse theory, impasse clarification and impasse resolution (Goulding and Goulding, 1979; Mellor, 1980) (see Point 85).

5

The redecision school: methods

Methods

Redecision therapy begins with a clear and focused contracting approach, where the therapist facilitates the development of a clear contract for change. Passive language is confronted in the client's discussion of their problems/situation or contract goals, and the 'language of response-ability' is encouraged (such as changing 'can't' to 'won't') (Goulding and Goulding, 1979).

The client is then often invited to use a range of fantasy and visualization techniques, such as two-chair work. This involves the visualizing of one or more of the client's Parents, or the client's Child as being in an empty chair. The therapist then facilitates a dialogue between the two different parts of the self to clarify and resolve ego state conflicts. Other fantasy methods used include early scene work, where the client is invited to mentally go back in time, and recall the time they made the original script decision or to go back to a prototypical ('screen') memory of an event that in some way encapsulates the essence of the script decision or the environment in which the decision was made. In the event that the client cannot remember a specific scene, they are invited to invent one, as it is believed that the imagined scene, being a product of the client's psyche, will contain all the relevant aspects needed to facilitate a redecision. Passive language, or magical thinking, is confronted while the client verbalizes the dialogue in the visualized scene. The affective charge is developed through the use of heighteners (McNeel, 1976) or other gestalt methods. These are used to increase the discomfort in a particular scene to emphasize the limiting nature of the decision. Further, this stimulates an organismic disgust reaction which mobilizes the client's physis and helps the client to throw off or reject the old limiting script decision. At this point the client is invited to bring their Adult awareness and resources into the scene, or the therapist may provide new information to help the client make a new decision.

After a redecision piece, the therapist invites the client to generate a series of behavioural contracts regarding how they will maintain their redecision in their everyday life (McCormick and Pulleyblank, 1985). Although a redecision piece is a significant change event, redecision itself is considered to be an ongoing process and one which needs reinforcement to help the client maintain new healthy ways of living rather than slide back into familiar scripty ways of being.

Critique

The Gouldings model was developed primarily in a residential therapy marathon setting, whereby clients would attend for at least a week, and commonly as much as a month. The intense atmosphere of an extended residential marathon format and the protection this afforded participants provided a good setting for rapid and deep change work. This option is generally not open to the therapist working with individual clients in private practice. Most clients attending the marathons were therapy trainees, and all clients were in ongoing therapy and so were ostensibly 'couch broken' and well engaged with their own process of change. Therefore to presume that the Gouldings methods provide rapid change without substantial preparatory work is incorrect. The intense catharsis resulting from many of these methods could indeed trigger quite intense and unwanted reactions, which could be attended to in a residential setting in a way that they cannot in regular clinical practice.

The techniques of redecision therapy are often dramatic and engaging and can involve deep catharsis. This can be very seductive and a therapist can mistake catharsis for real change. It is possible that some clients effectively 'go through the motions' and engage in redecision pieces as an overadaptation to the therapist without any change taking place. It may also be the case that with overadapted clients their script is inadvertently reinforced. The Gouldings were well aware of this potential problem in (mis)use of their techniques and advised against cathartic ventilation of feelings done for its own sake.

Redecision therapists actively seek to 'sidestep the transference', and deliberately avoid taking on a transferential role in the therapeutic relationship (Goulding and Goulding, 1979). This approach is not suitable for all clients and can be misused by therapists who are not comfortable with accepting or containing a client's strong transferential feelings. Similarly this can be misused by therapists who struggle with accepting personal responsibility for making mistakes. This is not a critique of the redecision approach per se, but is a potential pitfall if used badly or by therapists who have not engaged with their own personal therapy.

The therapist needs to be mindful of the double message inherent in some methods of redecision therapy – 'Assume responsibility the patient is told . . . and I'll tell you precisely how, when and why to do it' (Yalom, 1980: 250).

6

The cathexis school: foundations

Background

The cathexis approach was originally developed by Jacqui Schiff – one of the early transactional analysts in Berne's seminars. Shortly after taking into her home a young schizophrenic man and beginning residential therapy, she established a residential treatment centre for clients in psychosis. Their centre was originally based in Fredericksburg, Virginia, USA, and then because of controversy, moved to Oakland, California, where in addition to the residential centre, they opened a day treatment facility. Following the success of the Oakland project Schiff opened another centre in Hollywood. The theory and methods of the cathexis approach were developed by Jacqui and her colleagues who joined her at the Cathexis Institute. Within the relatively protected residential setting for therapy, the Schiffs experimented with 'allowing' the clients to regress, and 'redo' early developmental deficits and cathect new Parent ego states. The Cathexis Institute programme experienced huge problems (and Jacqui was expelled from the International Transactional Analysis Association [ITAA]) amid controversy relating to breaches of ethics including physical punishment of clients. Eventually a young man in treatment at The Cathexis Institute died following injuries sustained while at the institute and the Californian authorities closed down the programme. Despite this controversy and problems in methodology, many of the insights and methods developed at The Cathexis Institute have been successfully and ethically adapted by TA therapists and used with a wide range of clients. In a particularly interesting development a form of cognitive-behavioural therapy called schema-based therapy now utilizes procedures it refers to as 'limited reparenting' (Young *et al.*, 2003).

Philosophy and approach

The Schiffs saw the nature of psychopathology as being twofold: the first being issues related to developmental deficit; and the second as being issues related to having 'defective' or pathological Parent ego states. Their methods were developed to both deal with the developmental deficits in the Child ego state through provision of a reparative experience and also to systematically decathect 'crazy' Parent ego states and then reintroject new, positive Parent ego states. Clients were not on medication while at Cathexis and treatment was purely psychotherapy (Schiff *et al.*, 1975). The Schiffs created an environment which was *reactive*, and one which (in theory) invited clients to think about their problems (see critique below).

The cathexis approach is a one-and-a-half-person approach when the emphasis is on corrective experience, or one-person if the focus is on discounting and redefining (Stark, 2000). Defective parenting is considered to be the primary cause of psychopathology and the cathexis approach utilizes a deficit model (Lapworth *et al.*, 1993) for understanding and treating psychological problems.

Key theoretical concepts

The Schiffs developed a range of theoretical concepts that have been integrated into a TA approach, particularly concepts relating to how clients 'distort' reality, or make the world fit their script. The key concepts developed by the Schiffs include the following:

Passivity and the four passive behaviours (Schiff and Schiff, 1971).
Discounting and grandiosity (Mellor and Schiff, 1975; Schiff *et al.*, 1975).
Redefining (Schiff *et al.*, 1975).
Symbiosis (Schiff *et al.*, 1975).
Cycles of power and developmental affirmations (Levin-Landheer, 1982). Pamela Levin formulated her 'cycles of power' child

development theory and associated developmental affirmations from her experiences at The Cathexis Institute and it is clearly based on a reparative–deficit model.

7

The cathexis school: methods

Methods

A key method of the cathexis approach to TA therapy is the repeated confrontation of discounting, grandiosity and passivity. It is possible that this emphasis accounts for some of the success of this model with clients with borderline personality disorder where consistent confrontation is recommended (see Point 88).

The cathexis approach relies also on the use of a reparenting/ reparative model of psychotherapy (Clarkson, 2003). The principle behind this is that if the client is given a boundaried, reparative experience then the original need and developmental deficit is repaired. The therapist is deliberately used as a replacement 'parent' for the client. The practicalities and reality of this can be extremely draining for the therapist.

Critique

Despite the emphasis on clear thinking and the social level message to 'get into Adult', the environment at Cathexis gave a clear psychological-level invitation to stay in Child ego states. Indeed, some participants in the Cathexis programme have stated that there was enormous pressure on individuals to regress. This apparent contradiction will no doubt have been confusing to a number of clients.

The approach of providing a reparative, corrective emotional experience (Alexander *et al.*, 1946) is also particularly seductive to therapists who have rescuer fantasies or who have not relinquished fantasies of having a new perfect childhood to make up for their own problematic childhood (Davies and Frawley, 1994). Furthermore, the provision of gratification of a client's 'needs' can keep the therapist in a permanent 'good object' position, and not provide scope for the development of a negative transference, and the dealing with optimal frustration that is necessary for full structural change. In practice the provision of such 'good experience' can also set up situations whereby the therapist becomes burnt out by ever-increasing and escalating client demands for more. Cornell and Bonds-White (2001) develop this critique further, and are particularly critical of how such reparative approaches can reinforce unhealthy merger fantasies. This reinforcement of such fantasies can also apply to the therapist who is susceptible to enacting their own needs in the therapeutic relationship.

Jacobs (1994) has also extensively critiqued The Cathexis Institute reparenting approach as being based on thought control with features of a psychotherapy 'cult' and therefore inherently unethical and problematic. The Schiffs relied heavily on the concept of *consensual reality*, that is, a version of reality that was determined by popular consensus. Although such definition can have use in confronting crazy or distorted thinking, the concept of consensual reality is problematic in that general consensus, even wider social perspectives, can be 'wrong', and as an approach it does not account for multiple realities, or multiple construction of differing realities. This concept can also be problematic in working transculturally with unfamiliar and culturally embedded frames of reference (Hargaden and Sills, 2002).

Levin's cycles of power theory and the use of developmental affirmations is also problematic in that it does not relate to and is inconsistent with established and researched child development theory (Cornell, 1988; Matze, 1988) and is critiqued for being too prescriptive, oversimplified and deterministic (Cornell, 1988). The use of giving developmental affirmations by the therapist is also problematic in that they implicitly infantilize the client (partly in their construction which emphasizes the 'giving of permission'), and also suggests an oversimplified approach to therapeutic change; if only therapy were as simple as giving clients a few key messages!

There is no doubt that many people were helped, either by the Schiffs, or by therapists who have used cathexis concepts or methodology. However, the use of reparenting strategies is not recommended, and concepts and methods need to be used in the light of critique and with clear supervision. Concepts such as discounting and grandiosity, however, will continue to be potent tools for therapists working with clients with all levels of problems, and can be used effectively and ethically for the expansion of awareness and confrontation of contaminations and script beliefs.

8

Radical psychiatry: foundations

Background

'Radical Psychiatry is a theory of human emotional disturbance and a method designed to deal with it' (Steiner, 2000).

Radical psychiatry was developed by Claude Steiner and Hogie Wyckoff in Berkeley, California in the late 1960s. It was heavily influenced by the works of Karl Marx, Wilhelm Reich and R. D. Laing (who wrote about the negative impact of oppression on the psyche) which were combined with TA theory, particularly its tools for analysing the transactional, person-to-person mechanisms of oppression and liberation.

Philosophy and approach

The central principle of radical psychiatry is that psychiatric problems are manifestations of alienation that results from oppression that has been mystified in the isolated individual. Mystification involves cultural discounting or justification of oppression. Oppressive social structures and mystifying myths promote emotional isolation of the individual. The formula given for alienation is:

Alienation = Oppression + Mystification + Isolation

The radical psychiatry antidote to alienation is: contact to undo isolation, awareness to demystify oppression and action to combat it. The resulting formula is:

Power in the world = Contact + Awareness + Action

Radical psychiatry opposes the medicalization of psychotherapy and the use of psychiatric jargon and diagnostic labels and sees such usage as an example of oppression and alienation of isolated individuals in emotional distress.

The accounting of the context of the person, and the impact of social and political factors on the individual and their way of relating to others locates radical psychiatry as what might be called a 'two-and-a-half'-person approach (Tudor, 2009).

Key theoretical concepts

Alienation

There are three principal forms of alienation each one representing a script type. The script of *lovelessness* comes from the alienation from our loving capacities, leading to depression due to stroke starvation. The script of *joylessness* originates from alienation from our bodies and can lead to addiction. The script of *mindlessness* results from alienation from our minds due to mystification and lies, and the alienation from work due to workers' exploitation.

Pig Parent

The Pig Parent, later renamed as the *Critical Parent*, refers to the Parent in the Child (P1) ego state. The Critical Parent is seen as the internalization of oppressive messages that perpetuate alienation. Radical psychiatry seeks to radically decommission the influence of the Critical Parent.

The stroke economy

The stroke economy (Steiner, 1971) is a set of restrictive internal rules about giving and taking strokes. The stroke economy rules, enforced by the Critical Parent, are considered to be the source of alienation from love. The antidote to the stroke economy is the free exchange of strokes.

Lies and discounts

These are seen as a principal source of alienation from the mind and rational thinking. The antidote to lies and discounts is *radical truthfulness*.

Power plays

Power plays are the transactions that people use to coerce and oppress each other. Power plays can be physical or psychological, crude or subtle: from murder and rape to lies and propaganda.

9

Radical psychiatry: methods

Methods

Group psychotherapy is the main therapeutic method in the radical psychiatry approach. Exploring oppression and the mystifications that support oppression through 'consciousness raising' (awareness) is a key method. Demsytification of the oppressiveness of racism, sexism, homophobia, ageism, class prejudice and other oppressive systems involving developing awareness of discounting and power plays as they manifest in the activities of the group is also used.

The promotion of egalitarian and cooperative relationships between group participants is an important goal in radical psychiatry groups. Groups maintain cooperative contracts as 'rules of engagement'. The cooperative contract involves an agreement not to power play, especially not to use lies of omission or commission, and avoiding the roles (Rescuer, Persecutor and Victim) of the drama triangle (Karpman, 1968). Awareness of oppression and action against it is promoted inside and outside the group. Social action is considered essential since society requires improvement if people are to be empowered within it. In the mutually supportive environment of the group participants are encouraged to confront and overthrow their Critical Parent and script.

Groups can take several forms: problem-solving groups, bodywork groups using methods to increase body awareness and enhance permission to feel; and finally mediations, where the therapist is a facilitator to help resolve conflict.

Critique

Many of the concepts of radical psychiatry have now been adopted in wider society, partly as a result of the influence of feminism, an awareness of abuse of patients of medical and psychiatric practitioners, the formation of patient groups and wider social initiatives which promote equality and political awareness. As a result, some of the ideas of radical psychiatry can be seen to be somewhat outdated, and culturally and historically located within a radical, 1960s Californian frame of reference. Although victim behaviour is discouraged and confronted in the radical psychiatry approach, critics suggest that it overly focuses on external and wider social circumstances and can result in users 'blaming the system' rather than taking personal responsibility for their situation. Considered as a whole, radical psychiatry has been criticized for being overly theoretical and not leading to easily accessible techniques in psychotherapy. (For more information see www.claudesteiner.com/rpprin.htm)

10

Integrative TA: foundations

Background

Integrative TA was developed primarily by Richard Erskine, in conjunction with his colleagues Rebecca Trautmann and Janet Moursund. Erksine, Trautmann and Moursund developed a synthesis of a range of theoretical concepts and methods, selecting concepts which were theoretically congruent and compatible with each other.

Philosophy and approach

The main external theoretical influences of integrative TA include self-psychology, gestalt and person-centred therapy. Integrative TA, like other TA approaches, considers the need for attachment and relationship to be a primary human need. Lack of contactful relationship, or disruption in relational contact or relational trauma, is the primary source of psychopathology. Just as relationships or problems in relationships are seen as the primary source of pain, relationships and particularly the therapeutic relationship are considered the primary vessel for change and recovery. The therapist seeks to provide a contactful relationship with the client that provides an environment which increases the client's awareness. 'Within this contactful relationship, each newly discovered piece can be integrated into the self, and the split-off parts reclaimed and reowned' (Erskine *et al.*, 1999: 13). In some of Berne's writings he defines Child and Parent ego states as fixated ego states (although in others he appears to contradict this position). Erskine has taken this position, and views Child and Parent ego states as fixated and unintegrated ego states, and that in the process of change, the individual needs to deal with the trauma that triggered the fixation and integrate the experience into the Adult ego state (Erskine, 1988).

Integrative TA acknowledges that humans are fundamentally relationship seeking and interdependent throughout life. Needs for relationship and contact are normalized and the integration of self-psychology concepts of selfobject transferences (Kohut, 1984) in the relational needs affirms this interdependence and the ongoing development of the self. Both internal and external contact are considered to be essential features of healthy human functioning.

With its emphasis on the provision of an empathic, corrective experience and addressing developmental and relational deficits, integrative TA is generally a one-and-a-half-person approach (Stark, 2000). However, when the emphasis is on fixation, it is a one-person approach. Psychopathology is understood using a deficit model (Lapworth *et al.*, 1993), whereby pathology arises from a deficit of internal and interpersonal contact.

Key theoretical concepts

Key transactional analysis concepts primarily used in integrative TA are: ego states, scripts and the racket system (referred to in the integrative TA literature and throughout this book as the script system). Integrative TA also draws upon a number of theories from other theoretical approaches.

Contact

The concept of contact is taken from gestalt therapy and also draws upon person-centred theory, particularly Rogers' six necessary and sufficient conditions (Rogers, 1957). Integrative TA emphasizes the importance of both internal contact and interpersonal contact. Internal contact can be seen as a state of being whereby the individual is in relatively full awareness of their internal experience. In TA terms it could be considered to be a state of minimal discounting of internal experience. Contact is seen as a dynamic state of continual flux. Interpersonal contact is seen as a primary motivating force, and is characterized by intimacy, an absence of defensiveness and is satisfying. The individual who experiences repetitive lack of interpersonal contact processes these experiences and the resulting cognitive dissonance by forming script decisions in order to make sense of the lack of contact.

Attunement

Drawing upon Stern's (1985) work on attunement, integrative TA considers lack of attunement to be experienced traumatically. Consistent and repeated lack of attunement and the resulting cumulative trauma is seen as a determining factor in development of script beliefs. Attunement has similarities to empathy, in that close attention is paid to the client's subjective experience. However, in attunement, the therapist responds with a reciprocal appropriate affect (Erskine *et al.*, 1999).

Relational needs

Erskine and Trautmann (1996) developed their eight relational needs. These needs are not considered pathological, but are seen as ongoing needs in relationship which occur throughout the life span. The relational needs can be seen as an elaboration on Heinz Kohut's selfobject transferences (Kohut, 1984) of mirroring, idealization and twinship selfobject transferences which were considered also as ongoing needs. Of course, humans have a great many relational needs and are not limited to just eight. However, the eight relational needs presently described were identified by Erskine and Trautmann (1996) as recurring themes emerging in psychotherapy. The eight relational needs are:

- security;
- valuing;
- acceptance;
- mutuality;
- self-definition;
- making an impact;
- having the other initiate;
- to express love.

Erskine's position is that frustrated, or unmet relational needs not only result in script decisions, but also in games and other pathological processes as the individual is seeking a means of getting the needs met, albeit in a way which is scripty and painful. The diagnosis of, and attention to meeting of, these relational needs in turn reduces the need for engagement in games (Erskine *et al.*, 1999).

The script system

The script (racket) system is used to understand the dynamic and mutually supporting nature of the individual's script (Erskine and Zalcman, 1979).

Juxtaposition

Erskine and Trautmann (1996) identified the juxtaposition reaction. In juxtaposition, the experience of deeply empathic, attuned contact can be profoundly painful for clients as it contrasts with their experiences of misattunement and can activate different Child responses and reactions which were hitherto buried. The therapist needs to watch for juxtaposition reactions, and to slow the pace of the therapy down if the client is experiencing a painful juxtaposition.

11

Integrative TA: methods

Methods

The principal methods of integrative TA are *enquiry*, *attunement* and *involvement* (Erskine *et al.*, 1999). The combination of these in integrative TA creates a sensitive, empathic therapy.

Enquiry

Enquiry is subdivided into areas of enquiry: phenomenological enquiry, enquiry into the client's history and expectations, enquiry into coping strategies, choices and script decisions and also enquiry into the client's sense of vulnerability (see also Point 19) (Erskine *et al.*, 1999). Enquiry is done from a position of respect for the client and their process and from a place of genuine interest in the client. The purpose of enquiry is to generate increasing awareness and to promote internal and interpersonal contact (Erskine *et al.*, 1999).

Attunement

Attunement is a key therapeutic technique and begins with an empathic resonance with the client, but is added to in that the therapist remains open to responding accordingly to the client. The foci of attunement include attunement to the client's relational needs (an attuned response seeks to meet the relational needs in the therapeutic relationship), their developmental issues (related to developmental arrest or deficit; this may be addressed through setting up regressive work), cognitive processes (seeking to enter the client's frame of reference and understand *how* they think, as well as *what* they think), rhythms (this involves timing and pacing the work carefully) and affective attunement (which involves responding with a corresponding affect, such as compassion in response to sadness).

Involvement

Involvement is a less tangible and more attitudinal therapist activity. 'Inquiry is about what a therapist *does*; involvement is not about *doing* so much as about *being*' (Erskine *et al.*, 1999: 83). Involvement requires the therapist to be willing to be impacted by their client, and the therapist's commitment to do their utmost to help each client. A commitment to continual professional development is another feature of involvement. The expression of involvement in practical terms is demonstrated primarily through the use of several therapeutic strategies: acknowledgement of the client, their experience and of who they are as a person; validation of the client and their emotional reality, normalization ('that sounds like a very normal and understandable reaction to a very difficult situation'); and finally, through the therapist's presence. Presence is perhaps the least tangible quality, in that one can either feel someone's presence, or one cannot. Erskine *et al.* (1999) invite the therapist to remain curious about the client, to maintain internal and interpersonal contact, to be patient and consistent and to remain open and willing to be emotionally impacted by the client.

The integrative approach as described by Erskine *et al.* draws heavily upon gestalt two-chair methods, familiar to transactional analysts who use similar methods within a redecision therapy framework. Other methods used by some integrative transactional analysts include regressive techniques.

Critique

The use of regressive techniques in integrative TA is criticized by some, who see this as an infantilizing approach. The 'provision' of empathy can invite or perpetuate an idealizing transference, which would increase the potential for infantilization of clients. This is particularly the case with therapists who struggle with receiving negative transference or hostility from their clients, and who wish to remain in a 'good object' position (Cornell and Bonds-White, 2001).

Despite being based on TA theories of ego states and scripts (particularly the script system) and using Berne's human hungers as a motivational theory, some critics of integrative TA consider it to deviate too markedly from TA theory and practice.

12

Cognitive-behavioural TA: foundations

Background

Cognitive therapy was pioneered by Albert Ellis and Aaron Beck, who, like Berne, both originally trained as psychoanalysts, but abandoned psychoanalysis in favour of other methods for effective therapeutic change.

The active approach of the therapist, from challenging unhelpful thinking (contaminations) to the emphasis on behavioural change, that was emphasized in early TA clearly marks TA as a therapy which has a strong cognitive-behavioural component. The cognitive-behavioural therapy (CBT) approach to TA is not generally considered within the traditional 'schools' of TA, and yet represents a very clear and distinct application of TA as it is practised by a large number of transactional analysts.

> Conceptually, Berne provided us with an instrument for interpersonal behavioural analysis that is consistent with a therapy of social control. . . . On reading Berne's writings, one has the impression that unconscious processes were accepted through the front door and then thrown out the window. Bernean methodology remains psychoanalytic, but its conceptual apparatus seems more pertinent to a model of cognitive-behavioural therapy or communication training.
>
> (Terlato, 2001: 106)

In the current climate, CBT is favoured over many other approaches to therapy, and brief therapy is often considered to be the norm. A number of transactional analysts now identify as cognitive transactional analysts (English, 2007), and certainly some TA therapists will tell prospective clients that they can offer a version of CBT.

Philosophy and approach

Cognitive approaches to therapy make the assumption that much psychological distress has its origin in unhelpful patterns of thinking that individuals develop. Events in and of themselves are not considered distressing, rather it is our response to situations or how we construe them which determines our distress. Cognitive therapists seek to uncover such unhelpful thought processes (which may be clear or may operate out of awareness, or on the edge of awareness) and to systematically change them. Deliberate changing of thinking patterns is believed to result in less emotional distress. Similarly, behavioural change is also believed to promote positive change globally, particularly if positive actions are supplemented with a corresponding positive change in thought content. For example, someone who is depressed and has spent several months doing less and less generates a list of tasks with their therapist, ranging from simplest to most difficult. The client then engages in the simplest task, and then through internal dialogue praises themselves for having completed a task, and as such makes an improvement in their situation.

Berne developed TA independently of the cognitive therapists. However, Berne's concepts of the Adult ego state and contaminations of the Adult gave TA a framework for working cognitively (Schlegel, 1998). Similarly, the emphasis on contracts and behavioural change in TA gave TA a framework for incorporating behavioural therapy. Berne's concept of 'voices in the head' (Berne, 1972) provided therapists with a means to begin to understand and work with internal dialogue. Using this concept, TA therapists invite clients to become aware of their internal dialogue, or to make conscious the dialogue that one might infer is happening if the dialogue is not consciously available and clearly identifiable. This concept has similarity to the process used in cognitive therapy to identify negative automatic thoughts (Sanders and Wills, 2005). The approach Berne took to the change process was 'change now, analyse later', and is identical to the cognitive-behavioural approach to change. The CBT approach believes that behavioural change can occur without the need for internal, intrapsychic change and that it is possible for internal change to occur through making behavioural changes. Social control and symptomatic relief may provide enough change that can be sustained, and which may in turn provide the client with a springboard into script change. Certainly the emphasis on structured, focused interventions makes cognitive-behavioural TA appropriate for time-limited therapy.

Cognitive-behavioural TA, with its emphasis on knowledge and resolution of internal conflicts, and the stance of the therapist as an objective observer places cognitive-behavioural TA as a one-person psychology approach (Stark, 2000).

Key theoretical concepts

The majority of the key cognitive-behavioural TA concepts are drawn from the classical approach to TA, and can be used to develop CBT-style interventions.

13

Cognitive-behavioural TA: methods

Methods

Decontamination

Contaminated beliefs are scrutinized and challenged in the process of decontamination (Berne, 1961). A cognitive therapist will invite clients to be aware of the implicit 'oughts' and 'shoulds' they are living by and systematically challenge them (Harper and Ellis, 1969), in the same way a transactional analyst would challenge similar Parent contaminations (James and Jongeward, 1971). Child contaminations are also held up for reality testing, and the validity of the beliefs and experiences which act as 'supporting evidence' for the maintenance of the contamination is examined. 'The great profit that a transactional analyst can derive from the explanations of Ellis and Beck is a method for decontamination' (Schlegel, 1998: 273).

Behavioural contracts and homework

TA therapists and their clients often collaborate to generate a range of behavioural contracts and homework assignments that are undertaken as steps towards the achievement of the overall treatment contract.

Egograms

Dusay's (1972) method of egograms is a cognitive-behavioural approach, focusing on behavioural change. The individual identifies which of the functional ego states they want to reduce, and which they want to increase. The method involves deliberately and systematically increasing behaviours associated with the area of desired growth, working on the principle that the ego state behaviours one is seeking to reduce will automatically decrease.

Script (racket) system

Identifying script beliefs can make them amenable to direct modification (Erskine and Zalcman, 1979). Similarly, developing awareness of internal manifestations of the racket/script process and observable behaviours can be used to develop strategies for moving off (and not reinforcing) the system. Also, racket/scripty fantasies can be explored and modified using a range of cognitive-behavioural methods. Although this approach will develop movement off the script system, it does not resolve the underlying issues that fuel the racket. Deconfusion and redecision are needed for full resolution of the script system. The script system is not necessarily a cognitive-behavioural concept, although it can be used in a cognitive-behavioural way. Interestingly, modern cognitive-behavioural therapists are using a method of formulation of client beliefs that includes beliefs about self, others and the world which has a striking resemblance to the script system (Sanders and Wills, 2005).

Self-reparenting

Muriel James (1974, 1981, 2002) has developed the approach of self-reparenting, which involves an individual identifying deficits in the parenting they received. The individual then engages in a range of self-nurturing behaviours. James' position is that the behaviour will create changes in the Parent ego state. It is, however, doubtful that consciously engaging in certain behaviours will result in an individual substantially changing their Parent ego state. This method probably works by modifying internal critical dialogue (challenging negative automatic thoughts) which is considered a Parent ego state-driven process, and replacing it with more positive Adult-based self-talk: clearly a cognitive strategy. Consistent reinforcement of self-nurturing behaviours may generate new self-soothing behaviours for clients, and may change ingrained patterns of self-neglect.

Confrontation of discounting

The Schiffs (Mellor and Schiff, 1975; Schiff *et al.*, 1975) developed the concept of discounting and the discount matrix as a tool for dealing with distorted thinking processes and limiting frames of reference.

> Working with the discount matrix can be viewed as parallel to decontamination work as described by Berne, which serves to free and empower the Adult ego state. It provides an elegant cognitive-psychotherapeutic method that can be used for problematic situations.
>
> (Schlegel, 1998: 274)

Critique

One critique of the cognitive-behavioural approach to TA is that it can be a 'surface' approach, in that emphasis on behavioural change does not necessarily result in internal structural change or resolve the unconscious aspects of an individual's script. The approach also relies on a degree of sufficient Adult functioning from the start and the ability of the client to enter into a cooperative relationship, which may be rather difficult for clients with significant disturbance or psychological injury.

> When the psychotherapist emphasises only cognitive or behavioural change – such as confronting games or rackets . . . or determining how a person should behave or think – then the process of psychotherapy replaces one overused and rigid structure with another.
>
> (Erskine, 1998: 138)

The premise that we experience thoughts first, and then feelings spring from thoughts is not supported by neuroscience, as all stimuli are processed first by emotional centres within the brain before being processed in areas of the brain which are associated with rational thought. Furthermore, the separation of thoughts and feelings into two distinct categories of functioning 'is an oversimplification of little heuristic value and one that has no credibility either within philosophical tradition or in modern cognitive science' (Roth and Fonagy, 1996: 6). Granted, modern CBT is making changes to its theories in the light of developments in neuroscience and from psychotherapy research. Nevertheless, therapists need to be cautious about the championing of thought over emotions as the primary method of change. Similarly, behavioural changes and knowledge are unlikely to generate permanent intrapsychic change and must not be mistaken for solid evidence that change has indeed taken place without a period of time elapsing and the changes remaining 'stable under stress' (Woollams and Brown, 1978).

14

Psychodynamic TA: foundations

Background

In his 'Minimal basic science curriculum for clinical membership in the ITAA', Berne (ITAA Education Committee, 1969) explicitly stated that TA psychotherapists must have a basic grounding in psychoanalytic theory. Indeed, most of Berne's writings assume the reader has a degree of familiarity with psychoanalytic theory. In Berne's early writing he referred to both deconfusion of Child ego states and script cure in psychoanalytic terms.

> From psychoanalysis, Berne drew his understanding of intrapsychic forces acting upon the person. His major works . . . are only truly well understood given a sufficiently thorough grounding in psychoanalytic thinking . . . later readers, who may lack such background, may have missed some of this depth.
>
> (Clarkson, 1992: 4)

> Right up until his death in 1972, Berne asserted that transactional analysts are 'para-freudian'. They work through analysis of childhood experiences and script which have become unconscious, and lead the individual to follow repetitive and predictable interpersonal behaviour patterns.
>
> (Novellino, 2003: 152)

Berne was hugely influenced by his analysts, Paul Federn and Eduardo Weiss, both psychoanalysts who were prominent ego psychologists. The ego psychology perspective of TA remains in the concept of ego states (a term originally used by Federn), as well as TA's interest in 'adaptation, reality testing, autonomy (and) self-responsibility' (Sills and Hargaden, 2003: xvi). TA is also in many respects an object relations therapy, in that the primary motivation for individuals is the need for connection and relationships (Berne, 1964, 1972; Novellino, 2003) and that people are by very nature relationship (stroke) seeking from birth.

Philosophy and approach

The psychodynamic approach to therapy makes certain basic assumptions:

1   psychopathology and psychological/emotional conflict have their origins in childhood experiences;
2   people are usually not aware of these conflicts, as they are contained within the unconscious;
3   unconscious material surfaces in therapy, usually indirectly through transference and symbolism (McLeod, 1998).

The above points McLeod makes will not be new to trans-actional analysts; indeed, concepts such as script are based on the assumption that the script was primarily formed in child-hood and operates largely unconsciously and surfaces indirectly (Berne, 1966; Woollams and Brown, 1978; Stewart and Joines, 1987).

Psychodynamic TA is generally a one-person approach (Stark, 2000), although it may have elements of one-and-a-half-person or two-person approaches within it depending on the practitioner. Similarly, psychodynamic TA most commonly uses a conflict model for understanding psychopathology and con-ducting treatment, although the individual practitioner may also use deficit or confusion models in their work (Lapworth et al., 1993).

Key theoretical concepts

Many of TA's core theories are useful in understanding uncon-scious processes (see Points 26–28) in a directly observable manner. Many key concepts from psychodynamic therapy are incorporated into TA, such as repression. There are no particular theoretical concepts that have originated in psychodynamic TA, as the emphasis is on the application and use of TA theory and methods rather than generating new concepts per se. Essentially, concepts such as confusion and subsequent deconfusion and the emphasis of the past contained in Berne's analogy of the 'bent pennies' (Berne, 1961) contains the psychodynamic concept of the importance of the past in the formation of the personality.

15

Psychodynamic TA: methods

Methods

The triangle of insight: in here – out there – back then (Jacobs, 1988)

A psychodynamic approach explores the client's feelings and experiences that are related to the experience 'in here' in the therapeutic relationship, 'out there' in relation to other current relationships outside the therapy room, and 'back then' in historical relationships and experiences. The therapist will focus, generally in each session, on all three aspects of experience and linkage is made between different points on this triangle of insight (Jacobs, 1988; Luborsky, 1984). Interpretations are made to link these points and the feelings evoked by two or three of these points repeatedly throughout therapy to generate insight and promote resolution of unresolved feelings. In TA terms, this linkage facilitates the exploration of rubberbands (Kupfer and Haimowitz, 1971) and promotes deconfusion.

Interpretation

[An] interpretative intervention is to some extent a development of the empathic response: that response which tries to highlight half-expressed feelings and thoughts. There is however a difference in that an empathic response points to a conscious or semi-conscious feeling, of which the client is aware, although cannot verbalize to himself or the counsellor. An interpretative response is aimed more at elucidating unconscious feelings or ideas, of which the client is unaware. A skilful interpretation observes feelings which are close enough to the surface, and allows them into consciousness.

(Jacobs, 1988: 35)

Interpretation can also be of 'bilogical transactions' (Novellino, 2003) and the unconscious content they contain. It is assumed that clients will unconsciously defend against certain feelings, particularly those evoked by the therapeutic relationship, and so will discuss them indirectly in the therapy by discussing problems in relationships with others. For example, following a break in therapy due to the therapist going on holiday, the client in the first session after the break discusses how they felt angry, hurt and excluded by some friends who went for a meal together without inviting the client. The therapist might wonder out loud if the client also has some of those same feelings about the therapist and their relationship (Gill, 1979).

Psychodynamic TA, although sharing many commonalities with relational TA, is different. In psychodynamic TA, the transference is considered to be about the client's structure and pathology, and the therapist positions themselves as an observer and interpreter of this process (one-person approach). In relational TA, transference is considered to be co-created and although it does contain elements relating to the client's structure and pathology, it is also considered in part to be stimulated by the real, here-and-now interaction of client and therapist (two-person approach).

Critique

Some TA practitioners are deeply critical of developments in psychodynamic TA, as they consider TA to have been originally developed by Berne as a move away from psychoanalysis, and that any movement back to a more psychodynamic perspective is a regressive tendency. In response to this critique, psychodynamic TA practitioners see that psychodynamic concepts can add incredible richness and depth to TA and consider the wholesale rejection of psychoanalytic insights by many of the early transactional analysts as being a reactionary move, which at the time was important in forging a separate identity for TA, but is now outdated and inappropriate in a post-modern, pluralistic world.

16

Relational TA: foundations

Background

The relational approach to TA has developed over the last twenty years as an emerging tradition (Cornell and Hargaden, 2005). Hargaden and Sills (2002) describe their own journey to relational therapy as being driven out of recognizing a change in the typical presenting profile of clients and an increase in clients presenting with disorders of the self such as borderline, narcissistic and schizoid structures (Masterson and Lieberman, 2004).

> When Berne first wrote, the common client was putatively an inhibited, rule-bound individual who needed the metaphorical 'solvent' of therapy to loosen the confines of his or her script. As we move into the twenty-first century, the 'typical' client is one who needs not solvent but 'glue'.
>
> (Hargaden and Sills, 2002: 2)

In response to this need, they revisited psychoanalytic concepts and began a process of developing TA models that matched the experience of themselves and their clients and which integrated modern developments in psychoanalysis from the relational and intersubjective movements and from developments in child development theory such as the work of Daniel Stern (Stern, 1985).

Philosophy and approach

The relational approach to TA emphasizes the emergence and analysis of unconscious processes in the therapy. As opposed to more goal-oriented, behavioural forms of TA, relational TA therapists consider the deeper processes of change occur when the therapist and client pay attention to the emergence of these unconscious processes on a moment-to-moment basis in the dynamics between therapist and client. In line with mounting current research on curative factors in psychotherapy, relational TA therapists champion the therapeutic relationship as being the primary agent for change.

The relational approach to TA also accounts for what the therapist brings to the therapeutic encounter, and the therapist's own script issues and unconscious process. A relational TA therapist will be mindful of their own process and how this impacts the relationship and their client, and will remain receptive to learning more about their own unconscious process in an ongoing and unfolding way. A key principle in relational TA is the idea that the therapist is also changed by the therapeutic encounter. This makes sense when we consider that our own scripts will invariably limit our own ways of relating, and the process of honest, intimate communication characterized by mutuality with our clients will repeatedly push us as therapists to move beyond and outside our own script into new patterns of relating. Stark (2000) beautifully summarizes the relational approach to psychotherapy and the relational perspective on the mechanisms of change:

> In the relational model, it is the negotiation of the relationship and its vicissitudes (a relationship that is continuously evolving as patient and therapist act/react/interact) that constitutes the locus of the therapeutic action. It is what transpires in the here-and-now engagement between patient and therapist that is thought to be transformative . . . [in the relational model] the focus is on the therapist as subject – an authentic subject who uses the self (that is, uses her countertransference) to engage, and to be engaged by, the patient.
>
> (Stark, 2000: xxi–ii)

To use Stark's model, relational TA is a two-person approach.

Another feature of the relational approach is an appreciation of 'the co-construction and multiplicity of meaning' (Hargaden, 2007: 10) that in real terms means 'it is important to learn to play with possibilities and not to get fixed on just one meaning' (Hargaden, 2007: 10). Dialogue and exploration into the

manifestation of relational dialectics in the therapeutic relationship, and how the client manages the core tensions of relational
dialectics in other outside relationships is often on the therapeutic agenda in a relational approach. In the original model of
relational dialectics the core tensions that exist within any
relationship are the apparently contradictory needs of *privacy
versus transparency, novelty versus predictability* and *autonomy
versus connectedness* (Griffin, 2003). It is possible to be simultaneously pulled by both poles of one or more of these dimensions and this conflict and tension can feel disorientating. In any
relationship, both persons are influenced by their own ongoing
tensions relating to these poles, and the interaction of two
people will require they find some kind of balance of managing
their interacting core tensions. It could be considered that many
script decisions originate in the historical interaction of two
people's core tensions, with the more vulnerable person (child)
subjugating their needs to the more dominant one (the parent)
and developing an implicit set of beliefs and expectations to
make sense of this process.

Relational TA is interested not only in how the client replays
their script both within and outside the therapy room, but in
examining features of the therapeutic relationship that are
unique and a product of the interaction of this unique client and
this unique therapist. Enhancing the client's relationships in all
areas of their life is a central concern in relational therapy.

Key theoretical concepts

Hargaden and Sills (2002) present an alternative model of the
third order structure of the Child ego state. One key difference is
they diagram the C0 and P0 ego states as overlapping, with the
intersection between the two as being the A0 ego state. Their
inspiration for this amendment is the work of child development
theorist Daniel Stern (Stern, 1985). In Stern's work, the 'self'
emerges (Stern calls this the emergent self) from the interaction
between the infant and the primary caregiver(s). The self does
not develop independently or spontaneously but is entirely
shaped by interactional processes. The overlapping of the circles
is a play with the visual metaphor of the ego state model to

illustrate this process. The primary caregiver(s) provides an essential affect-regulating function (Stern, 1985) for the infant. For the infant, the source of this affective regulation is not identified as being external to the self, and over time, the regulating function of the other becomes part of the self (as key brain structures such as the orbito-frontal cortex mature). The mutually influencing processes of development, together with a relative lack of differentiation between self and other, mean that at these early stages the self–other boundary is not clear and the qualitative, affective nature of the interaction will become part of the individual's developing sense of self by internalization which is recorded in the early Parent ego states.

Both infant and primary caregiver(s) mutually influence each other, and it is the quality of the relationship which is internalized and recorded in the individual's protocol. The protocol forms the basis of our script and in therapy attention is paid to the interaction of transference and countertransference to shed light on and rework the protocol and its unconscious processes.

17

Relational TA: methods

Methods

The primary therapeutic interventions used in relational TA are empathic transactions (Clark, 1991; Hargaden and Sills, 2002). A revised version of Berne's eight therapeutic operations is offered that provide the basic empathic backdrop for the work. Interpretation is also used; however, empathic and interpretive interventions are primarily used to analyse, explain, highlight and work with the here-and-now processes occurring in the therapy. The relationally oriented therapist will regularly focus on the client's impact upon the therapist, the therapist's impact upon the client, and the here-and-now engagement between them (Stark, 2000).

A relational TA therapist may explore the significance in the therapeutic relationship of parallels in experiences the client reports in other relationships (see bilogical transactions in Point 15). Clients may reveal the hidden or repressed feelings they hold about the therapist but cannot express directly in an indirect, coded manner by discussing events with other people outside the therapy. The therapist invites the client into exploration of whether they hold the same feelings towards the therapist (Hargaden and Sills, 2003; Novellino, 2003; Gill, 1979).

All transactional analysts seek to detoxify the toxic introjects of their clients. With approaches such as redecision TA, the therapist joins the client in fighting back against these introjects, mobilizing Child and Adult energy to challenge these introjects, and possibly decathect significant aspects of the introjects. Relational TA takes a different approach. In relational TA, the therapist considers that it is not enough to simply provide a good, corrective experience, or to engage in analysis or seeking to mobilize forces against these introjects as, even if significant change takes place, the introjects are still there. A relational approach to working with such introjects is to metaphorically make space for them to emerge in the therapy via the transference/countertransference matrix. In this instance, the therapist takes on the client's transferential projection of the negative, bad object introjects and re-works them. In this process, relational therapists consider that the existing introject is detoxified and re-worked and the relational conflict that was bound up with the introject is resolved in the relational process.

Critique

Some of the theory of relational TA can be difficult for beginning students to understand, and some of the articles published on the relational approach can be dense and heavy in their use of advanced and psychoanalytic concepts, and also light on practical recommendations which those who are interested in developing their work in this way can use readily. Hargaden and Sills' (2002) book is, however, full of practical advice and narrative to explain and illustrate the theory discussed. Not all relational therapy is psychodynamic in origin; Summers and Tudor (2000) developed co-creative TA, a relational therapy which is not psychodynamically based but is based on present-centred approaches, such as gestalt therapy. Critics of the relational approach believe the often complex language of relational TA is contrary to the spirit of TA. However, relational TA therapists argue in response that some processes are not simple to understand or describe, and that the language used reflects the complexity of these phenomena and greater refinement in our understanding.

Part 2

THE THERAPEUTIC RELATIONSHIP

18

The initial sessions

The initial sessions of therapy set the scene for the work that follows and acclimatize the client to the unusual situation of therapy. There is now considerable evidence to suggest that a strong working alliance is the most reliable predictor of successful therapy (Orlinsky *et al.*, 1994). It is during the initial sessions that the working alliance is formed and these sessions are therefore critical to the outcome of the therapy.

Cornell describes the tasks of the initial sessions as being engagement and collaboration, clarifying with the client how the therapy will work (what is involved in therapy) and assessment (Cornell, 1986). One key aspect of the initial sessions is letting the client tell their story. The therapist's job is to listen carefully, incorporating sensitive use of questioning and clarifying questions to facilitate gaining the necessary information about the client, their situation and their process. The client will generally present with a great need to feel understood, and to feel emotionally safe. To this end, the therapist needs to offer regular empathic responses that communicate their understanding to the client. The emphasis is on establishing 'contact before contract' (Lee, 1998) and as such the therapist's interventions are likely to be simple, and minimal. All through this stage, the therapist is building up a detailed picture of the client's process, and is noticing emerging patterns, both in the client's life, and in their manner of presenting in therapy.

My own preferred opening invitation is 'So tell me a little about what it is that brings you here', which is an open question that leaves the space clear for the client to discuss their concerns, reasons for coming for therapy and a little history. Some therapists prefer the more direct 'Why have you come to therapy?' It is sometimes necessary to interrupt and seek clarification, particularly with clients who give extremely long, complicated and involved stories. The opening invitation can be followed with questioning that invites the client to discuss their therapy goals, which can then be used to establish an initial working contract. An example of such a question might be 'Tell me a little about what you want to get out of therapy'. Responses here are often phrased in terms of what the client wants to stop, or get rid of ('to get rid of my depression', 'to stop feeling anxious'). At this stage, this is sufficient for an initial sense of what the client wants. The contract can be firmed up in positive, specific language later in the therapy. It is also often useful to enquire about the client's expectations of the therapist, therapy in general and what will happen in therapy. The therapy can get off to a rocky start if client and therapist have very different views about what the tasks of therapy are.

Cornell advocates asking the client 'What do you need to know about me?' (Cornell, 1986), which avoids the situation whereby the therapist (with the best of intentions) overwhelms the client with information that the client neither wants to know nor needs to know. The client needs to leave the session feeling that the therapist has made a real attempt to get to know them, and to find out about their problems, rather than feeling that they know more about the therapist than the therapist does about them!

The client needs to experience some of what therapy is about, and how the therapy will work during this opening stage. To this end the therapist does need to introduce some interventions and find the right balance between challenge and support. If clients feel too challenged they will get scared or feel offended and leave therapy; if there is not enough challenge, they will not experience the therapist as potent enough to help them change. At the end of the session, the client will need to leave with some sense about how the therapist works and what 'doing therapy' will involve. This is best done experientially, rather than via explanation. Cornell also recommends that the therapist pay attention to the 'triangle of insight' (see Point 15) in the initial sessions. I agree with his position that doing so invites the client from the outset into a collaborative process and in terms of contracting, gives the client a real flavour of the nature of the work of psychotherapy, and as such, promotes informed consent (Cornell, 1986; Steiner, 1974). It is also wise to draw upon the therapeutic relationship from the outset. Yalom (2001) also advocates contracting for this in the very first session by raising the following with a client:

> It's clear that one of the areas we need to address is your relationship with others. It's difficult for me to know the precise nature of your difficulties in relationships because I, of course, know the other persons in your life only through your eyes. Sometimes your descriptions may be unintentionally biased, and I've found that I can be more helpful to you by focusing on the one relationship where I have the most accurate information – the relationship between you and me. It is for this reason I shall often ask you to examine what is happening between the two of us.
>
> (Yalom, 2001: 85–6)

In my experience, the overwhelming majority of clients are receptive to such an approach.

In terms of assessment, a more holistic view of assessment is recommended, as opposed to one which focuses entirely on problems and the client's pathology (Cornell, 1986). It is very easy to focus on problem areas, and gaining some sense of the client's strengths is useful in orienting the therapy towards health and the promotion of strengths.

19

Therapeutic enquiry

Use of enquiry is probably every therapist's second tool, after listening. Even if, as a therapist, all you do is use enquiry, you can have some degree of success (Erskine *et al.*, 1999). The backdrop of therapeutic enquiry is a genuine interest in the client and their process and is done respectfully and sensitively (Hargaden and Sills, 2002). The intention behind the enquiry process is to deepen awareness – both for the client and the therapist. Sensitive, and carefully attended to, enquiry will often enable the client to see their own meanings and generate solutions to their problems with the minimum of therapist intervention. Elegant therapeutic enquiry leads to ever-increasing awareness and greater integration for the client. For the therapist, skilful enquiry helps to create a knowledge base of information about our client, and in terms of the overall process of therapy, it facilitates our clients talking about themselves and their deepest processes, and it enhances the owning of responsibility and implies the potential for problem solving.

Erskine *et al.* (1999) offer a 'menu' of areas for enquiry, including: physical sensations and reactions; emotions; memories; thoughts; conclusions and 'as if' script decisions; the meaning the client makes of experiences; hopes and fantasies. This list is not exhaustive, but is rather used as a prompt of suggestions for the therapist to consider. Erskine *et al.* (1999) also emphasize the importance in enquiry of promoting contact – both internal contact, and interpersonal contact.

Recently the therapy world has turned its attention to concepts such as mentalization (Fonagy *et al.*, 2002). Mentalization is the ability to make inferences about the internal states and intentions (such as goals, feelings, purposes, reasons) of others that inform their behaviour. It involves 'imaginative empathy' (Bateman and Fonagy, 2006). Mentalization is considered a key life skill, and is an aspect of emotional regulation. The deliberate use of mentalization as an intervention, and developing the client's mentalizing capacity, is an important part in the therapy of a wide range of presenting problems. Mentalizing is significantly enhanced through the use of therapeutic enquiry. Enquiry helps the therapist to mentalize the client, and invites the client to mentalize about their own internal experience (see Point 92).

Enquiry plays a central role in many other interventions, for example decontamination can be effectively done using the cognitive therapy method of the 'downward arrow' (Burns, 2000). Specification is one of Berne's eight therapeutic operations (Berne, 1966) that can support and follow enquiry: 'The object is to fix certain information in his mind and in the patient's mind, so that it can be referred to later' (Berne, 1966: 234–5). A specification can be highly effective at summarizing or highlighting key points emerging from the enquiry. It does not involve interpretation, and focuses solely on what the client has expressed and is a form of empathic enquiry (Hargaden and Sills, 2002).

20

The centrality of empathy

Empathy has been firmly placed on the TA map since Barbara Clark's paper on empathy and its role in deconfusion (Clark, 1991). This has been subsequently developed by a number of other TA authors, including Erskine (1993), Erskine and Trautmann (1996), Hargaden and Sills (2002) and Tudor (2009).

Berne made little reference to emotions in his work, or how to work with emotions, yet Berne was firmly interested in the therapist working with the client's phenomenology – the client's construction of meanings and internal experience of themselves, others and the world. In approaching phenomenological enquiry, the therapist would need to account for and enquire into the client's emotional world. It is now widely accepted that experiencing empathy is essential for the development of a cohesive sense of self (Hargaden and Sills, 2002). Stern (1985) has written extensively on the importance and centrality of affective attunement in the development of the self in child development.

So what is empathy? To be empathic means to move outside our judgement frameworks, our sense of what is right or wrong or how things 'should be'. Empathy is to enter our client's frame of reference and see and experience the world as they do. When we are empathic, we learn about the client's experience and their reality. Empathy is not about agreeing, or disagreeing with our clients, it is not about reassuring them, or comforting them or providing them with support. Empathy might be gratifying, but the intention in an empathic response is not necessarily to be gratifying, it is simply to resonate with the client's experience. For example, in a situation where a client is directly seeking reassurance from their therapist, the empathic therapist will not provide the reassurance, but will empathize with the client's experience of need and the emotions which are fuelling the requests for reassurance.

Empathy is composed of two aspects – empathic understanding (listening) and empathic responding. In many respects empathic understanding is useless unless it can be effectively communicated to the client (Rogers, 1957; Clark, 1991). Stern (2004: 241) refers to *affect attunement* as 'a way of imitating, from the inside, what an experience feels like, not how it was expressed in action' and includes attention to the temporal dynamics of the affect in terms of intensity, form or rhythm.

> [To be empathic] means entering the private perceptual world of the other and becoming thoroughly at home in it. It involves being sensitive, moment by moment, to the changing felt meanings which flow in this other person, to the fear or rage or tenderness or confusion or whatever that he or she is experiencing. It means temporarily living in the other's life, moving about in it delicately without making judgments.
>
> (Rogers, 1980: 142)

Empathy requires attending to, and resonating with the client's 'felt' experience. When we are empathic, we tune in to where the client is emotionally at. The emotions we resonate with will be within the client's sphere of awareness, or partially within their awareness, but nevertheless part of their experience. This is the key difference between empathy and interpretation: empathy addresses the client's affective experience – it is experience-near; interpretation draws the client's attention to where they are currently unaware and emotions that are not presently part of the client's experience – it is experience-distant (Jacobs, 1988; Stark, 2000).

Accurate empathy is not always the warm, pleasant experience we might expect it to be. To be truly empathic requires that the therapist be prepared to tolerate and contain intense and possibly confusing unpleasant emotions. If we are to have some real appreciation of what it is like to be in our client's skin, an empathic therapist will regularly feel high levels of fear, hatred, depression, despair, doubt, grief and shame to name just some of the possibilities. Such attunement distinguishes empathy from compassion or sympathy.

In terms of treatment planning, emphasizing empathy forms a crucial aspect of the formation and maintenance of the therapeutic relationship, and certainly helps cement the 'therapeutic bond' aspect of the relationship (Bordin, 1979). Clients generally present in therapy initially with an intense need to be understood, to unburden, to feel safe, knowing that their experience makes sense to someone. In many respects interventions other than inquiry will have limited effectiveness until the client experiences the therapist's empathy.

> Nearer the beginning of treatment, it may well be that the patient will respond especially well to empathic interventions that validate the patient's experience and enable her to feel understood. In fact, the patient may not be receptive to interpretations that highlight recurring themes, patterns and repetitions in her life until she becomes more comfortable in the therapy.
>
> (Stark, 2000: 162)

In terms of later stages of therapy:

> the therapist must decide from moment to moment whether to be with the patient where she is or to direct the patient's attention elsewhere. . . . There are times when the therapist senses that the patient is open to the possibility of acquiring insight. There are other times, however, when the therapist senses that what the patient wants is, simply, empathic recognition of who she is and what she is feeling.
>
> (Stark, 2000: 16)

Although indicated in early stages of treatment, empathy is a vital ingredient throughout.

> The empathic bond is imperative when working toward deconfusion of the Child ego states. At this stage, the person has to believe that his or her most profound emotional states and needs can be understood by the therapist.

In the empathic ambience, the patient and therapist will be able to access the early developmental levels of the Child ego states which is necessary for deconfusion to occur.

(Clark, 1991: 93)

21

Accounting for the impact of diversity in the therapeutic relationship

Our identity, who we are, is a culturally embedded concept and one that plays a part in our unconscious process.

> Transferential and countertransferential responses stem from frames of reference that include who we are racially, culturally and individually. It is important for all therapists to have an understanding and awareness of all their ego state responses so that we become aware of our impact on a client who may represent the 'other'. This includes having an awareness of our own racial identity, prejudices and biases.
>
> (Shivanath and Hiremath, 2003: 171)

The same authors continue to highlight the therapist's commitment to self-awareness and personal exploration of such issues: 'as psychotherapists it is our responsibility to explore all our ego state responses to race and racism' (Shivanath and Hiremath, 2003: 177). I agree, and would extend this to include other forms of diversity including gender, sexual orientation and class.

Acknowledging and accounting for differences between the therapist and client is essential to developing empathic sensitivity and in beginning the process of understanding the frame of reference of the client, and how the therapist's frame of reference may be in accord with or discordant with the client's frame of reference. Oppression subtly but powerfully shapes the frame of reference of every single person. People from a culturally dominant background can easily take for granted their privileges, and can discount the impact that growing up and living life as part of a culturally less powerful and oppressed group can have in the shaping of the frame of reference and script of an individual who has had, and continues to live with, such experiences on a day-to-day basis.

Awareness of cultural and social differences is a key feature in working across difference. Understanding, and accepting cultural (and subcultural) differences avoids pathologizing behaviours and ways of living that are not part of the usual cultural frame of reference for the therapist and helps the therapist to practise in anti-oppressive ways.

> It is sometimes more important, at least in the early phases of developing a therapeutic relationship, to consider the emotional implications of a person's age, race, ethnicity, class background, physical disability, political attitudes, or sexual orientation than it is to appreciate his or her appropriate diagnostic category.
>
> (McWilliams, 1994: 18)

Working with difference can be disturbing for therapists from the more culturally powerful background (white, heterosexual, educated, middle class) and who are relatively culturally aware and sensitive at some levels to issues of oppression. This disturbance and the associated guilt, shame or even denial can manifest subtly in the therapeutic relationship and significantly impair the therapist's capacity to be potent (Hargaden and Sills, 2002; Shivanath and Hiremath, 2003). Similarly a refusal to acknowledge the role of difference or similarity between the therapist and client, and the potential impact it is having on the therapy is to discount entire areas of exploration of meaning and unconscious process and associated experiences and script decisions as well as large areas of the client's experience. Shadbolt (2004) describes the importance of accounting for our countertransference responses to our clients in relation to working with gay clients; however, her position is one which is very relevant when working with all clients and one which it is wise to pay special attention to when working with clients who are different from ourselves, or clients from minority cultures. Our countertransference feelings, particularly the more 'negative' ones, may contain vital information about the client's experience and may result in a 'detoxification' of the oppressive introjects, through processes of working with the projective or transformational transference. 'By owning and identifying such countertransference feelings, therapists understand, hold, manage and transform them for clients who have, as yet, been unable to do so intrapsychically' (Shadbolt, 2004: 121).

Another consideration for the therapist in accounting for how difference between therapist and client interacts and influences the therapeutic relationship is in the experience of empathy. Stark (2000) draws a distinction between 'easy' and 'difficult' empathy. In easy empathy, aspects of the client's experience are similar or close to the therapist's own experience, or how the therapist would experience the same situation. Difficult empathy 'involves understanding aspects of the patient's experience that are at variance with the therapist's worldview, aspects that are discrepant from the therapist's experience' (Stark, 2000: 179). It can be very difficult to empathize with clients who have very different social, political and cultural experiences from us, and to account for the significance of, and respect culturally accepted etiquette, technicalities and characteristics (Drego, 1983) which are at variance with our own.

22

Conceptualizing the therapeutic relationship

The therapeutic relationship is different from any other type of relationship. Repeated studies have demonstrated that the most curative factor in psychotherapy is not the techniques the therapist uses, or their theoretical orientation, but the strength of the therapeutic relationship (Horvath and Greenberg, 1994). The therapeutic relationship in many respects is a relationship of potentiality. It can be likened to a relationship laboratory, with client and therapist engaged in experimentation with different means of relating to each other and reflection upon these relational experiments. The potentiality includes the potential to relate to each other from a range of ego states, from scripted positions, and autonomous positions. The length of time needed to establish a strong therapeutic alliance can vary quite considerably and is substantially influenced by the client's level of organization and integration. More seriously disturbed clients, such as those with personality disorders, may require over a year before the alliance can be considered to be properly formed. Clients with neurotic-level problems, where there is the discernible presence of both an observing and an experiencing ego, are likely to form an alliance with the therapist more readily, maybe only requiring a few sessions before a sufficiently strong alliance can be considered to be established, whereas those with less or even no observing ego are likely to need extensive therapeutic input to get to the stage where such an alliance between the therapist and the observing ego is possible (McWilliams, 1994).

A particular feature of the therapeutic relationship is the therapist's willingness to be 'recruited' (Barr, 1987) by the client as a participant in the client's (transferential) drama. In TA terms, this means the therapist being willing to be stimulated into entering the client's games, so that these games can be understood and analysed and so the underlying script issues can be healed within the context of a relationship. Therapists bring their own relational experiences (and associated script) to the therapeutic encounter, and these interact with our client's to generate the sum total of immediate relational potential at the outset. As the therapy proceeds, this potential increases. Berne (1961) analysed relationships by their transactional possibilities, that is, the transactional vectors and ego states that are activated in the relationship, out of the nine types of transaction that are possible between two people. In TA psychotherapy, the transactional analyst takes time to consider the type and nature of the therapeutic relationship and transactions between them and their client(s), and will actually analyse transactions and transactional sequences that emerge in the therapeutic interaction. This analysis is done both to strengthen the quality of the therapeutic relationship, and also to help illuminate the client's internal dynamics and their manifestation and enhance their interactions with others (see also Point 100). The relationship is also analysed with reference to Berne's six categories of time structuring (Berne, 1961): withdrawal, rituals, pastimes, activity, games and intimacy.

Many therapists believe that it is the intensity of the therapeutic relationship which creates the necessary conditions for therapeutic change. Perhaps the intensity of the relationship encourages the growth of new neural patterns and ways of relating. Some therapists who work with a deficit model (Lapworth et al., 1993) see that this intensity is needed to act as an 'antidote' to previous relational trauma:

> . . . it is thought that part of what enables the therapist to be deeply effective is that she comes (by way of the patient's regression) to assume the importance of the original parent. When the therapist has been vested with such power, then and only then is the therapy relationship able to serve as a corrective for damage sustained during the patient's formative years.
>
> (Stark, 2000: 11)

Each therapist over time forms their own conceptualization of the nature and role of the therapeutic relationship and of the therapist's key tasks. This is part of creating a personalized approach to psychotherapy, and making personal meaning of theories and models. Erskine (1998) beautifully paraphrases Berne on the task of the therapist and the nature of the therapeutic relationship:

> The psychotherapist's task is to create a contactful therapeutic relationship that facilitates decoding of the client's transferential expression of past experiences, detoxifying introjections and rectifying fixated script beliefs and defensive structures, and helping the client identify relational needs and opportunities for need fulfilment through enhancing the client's capacity for internal and external contact.
>
> (Erskine, 1998: 139–40)

23

Strengthening the working alliance by attention to tasks, goals and bonds

Bordin (1979) developed a formulation of the dimensions of the working alliance in psychotherapy, which he identified as comprising three main components: tasks, goals and bonds (Bordin, 1994). There has been considerable research on this formulation and it is now widely accepted that therapist–client agreement on the tasks, goals and bonds is a reliable predictor of strength of working alliance and as such can be seen as a reliable predictor of positive outcome and successful therapy (Horvath and Greenberg, 1994). Bordin's formulation can be used to establish, enhance and develop the working alliance.

Tasks

'What do we do here?' There needs to be agreement regarding the nature of the tasks of therapy. At the beginning, the client who is new to therapy is looking to the therapist for the therapist to provide structure and to indicate to the client what the tasks of therapy are, how the therapy will be done, what kind of things they can expect and so on. This is true also for clients who have already experienced some previous therapy as they need to work out how this new therapist works. Agreement on tasks also provides a degree of emotional containment as total lack of structure can be profoundly disturbing. Agreement on tasks can provide a sense of the boundaries of the therapy on an emotional level. Exploration of the client's expectation of therapy, and what they anticipate the therapist will do is often very helpful in establishing agreement on therapeutic tasks. Where the client has unspoken expectations of the therapy that conflict with the therapist's expectations of therapy and the different methods which will be used in the therapy, the alliance will be placed under enormous strain, and may not develop quickly enough unless the tasks are clarified. Explicitly discussing this aspect and the client's expectations is often particularly helpful. This also has an ethical and contractual dimension, in that when a client has information regarding the nature of therapy and the 'nuts and bolts' of how it works they are in a position to make an Adult informed choice, which meets Steiner's requirement of mutual consent (Steiner, 1974).

Goals

'Why are we here?' In many respects, transactional analysts are incredibly thorough in seeking agreement regarding the goals aspect of the working alliance with their attention to contracting, and getting a clear agreement on the focus of the work. This needs to be balanced carefully – an excessive focus on goals can imbalance the work, and can leave clients feeling misunderstood. In the process of empathic enquiry the therapist will note, and often articulate, areas that the client will want to change and will check them out with the client as some initial therapy goals. The contract at the early stages should also always include a general 'exploration contract' for both therapist and client to use the space to explore the client's problems further with a view to developing more clearly defined goals in time. The therapist's own conceptualization of the overall and more general goals of therapy (usually rooted in their theoretical perspective) is also relevant here.

Bonds

'How will we be with each other?' This includes from the client's perspective an Adult assessment regarding the therapist's degree of perceived potency and credibility. The bonds also include a Child component – 'Will the therapist provide sufficient safety for me to do the work I need to?' It is essential that the client experiences sufficient empathy from the therapist and also feels that the therapist is warm and genuinely interested in them. The client needs to feel understood, respected, valued and so on. *How* the client attaches or does not attach to the therapist is also important. The therapist can gain useful significant (often at this stage, inferential and tentative) information regarding the client's attachment pattern, relational scripts, and script beliefs about self, others and the world. The client will be showing the therapist how they attach to others. Often there will be some element of distrust from the client towards the therapist. This is to be accepted and understood as being appropriate and having a protective function for the client. In many respects, the bond forms over time and attention to the goals and tasks; an empathic stance which is supportive and appropriately challenging will help forge this bond.

24

Considering Adapted Child responses as indicators of alliance rupture

Relational approaches to TA psychotherapy pay particular attention to instances of therapeutic alliance rupture. A rupture is a moment where the therapeutic alliance comes under some sort of strain. The genesis of pathology is considered primarily as a result of repeated relational rupture, and the enactment of relational ruptures in the therapy is viewed as inevitable (Guistolise, 1996). The subsequent consistent and repeated repair of these therapeutic alliance ruptures is considered to be a primary healing process in psychotherapy (see point 77).

Safran and Muran (2003) explored various client behaviours as indicative of alliance rupture. Their observations can easily be translated into TA terms giving the transactional analyst solid clues as to the potential presence of an alliance rupture and clear indicators for immediate treatment planning. Their framework presents two main categories of rupture markers: withdrawal and confrontation. In their framework, compliance/adaptation is linked to withdrawal. This classification of responses is consistent with a TA framework regarding Adapted Child (functional) responses, and also incorporates withdrawing as an additional type of Adapted Child response (Oller Vallejo, 1986). The rupture marker is determined by the individual's protocol and their stereotypical *response of self*, and the expected *response of other*. Below is a list of observable behaviours or ways of interacting that the therapist can use to identify a potential alliance rupture. This list is not exhaustive, and it is probable that each person will have their own set of rupture markers that are unique to that person. The therapist is advised to develop their sensitivity in noticing rupture markers, both observable and on the basis of their countertransference and subjective reaction to their client.

Adaptation/compliance

Client begins describing what they think the therapist wants to hear; the client becomes overly accommodating or solicitous; the client offers many strokes to the therapist; accepting therapist interpretations or explanations too readily; submissive behaviour; 'Gee, you're wonderful'; client 'softens the blow' by qualifying or minimizing (discounting) negative feelings towards the therapist; client begins long over-detailed story.

Withdrawing

Minimal answers to open-ended questions; intellectualization, discussing problems or painful experiences in a non-emotional or dispassionate manner; silence; avoiding eye contact; client begins 'talking about' others.

Rebellious/confrontational

Client attacks the therapist as a person; the client criticizes the therapist's skills; the client expresses doubts about being in therapy; the client attempts to rearrange sessions; client expresses irritation about the therapist's questions or suggested tasks. (Adapted from Safran and Muran, 2003.)

Deflection is also a key indicator of alliance rupture. In TA terms this would involve the use of tangential redefining transactions (Schiff *et al.*, 1975). The cathexis approach would suggest that clients use redefining to preserve central aspects of their script-bound frame of reference. In this example, the relational context is relevant and the client can be seen to be defending or reinforcing their relational script beliefs, in terms of beliefs about both self and others. In terms of the above framework, deflection/redefining could be an indicator of either withdrawal or rebellion and is a potential rupture marker.

25

The therapeutic alliance: rupture and repair

An alliance rupture is a moment where the therapeutic relationship is under strain in some way. There is mounting agreement amongst therapists of all orientations that such ruptures are inevitable (Guistolise, 1996), and that learning how to identify and respond to such alliance ruptures are key skills for therapists (Safran and Muran, 2003). Transactional analysts pay attention to each transaction, and note both their own response to each transactional stimulus and the impact of their transactions upon their client and the therapeutic relationship. Analysis of transactions can suggest an alliance rupture, for example an unexpected, jarring crossed transaction may suggest the presence of a rupture (although do bear in mind much therapy is done when a therapist deliberately crosses transactions). If the therapist suspects a rupture, or experiences some strain in the relationship, naming the tension and openly exploring it begins the process of rupture repair. Inviting the client into exploring how he or she has experienced a particular intervention can reveal rich information regarding their process and way of experiencing the world and others. The therapist here needs to adopt a stance of curiosity into their own experience, and also enquiry into the client's experience and historical or phenomenological diagnosis of recurring patterns. In identifying and deliberately seeking to repair an alliance rupture, the therapist is acting differently from the expected re-enactment of the client's relational protocol. In some respects this is the equivalent of providing the therapeutically needed relationship and may act as an antidote to some of the more toxic introjects and relational script issues the client holds. The sensitive but frank manner in which the rupture is attended to, and the client's feelings empathized with, combined with the absence of defensive responses (blame, justify, defend, etc.) from the therapist may well be a deeply healing experience for the client.

There are many ways ruptures can be attended to and repaired. I offer a few examples of the process of rupture repair below.

Exploring relational affective significance of rupture

The current transactions that triggered the rupture need to be identified and explored. The nature and process of the rupture, together with the client's emotional experience of the rupture, needs to be accounted for and explored. It is worth enquiring whether the relational and affective experience of the rupture is in any way familiar for the client. For example, a client who does not complete 'homework' assignments may have a sensitivity to feeling dominated, or may fear criticism (and out of awareness, invite criticism) or a reluctant client may evoke an intrusive, 'digging' response from their therapist, which in turn provokes further withdrawal and resistance. A rupture around a misattuned response from the therapist may lead the client into an exploration of their experience of being repeatedly misunderstood, or a therapist feeling cautious around a client's anger and being willing to share and discuss their sense of cautiousness may result in the client exploring how others experience them as angry and avoid contact with them. Exploring the relational significance of the rupture can help the client gain insight into their relational patterns and how they are enacted in the therapy.

Changing direction to prevent further rupture

Sometimes as therapists we realize that a particular approach or line of conversation is 'off limits'. Perhaps the client has begun to get defensive or irritable with the therapist. Sometimes the best thing to do in these situations is to leave the particular topic and change conversational direction. The direction can be explicitly changed through stating a change in the therapist's direction, recontracting and negotiating with the client to pursue a different topic of discussion or can be done discreetly and without raising the matter. The therapist will need to reflect after the session as to whether to reintroduce the 'off limits' discussion at a later date or not. By being sensitive to a client's receptivity to a particular line of conversation the therapist demonstrates respect for the client.

Owning mistakes and taking responsibility for miscommunications

Sometimes, our clients misinterpret our intention or rationale behind a particular transaction. Reactions can be quite intense at these times, for both therapist and client. It is absolutely crucial that at these times the therapist seeks to maintain as non-defensive a position as is possible and has the humility to admit mistakes. As part of this, the therapist owns and acknowledges their part in any misunderstanding, by acknowledging that their communication was in this case not clear or effective. It is important that the client does not feel blamed or stupid for misunderstanding. Exploration of how the client came to their conclusions can also be productive in exploring his or her construal systems. Where a therapist has misinterpreted or mis-understood the client's meaning, it is wise for the therapist to simply apologize for misunderstanding. In the case where the misunderstanding is particularly significant and upsetting for the client, the therapist is advised to seek to empathically under-stand the feelings the client is experiencing in relation to feeling misunderstood. Often in relationships, individuals seek to blame each other for misunderstandings. By taking a non-defensive position, the therapist provides the client with a new, healing and healthy model for relating.

26

Important TA concepts relating to transference and countertransference

Transference is an important concept in psychotherapy, as well as everyday life. It colours all of our interactions. It is how we relate to others in our present life as if they were figures from our past. In relating, we draw upon a vast internal repository of relational experiences and interactions with others. The quality of these interactions is recorded, together with an expected response of the other, a longed-for response of the other, and a particular outcome of how we end up feeling or experiencing ourselves. In the therapy relationship, transference takes on a special emphasis as the past gets replayed in the present with the therapist, making it available for healing. TA has a range of concepts that we can use to understand transference, and the manifestation of transference. Typically, TA takes complex concepts and presents them in ways that are simple to understand. Below I describe how some basic TA concepts relate to transference, to assist those new to understanding and working with transference.

Social diagnosis

The TA concept of social diagnosis (Berne, 1961) provides the therapist with a rudimentary framework for beginning to think about transference and countertransference. The therapist needs to pay attention to their own internal flow and their own ego state shifts on a moment-to-moment basis in the room with their client. This is a complex task, and one which is being constantly refined through attention to ongoing personal development and ever-deepening analysis of one's own ego states. Attention to our phenomenological flow in the room may provide the therapist with useful indicators as to their client's internal process.

In developing our use of social diagnosis as an accurate method of diagnosis we need to spend time reflecting upon our client and checking for the significance of our shifts from the perspective of our own history. 'Who in my history does this client remind me of?' or 'What aspects of this client resonate for me, and which person in my history shares similar aspects?' It is very likely that the client will indeed share features with significant people from our past – in terms of how they look, how they speak, even their posture and gestures. This also includes personality traits and emotional presentation. We also may not be fully conscious of this information as we may be aware of resonance only through our implicit memory system. The therapist is advised to spend time thinking about this in relation to each client, and also exploring this further in supervision and personal therapy.

Transactions

Berne (1972) used analysis of transactions to understand transference reactions. Berne identified crossed transactions, whereby one person transacts Adult to Adult, and the response which comes back is, for example, a Child to Parent transaction or alternatively, a response which is a Parent to Child transaction, the former being the most common form of transferential response. In response to a transactional stimulus some internal event takes place, and some feature of the stimulus resonates unconsciously and a shift of ego states takes place. The process of resonance with the past and the accompanying shift of ego states is a form of transference. Transference may not be so apparent or obvious for basic analysis of transactions and is often better understood transactionally through analysis of ulterior transactions. In ulterior transactions there are two levels of communication: the social-level transaction; and the psychological-level transaction. In practice, transference tends to operate at this psychological level. Reflection upon a therapy session and the types of ulterior transactions taking place can give the therapist a rich sense of the transference and its manifestations in the therapeutic relationship.

Rubberbands

Rubberbanding (Kupfer and Haimowitz, 1971) is another evocative phrase to describe how certain situations lead us to 'respond at times as though we had been catapulted back to early childhood scenes' (Stewart and Joines, 1987: 111). This rubberbanding is a transferential response. Learning about our ego state shifts gives us information about our own patterns of rubberbanding, and we may be able to identify triggers and features over time. TA therapy involves the recognition of rubberbanding, the identification of the triggers and the gradual healing of the original scenes we rubberband back to.

Sweatshirts

Berne (1972), in his ever creative manner, encouraged therapists to imagine that their clients had imaginary sweatshirts on, each bearing a slogan relating to the client's unconscious presentation to the world (the slogan on the front of the sweatshirt) and the client's script payoff, or required outcome (the slogan on the back of the sweatshirt). Berne believed that these operate out of awareness, possibly at an unconscious level, and that our unconscious will intuitively identify and respond to the slogans on both the front and back of the sweatshirts the people we meet are 'wearing'. How we react to these depends of course on our own script.

Games

Games are transferential phenomena. Individuals issue game invitations to repeat the past in some way. The 'gimmicks', or vulnerabilities (Berne, 1972), that trigger the response to the game invitation are also based on an individual's script. The interaction of these two transactions and the various moves of the game are all connected with transference and represent some unconscious desire to repeat the past. Games also include elements of projective identification (a form of transferential phenomenon) as the projector will behave and relate to the recipient of their projections in ways which provoke, or invite the recipient to act out the sought-out response (Woods 1996). This in turn reinforces the script and does not 'heal' the original issue, which will come back to haunt again and again. Understanding games provides the transactional analyst with a useful way of understanding transference interactions and enactments.

Hot potato

The 'hot potato' is a transgenerational script mechanism (English, 1969). It relies on a form of projective identification whereby the parent 'ejects' some unconscious conflict or script outcome, which the child internalizes and accepts to live out, on behalf of the parent. Many psychoanalytic writers believe that at some unconscious level, the child, being the focus of the parent's aspirations and unconscious longings, also becomes their psychological repository for the parent's unconscious conflicts.

27

The drama triangle as a tool to explore countertransference

The drama triangle (Karpman, 1968) is a widely used piece of TA theory that is easily grasped and readily applied in understanding and analysing games. The drama triangle describes three psychological roles that people adopt in the course of their games. The roles are: *Persecutor, Rescuer* and *Victim*. The words are capitalized to draw a distinction between a 'real life' rescuer, persecutor and victim, for example in the case of a person who has slipped into the water and is drowning and who gets pulled from the water; the person who was drowning would be a 'real-life victim' and their saviour would be a 'real-life rescuer'. Similarly, a mugger would be a real-life persecutor (although they would probably also be a psychological Persecutor!).

Berne understood and described games as transference phenomena (Berne, 1964). As the drama triangle is a method of game analysis, the drama triangle can be used in identification and analysis of the transference and countertransference dynamics aspects of the therapeutic relationship. Using the drama triangle to analyse the transference/countertransference provides the therapist with a simple but rapid method of exploring the subtle relationship dynamics unfolding in the therapy. At the simplest level, the therapist pays attention to their urges, or impulses with regard to which of the drama triangle positions they want to take up with their client at any given point. Noticing which position we want to take up in relation to the client is useful in beginning to explore our countertransference.

Countertransference never exists in isolation, and is usually woven up with the client's transference. Analysis of the therapist's drama triangle countertransference may well shed some light on the position the client is taking. It may be that this is characteristic of the client's way of relating; however, it will also have features which are unique, and which are being co-created by the therapist and client at this particular time. They may also relate to the therapist proactively projecting some aspect of their own script into the relationship.

One means of analysing the therapist's reactions is to explore whether we are adopting a *complementary* role to the client, for example, a desire to Rescue in response to the client adopting a Victim stance, or they may be *concordant* and represent the therapist identifying with and resonating at some level with some aspect of the client's psyche, for example by feeling like a victim in the same way the client did as a child (Racker, 1968; Clarkson, 1992). Generally, positions on the drama triangle are not static, and at some point in the process of a game, a switch of roles occurs. It is important that the therapist notices their own internal shift in relation to the drama triangle positions.

This, of course, presupposes that the therapist has a great deal of awareness of their own particular configuration of experiences, feelings, impulses and behaviours in relation to each of the drama triangle positions. The overwhelming majority of therapists are drawn to the profession by their tendency to Rescue, therefore identification of being drawn into a Rescuer position is not difficult for most therapists, but still needs careful attention paying to the textural differences between its different manifestations. Many therapists are also familiar with the Victim position, and can offer a great deal of understanding to the plight of others in this position. What is not so comfortable is exploring our tendencies towards Persecuting, and the many guises, variations and subtle differences between our differing Persecutory behaviours. It is prudent for the therapist to spend a great deal of time systematically gaining more information on their own particular brand of drama triangle manifestations, from each of the positions, and particularly to explore these in therapy. Group therapy is especially powerful at generating situations where we can explore our own tendencies. As we develop and change in terms of our sophistication, so do our games, and our manifestations of our games, and the therapist is therefore advised to periodically review and update their understanding of their drama triangle manifestations, and to undertake personal therapy. This self-awareness gives the therapist a greater understanding of the subtlety of their countertransference responses, which in turn can shed light on their client's transference and unconscious process, and also the client's patterns of relating to others.

28

Transference and countertransference: an *aide-mémoir* of TA models

There are essentially two aspects to transference: the *needed relationship* and the *repeated relationship*. All taxomomies of transference are ultimately differing ways of conceptualizing these two dimensions. The needed relationship relates to the client's (unconscious) desire to meet historical needs, and can be viewed from a humanistic perspective as being driven by the client's striving towards health; the client's urge to obtain the needed relationship experience which will 'heal' her script. The repeated relationship refers to the client's (unconscious) urge to repeat the original scenario, which is usually one that mirrors the client's early experiences with their caregivers/ parents. One perspective on this is that this repetition seeks to 'do it right' at last, and gain mastery over the original traumatic scenario.

Clarkson (1992), developing the material of Racker (1968), discusses two types of countertransference: complementary and concordant countertransference. Complementary counter-transference involves the therapist being 'recruited' to take a complementary role in the client's script, usually by taking on the projected experience of the client's Parent. The therapist experiencing complementary countertransference may find he feels subtly critical of his client or that he is distracted in sessions and is not paying attention to his client or taking her seriously.

With concordant countertransference, the client is somehow communicating to the therapist some aspect of her Child experience that the therapist resonates with in some way. The therapist experiences first hand the feelings the client felt as a child. This can be a deeply unsettling and disturbing experience. For example, in working with a client who was abused in childhood, the therapist may find in sessions she is left feeling powerless and despairing and filled with desires to make it all

OK for her client. She may be left questioning her self, and feeling inadequate. If understood as concordant countertransference, the therapist can be seen in this situation as taking on board, and understanding at a profound level, some important aspects of the client's internal experience.

Clarkson also discusses two additional types of countertransference: reactive countertransference and proactive countertransference. Reactive countertransference is where the therapist is reacting to the client's transferential material. Proactive countertransference is considered to originate in the therapist, and the therapist's transference towards the client. The relational approach to therapy considers that understanding countertransference includes examining both proactive (related to the therapist's own vulnerabilities and script) and reactive (reacting to the client's material) countertransference, and how the two interact. Countertransference is considered to be an interactive, co-constructed story that inevitably includes both proactive and reactive elements.

Moiso (1985) also developed TA thinking around transference by linking types of transference to the structural model of ego states. He categorized transference into P2 transferences, which are a relatively straightforward projection of the Parent onto the other, and P1 transferences, which involve the projection of earlier, more primitive, split (all good or all bad) Parent ego states onto the other. Hargaden and Sills (2002) developed Moiso's thinking and identified three types of transference: introjective, projective and transformational. Introjective transferences are deep relational longings, held and originating in the C0 ego state. They integrate Kohut's (1984) selfobject transferences of mirroring, idealizing and twinship as the varieties of introjective transference needs. Introjective transference is a variety of the therapeutically needed relationship. Introjective transference is considered to be always present, although it may be hidden by projective or transformational transferences as it relates to the emotional nourishment the client takes from therapy throughout (C. Sills, 2 May 2008, relational TA forum).

Projective transferences originate in the P1 ego state. They are defensive and splitting transferences. The projective transferences are aspects of the repeated relationship, whereby the client recapitulates aspects of the primary relational experience in the therapy in order to gain mastery over their unconscious process. For example experiencing the therapist as either hated or hateful or, conversely, as an object of idealization. The projection reduces their internal tension and can be seen as an attempt to re-work their early introjects.

Transformational transferences may originate from either the C1 or P0 ego states. They involve the projection of primitive affect *into* the therapist for the therapist to metabolize, process, detoxify and eventually, to re-present the experience back to the client in a form the client can assimilate. This is usually discussed as projective identification.

The approach to working with the transference varies, and is dependent upon careful diagnosis of the client's level of internal organization (McWilliams, 1994). More disturbed clients may need greater levels of disclosure and transparency from the therapist, to contrast with their projections. As clients with more severe problems often experience projections in global terms, it is important that these projections and distortions be corrected. Clients with higher levels of functioning may need the therapist to be more opaque so that their projective distortions emerge and become apparent and thus are able to be worked with in the therapy.

29

Ending TA therapy

Effective and therapeutic endings are a central part of the therapeutic journey, and need to be given due acknowledgement as an important part of the therapy process. The psychotherapy relationship is peculiar among relationships in that the ending of the relationship is at the very least implicit from the start; clients come expecting that the therapy will be effective and they will move beyond it and eventually have no need for therapy, or the therapist. The contracting and goal-setting process at the beginning generates an initial idea of what the criteria for ending the relationship will be. Generally, people do not enter relationships that are as intense or important in their lives as the psychotherapy relationship with the expectation that they will end, and yet as therapists this is exactly what we do with every new client we meet. Berne (1966) identified three types of endings in therapy:

1   *Accidental.* Sometimes changes in a client's work patterns or circumstances mean that they are no longer able to attend therapy. This is an interesting category in that, although such changes do take place, there is always the possibility that such changes are not as pressing as they might seem, and may well represent some kind of unconscious process whereby the client is at some level seeking to avoid or withdraw from therapy obliquely. It is very difficult for the therapist to explore such unconscious acting out, particularly as the reasons given for such endings are often so plausible and reasonable. Needless to say, endings can be enforced accidentally and regardless of the cause of the accidental ending, the therapist needs to be attentive to ending as satisfactorily as possible under the circumstances.

2   *Resistant.* A resistant ending would be seen in a client who suddenly and unexplainably withdraws from therapy.

Sometimes excuses or 'reasons' (as in the acting-out process described above) are given for this that mean that a formal ending process cannot take place.

3   *Therapeutic*. Obviously the most desirable type of ending is the therapeutic ending which 'occurs when the therapist and patient agree that the planned therapeutic goals have been attained, and that either an interruption or a final termination is in order' (Berne, 1966: 13).

Tudor (1995) adds a fourth type of ending: *enforced*. An example of an enforced ending might be where a therapist closes their practice, for instance when relocating to another city. Enforced endings can be very difficult to manage and must be done sensitively, and with due regard to the client's issues (for example 'abandonment wounds'). To some extent, enforced endings are likely to be difficult for therapists to manage in a maximally therapeutic way. The ethical therapist is wise to do all they can to conduct the ending in a way that minimizes reinforcement of the client's script wherever possible, although even with the best will in the world, a script-reinforcing ending may occur.

The ending process can also facilitate the surfacing of a range of issues that have not previously emerged in the therapy. Such issues need to be recognized and dealt with to enhance the ending as a significant part of the whole therapy. Clarkson (2003) offers some common client reactions to the ending of therapy. In summary, these themes that may require working through include: satisfaction and achievement; guilt and regrets; anger and disappointments; sadness and nostalgia; fear and trepidation; envy and gratitude; relief and release; anticipation; past losses; recycling; existential; archetypal (Clarkson, 2003). Working through these, or similar issues as they present in the final stages of the therapy will add to the value of the therapy, and provide for a more complete therapy process providing that in the ending process script issues are not inadvertently reinforced.

The ending may invite the client to reflect upon and evoke feelings related to past losses as part of the ending process and the therapist and client may wish to compare and contrast the current ending with these previous ones. It is important that wherever such reminiscing occurs the client is given the opportunity to explore their feelings as fully as time permits. Existential themes may well also emerge in the ending phase particularly those related to the four existential givens (Yalom, 1980) (see Point 99). Ending and grieving is not a one-off event and the ending of therapy will likely need revisiting many times in the course of the ending phase. The therapy, especially if it has been a long therapy, will require a period of mourning, so both client and therapist can end the relationship in a mutually satisfying, growthful way (Maroda, 1994).

Part 3

DIAGNOSIS

30

The importance of observation

> Observation is the basis of all good clinical work, and takes precedence even over technique.
>
> (Berne, 1966: 65–6)

All diagnosis begins with observation. Without observation the therapist cannot make any kind of diagnosis. Indeed, observation forms the backdrop for all interventions and treatment planning. Observation is more complex than simply noticing facets of the client's behaviour. It involves detailed observation of both self and the client and the maintenance of a curious, enquiring stance in relation to what we observe.

'The therapist should be aware of the probable physiological state of every one of his patients during every moment of the session' (Berne, 1966: 66). Although this is a rather unrealistic expectation of the therapist, the essence of what Berne appears to be saying here is that the therapist needs to develop their observational skills, going beyond the purely obvious, and to maintain this throughout therapy. Observation includes being sensitive to the client's facial expressions and fluctuations in facial muscular tone, facial colouring, gestures (even absent gestures), and wondering about the significance of these. The therapist needs to observe even minute changes on a moment-to-moment basis and maintain an attitude of curiosity about what these changes might indicate about each client's internal state. Listening forms a central part of the observational process in psychotherapy. The therapist is not just listening to the content of what the client is saying, but also to the words used, vocabulary, metaphors, sentence structure, breathing sounds, pitch, tone and rhythm (Berne, 1966, 1972). Beyond this the therapist is also listening to the client's process behind the words and the way they speak; is the client's language, for example, descriptive, evocative, brief, flat, precise, disjointed, or over-detailed? Observing and checking for inconsistency or incongruity between a client's words and their body language, or even how they say what they say is an important skill for TA therapists (Stewart, 2007) and can suggest the presence of areas of conflict which can then be sensitively brought into the therapy for discussion. Berne, however, cautioned against a 'navel gazing' approach to observation, and gave transactional analysts a clear instruction not to be complacent about the complex nature of communication when he said 'The therapist should not be beguiled by the currently fashionable talk about nonverbal communication into forgetting the fact that it will take years of study for him to master the subtleties of verbal communication' (Berne, 1966: 71).

It can be very fruitful for a therapist to sensitively share their observations, and their 'wonderings' about their observations. This is done in a spirit of curiosity and collaborative dialogue, to engage the client in the process of learning about their own mental states. Such an actively curious enquiring approach enhances both the therapist's and the client's capacity for mentalization (Bateman and Fonagy, 2006). To a transactional analyst, everything is important. Even seemingly insignificant details and ways the client presents or expresses their self are important (Erskine *et al.*, 1999). The same authors also highlight the importance of the therapist avoiding the temptation of making presuppositions about the client's experience, and suggest the therapist adopts a tentative stance in their inferences.

Berne invited transactional analysts to sensitively and unobtrusively find opportunities to observe people of all ages engaging in natural social interaction. Berne did not advise making inferences on the basis of these observations, but to simply note what behaviours the individuals engaged in, and what happened next. Such observation can reveal information about age-appropriate behaviours, which can be helpful in making behavioural diagnosis about an individual's ego states.

Observation should not be just of the client though – the therapist should pay close attention to observing themselves, their own internal state, their feelings, memories and thoughts that are evoked in the therapy and by the client when thinking about their client outside therapy sessions. Observation of one's own internal state is particularly useful in developing social diagnosis of the client, and in monitoring your counter-transference and analysing its significance (Novellino, 1984; Lammers, 1992; Hargaden and Sills, 2002; Widdowson, 2008).

Transactional analysts in the UK seeking certification as a transactional analyst and registration with the UK Council for Psychotherapy (UKCP) are required to undergo a mental health familiarization placement. An important part of this placement involves having an opportunity to sensitively observe people with a range of mental health problems. The placement can help the therapist develop skills in noticing what mental health professionals are looking for in determining severity of the client's problems. The placement can also help the therapist gain insight into what it is like having a range of mental disorders, including the cognitive and affective symptoms of various disorders. Taking time to find out what being a service user within mental health services is really like can be an eye-opening, and sometimes distressing experience. It is one that nevertheless is important for a therapist, who can then use this learning to increase their empathy towards clients who use such services. The insights from the placement can be especially important for lay people with no previous background in mental health.

From the therapist's observations, they begin to form tentative inferences about the client. The therapist then uses these tentative inferences to inform their next stage of diagnosis.

31

Intake assessment and case formulation

Developing a clear and thorough picture of the client is an essential part of the initial stages of any psychotherapy. The therapist needs to build up their picture of the client over the first few sessions. It is important to strike a good balance between letting the client tell their story, and 'offload' to some extent (for a number of clients, this will be the first time they have discussed many of their issues) and obtaining information that is useful in developing your case formulation, which includes your diagnosis and treatment plan for your client. I offer here areas of consideration that may be helpful to focus on to help develop a clear and thorough case formulation. Compiling a clear case formulation can also provide practitioners with an effective framework to present clients in supervision, and can be helpful also in determining cases where the therapist needs to refer the client on to another professional. These areas for reflection may suggest structural and dynamic (inter)relationships to self, others and the world and will help with accounting for the unique context and presentation of your client.

1   *Demographics.* Client age, gender, current living situation/ relationship, type of job (if relevant). Can also include information on the client's current class and the class they grew up in. It is important to account for the client's race, sexual orientation and any disability.
    Note: when presenting in supervision, it is worth obscuring some details to enhance the client's anonymity.

2   *Symptoms and presenting problems.* How does the client define the problem that brings them to therapy? What symptoms does the client experience? How can these symptoms be understood and categorized using a descriptive diagnostic system, such as Diagnostic and Statistical Manual

of Mental Disorder (DSM–IV–TR) diagnostic criteria (American Psychiatric Association, 2000)?

3   *Impression of presentation.* How did the client come into the room? How did they start? How did the client tell their story? Over-detailed? Impressionistic? Vague? What were the client's gestures? Was the client smartly dressed? Did the client appear not to be taking care over their appearance?

4   *Problem severity.* Is the problem mild, moderate or severe? To what extent is the client's overall functioning impaired? Is impairment limited to specific areas of the client's life?

5   *Precipitating factors.* What has brought the client to therapy right now? Were there any specific events or circumstances that led to the client's current problems or did the problems develop gradually, over a period of time?

6   *Psychiatric history/previous therapy.* Is the client currently on medication for mental health problems? Do they have a psychiatrist or have they seen a psychiatrist? Have they had any previous therapy or counselling? What was their experience of the previous therapy? What was helpful and what wasn't?

7   *Childhood.* How does the client describe their childhood? Was there any significant trauma or abuse? Was there cumulative trauma of repeated misattunement (Erskine *et al.*, 1999)? What is their historical view of their parents and their current view of their parents and the parenting they received?

8   *Adolescence.* What was adolescence like for your client? What were their social relationships like? What was school like for them? What about early sexual relationships? Was there any teenage rebellion?

9   *Past adult stressors.* This includes significant events, recent and also through the client's adult life. The impact of stress upon adults is well documented, and can indicate the degree of external stress the client faces which needs to be accounted for, and possibly may require work focused around adjustment. Repetitive patterns of stressors, or stressors which share similar features (for example acrimonious relationship breakups) can give important information regarding the client's games and script and script beliefs.

10 *Coping style, defence mechanisms and behaviours.* How does the client respond to stressful situations? What are their main coping strategies? Are these effective or appropriate? What defence mechanisms (for example: denial, splitting, projection, dissociation, etc.) (McWilliams, 1994) does the client exhibit? Are these mechanisms emblematic of any particular disorder or structure?

11 *Mental state.* Did the client seem focused or were they easily distracted and confused? Was there any agitation? Is there a slowness or a flight of thought? Is there a flatness of mood, or extreme emotional lability? Does the client appear to be 'psychologically minded' (this includes the client's self-awareness, capacity for reflection, insight, ability to understand problems as having a psychological or unconscious origin and capacity to consider the impact of the past on present problems)?

12 *Attachment style.* What is your impression of the client's attachment style? Secure, avoidant, ambivalent or disorganized? What do you use for evidence of this? What do you imagine the impact of this will be on the development of the working alliance? How does this impact upon your treatment planning and approach to therapy with this client?

13 *Obstacles to therapy.* What do you anticipate problems in therapy to be? Are there features of the client's presentation or perspective that may pose problems in the therapy process? What are the client's expectations of therapy and the role of the therapist? What is the client's expectation regarding length of therapy, and their engagement in the process? Are there external factors that may interfere with the therapy?

14 *Strengths and resources.* What strengths does the client have? What resources do they have that will be useful in the change process? This can include friends and family relationships, personal qualities, level of insight, and may also include additional factors, such as a client's economic situation (which can mean greater opportunities for change potentially available to the client). What personal qualities or perspectives does the client have that will be useful in therapy or in effecting change in their life?

15 *Motivation for therapy.* Does the client appear to be well motivated for therapy? Is the client being coerced or pushed into therapy by someone else?

16 *Transference and countertransference.* What is your impression of the transference and countertransference? How did the client feel towards you? How did they experience you? What role did they want to cast you in? What is your impression of what the client was trying to get you to do? What were your feelings towards this client, and what experiences made up your flow of feelings within the session? What engaged you? What disengaged you? What about this client disconcerts you, or attracts you?

17 *Prognosis.* What is your conclusion regarding the expected length and frequency of therapy? Does this match with the client's expectations? What do you imagine the client's problem severity will be at the end of therapy?

32

Assessing suitability for TA therapy

Limitations of the practitioner

Recognition of the limitations of one's training and experience is important in determining whether we should take on a particular client. It goes without saying that we should not work with clients who we do not have the skills or knowledge to work with effectively. The issue is where do we draw the line? We have to gain experience at some point, and sometimes it may not be apparent at the outset that we do not have the required skills or knowledge to work with someone. In this instance the primary determining factor has to be the principle of protection; is there sufficient safety to work with this client, at this time? If we cannot provide sufficient safety we must refer the client on appropriately. If in the course of working with someone the therapist discovers issues or problems they are unfamiliar in working with, it is important that the therapist seeks supervisory advice and makes serious attempts to extend their knowledge in the particular area, through reading and attending relevant workshops. To some extent therapists who regularly engage in a wide range of reading around different presenting issues will be in a better position to judge than those who do not.

Resources

Do you have the resources to work with this client at this time? It is not advisable to take on new clients who present in intense distress if you have a lot of holiday time coming up, or if you do not have the space in your diary to see them at least once a week. In deciding whether to take on a client, I ask myself whether I have *two* spaces free in my diary, to deal with the possibility that the client may need twice-weekly sessions. Unless you have specialist training, and immediate access to necessary medical back-up, generally therapists will not have the resources to work with someone presenting with drug or alcohol addiction until the client has completed a medically supervised withdrawal and detoxification programme.

Limitations of available service

Are there limitations in terms of the service the client can access? Therapists who work for agencies sometimes have to work with the constraints of maximum numbers of sessions, which can range from six to twenty sessions. In this case, it is important that the therapist be realistic regarding what change is possible for the client in such limited circumstances. Sometimes clients presenting in private practice also have limitations to their resources, and so may not be able to afford to come for weekly therapy. In general if a client is not able to afford to come weekly for at least three months, then it is perhaps better to refer the client on to a low-cost or free counselling service.

Psychological mindedness

Psychological mindedness refers to the individual's capacity for self-observation, self-reflection and a capacity to consider psychological factors as being significant in one's problems and present situation as well as the possibility that unconscious psychological forces impact upon our motivation. This includes a capacity to consider one's past as being significant in relation to how one is in the present. In order to engage in therapy a degree of psychological mindedness needs to be present from the outset.

Available Adult ego state

In the initial sessions the therapist needs to make an assessment of the client's available Adult ego state. This assessment is by nature subjective and needs to take account of the client's presenting problem and whether the client appears to have the Adult resources needed to engage in therapy at the level required. Clients who appear to have little Adult ego state to the extent that functioning is seriously impaired may need referral for psychiatric evaluation and possibly medication before therapy can proceed safely. With clients with little Adult ego state available, the therapist needs to determine, in consultation with their supervisor, whether they have the skills and resources to help the client develop and strengthen their Adult ego state.

Ability to enter a contract

Can the client reasonably consent to therapy? Is the client being coerced or otherwise being persuaded to enter into therapy? Is the client in a position to make a reasonably informed choice about whether to enter therapy or not? Is the stated contract goal realistic? This includes attending to the client's level of motivation for change (Woollams and Brown, 1978).

33

Using Berne's four methods of diagnosis

Berne identified four methods of diagnosis needed for accurate diagnosis of ego states (Berne, 1961). Although in practice behavioural diagnosis is the most commonly used for initial diagnostic purposes, to form or verify an accurate diagnosis, all four methods must be used. These methods were originally developed for diagnosis of ego states, but can be adapted for a range of diagnostic purposes.

Behavioural diagnosis

Often, our initial behavioural diagnosis is based on our first impression of our client, which can begin from the client's first telephone call to the therapist, as well as the client's behaviour in the first session. In forming a behavioural diagnosis the therapist needs to maintain an open-minded position and keep any diagnostic hypotheses as tentative. By nature, behavioural diagnosis is often generalized in that we make an inference about the ego state someone is 'in' based on generalized assumptions on how children or parents behave, for example. Due to the relatively universal way that both children and parents behave, and the experience we all have with children and parents in general, behavioural diagnosis can be somewhat reliable. Behavioural diagnosis may also include the therapist referring to child development theory in considering the developmental stage of presenting Child ego states in terms of how the displayed behaviour would be age appropriate for a particular age group. It is important, however, that behavioural diagnosis is not based simply on one behavioural clue, but is made up from detailed observation and behaviour clusters which together show a consistent pattern. Once an initial behavioural diagnosis is made, it is worth asking yourself 'What is your evidence for your conclusion? Would this diagnosis or hypothesis sound plausible to others?'

Social diagnosis

Social diagnosis is used when we draw upon our own reactions to a person, and notice our own ego state response to the individual to inform our diagnosis of the individual's ego state. Social diagnosis in therapy involves use of the therapist's countertransference. The use of the therapist's countertransference can add a degree of potency to the social diagnosis; however, the degree of self-awareness of the therapist making the diagnosis is absolutely critical. To effectively use one's own responses one has to have a good degree of understanding about the meaning of one's own responses and own shifts in ego states as well as having the ability to pay attention to one's own internal experience on a moment-to-moment basis. These responses must be acknowledged and reflected upon, rather than being immediately acted out. Some questions the practitioner can reflect upon include: 'What is my internal reaction to this person? What ego state do I go into? How do I want to respond to them? Would others have a similar reaction to the same stimulus?'

Historical diagnosis

In historical diagnosis we find out the historical significance of the behaviour, thought patterns or feeling(s). The therapist builds a picture of the historical diagnosis through the usual conversational flow of psychotherapy, but can establish or verify a historical diagnosis by asking 'Did you or anyone else do this in the past? Does this remind you of anyone or anything?' Such questioning can reveal sometimes surprising data, in that behaviour we had considered to be Child, is in fact Parent, which is established by a client for example describing how one of their parents, who was often in a Child ego state used the same behaviour. Similarly, behaviour we think of as Parent can in actual fact be Child in the case of people who were overly responsible, or even 'parentified' as children. Historical diagnosis also needs to be tentative, as it is possible that the client may not have certain information, or not be able to remember certain things in order to verify the historical diagnosis.

Phenomenological diagnosis

Phenomenological diagnosis is the subjective experience of an individual as being in a particular ego state *as if it was happening now*. This is most easily recognized with Child ego state, as we can all remember to some extent how we were and how we felt as children. Getting a subjective sense of what it felt like for one of our parents is more difficult, in that we have no way of knowing exactly how the individual was feeling at any one time, although we can have an intuitive sense that how we are feeling is *probably* how a particular parent felt in a particular situation. Phenomenological diagnosis also includes the transferential domain (Hargaden and Sills, 2002). In transference, the client is experiencing the therapist as if the therapist were in actual fact the transferential figure, although because of the unconscious nature of transference, the client may not be aware of the transference. Analysis of the transference can suggest the phenomenological diagnosis of a particular experience in that the client may be transferentially responding as they did as a child (complementary transference – seeking a complementary Parental response), or they may be responding as one of their parents did (concordant transference – seeking to replicate their parents or induce their child response in the other) (Clarkson, 1992). Clearly social diagnosis of the therapist's countertransference needs to be accounted for if diagnosis is made in this way.

Subjective, phenomenological diagnosis of Adult is also difficult in that most people would assume that most of the time they are in Adult ego state. This is complicated by the fact that when we are coming from a contaminated Adult ego state, by definition we are mistaking some Parent or Child content for Adult ego state. It is unfortunate, and perhaps a weakness in TA theory, that we form a diagnosis of the Adult by a process of elimination.

Diagnosis can also require the analysis and interpretation of vague, amorphous feeling, particularly when diagnosing early Child ego states (C1 or earlier structures). With such early Child ego states the client is unlikely to have a specific memory to verify historical diagnosis. At this level, diagnosis may be done using the therapist's knowledge of child development theory (behavioural diagnosis), the therapist's countertransference (responses to the client's use of primitive defences), and the client's affective, phenomenological experience that will probably be overwhelming, oceanic and unexplainable or 'irrational'. It is the nature of such experiencing which provides the phenomenological diagnosis, rather than being able to link it to a specific incident or period of life.

34

Applying the four methods of diagnosis

The four methods of diagnosis can be applied to a range of TA concepts, and not limited to ego state diagnosis. To illustrate how the four methods can be used to enhance our diagnoses, I use the example of the four methods applied to the diagnosis of injunctions.

In listening to our client, we may infer the presence of several injunctions from what he or she reports in relation to their situation and circumstances. The TA therapist is listening carefully to themes that emerge, which may indicate areas of experience and relating where the client feels somehow constricted. The client's behaviour provides us with clues we can use to develop a behavioural diagnosis of his or her script. For example, when a client presents with a restricted range of affective expression, we might behaviourally diagnose a 'don't feel' injunction (Goulding and Goulding, 1979). Similarly a client who reports a series of experiences whereby they gave up on projects such as courses right at the last minute can be behaviourally diagnosed with a 'don't succeed' injunction.

We may get a social diagnosis of our clients' injunction patterns by paying attention to our countertransference responses. It is important that we make space for and pay attention to our responses to our clients as they can yield enormous amounts of useful information. For example a client with a 'don't be important' injunction may be the client the therapist repeatedly 'forgets' to take to supervision, or who the therapist thinks to call first when they need to reschedule some work. The therapist may find themselves disconnected and lacking in vitality when working with a client with a 'don't feel' and a 'don't be close' injunction. Our urges may be ones that would seek to reinforce the injunction, or fight against it, and rescue the client. It is enormously valuable for the therapist to spend time carefully examining their range of responses to their clients, and not to take anything on face value without serious thought. Also relevant here is how others respond to the client – this could either be through observation in a group therapy context, or through careful attention to the client's stories about how others react to them.

Historical diagnosis of injunctions can be undertaken by inferential diagnosis from what the client reports of their life history, particularly their early experiences. For example it is widely viewed by transactional analysts that physical violence towards a child may result in the development of a 'don't exist' injunction (Stewart and Joines, 1987; Stewart, 2007). A client reporting being compared with other children or family members or being the less-favoured child in a family may be historically diagnosed as having a 'don't be you' injunction.

TA therapists often share their thoughts in relation to the client's injunction patterns with their client. Frequently clients appear rather shocked by this and confirm that they do in fact experience the injunctions internally. When this occurs, to some extent we can consider this to be a partial phenomenological diagnosis. However, phenomenological diagnosis is not just checking out the hypotheses about the injunctions with the client and asking for confirmation, but includes checking out how the client is experiencing the injunction *in the moment, in the therapy room.* As injunctions are generally considered to be pre-verbal and implicit messages, the client may well struggle immensely to verbalize the injunction, so it is the therapist's job to interpret the present difficulty, and sensitively, tentatively, and subtly check out their diagnosis with the client. If the client confirms the nature of their internal experience in a manner which is congruent with the particular injunction then a phenomenological diagnosis is verified.

The four methods of diagnosis have wide application. To take the example of ego states, rather than the rather dubious practice of saying to a client 'Oh, you're in your Parent ego state', the therapist could say 'I'm noticing a change in you [behavioural diagnosis], and you feel tense and a bit impatient to me [social diagnosis]. I'm wondering if this is familiar, in terms of how you or someone else was in the past? [historical diagnosis], and I'm also wondering what it feels like inside for you?' (phenomenological diagnosis).

35

Developing a conversational interviewing technique

A number of TA authors have presented detailed script analysis questionnaires that they recommend therapists use with their clients in a structured way. The reality is that the overwhelming majority of TA therapists do not do script analysis in such a structured format. I advise therapists *not* to follow formal, structured methods of script analysis, but rather encourage therapists to draw the information out in a more conversational and informal manner (Cornell, 1986). I am not advocating the total abolition of script questionnaires, but rather that the therapist takes a different approach to the information gathering needed for script analysis. Although some clients appreciate the formality and structure of the use of formal script questionnaire interviews, a large number of clients seem to find them an obstruction to the work, a hiatus in the flow of the therapy, and an uncomfortable formality which changes the balance of power in the therapeutic relationship, often at a time when they were beginning to feel more comfortable with their therapist.

One risk in using structured models, such as script questionnaires, is that the client's process can be obscured – the way the client tells their story, the consistencies, inconsistencies, jumping around from one area to another, aspects they focus on and aspects they minimize or discount, fractured or incoherent narrative (Holmes, 2001; Allen and Allen, 1995) all tell a story about the client. This includes the client's attachment style (Holmes, 2001), the client's level of developmental organization (McWilliams, 1994), their internal process and way of experiencing that world, which can be lost if the therapist is using a prescriptive and formal script questionnaire method. Using script questionnaires can also be a profoundly threatening and misattuned approach in working with clients with personality disorders/disorders of the self, who lack the necessary identity integration to be able to respond usefully. Such an approach with these clients may be experienced as so threatening as to provoke a hostile defensive reaction (McWilliams, 1994). One critique of traditional interview methods is that they can have a 'static' quality to them, in that the therapist uses them to gain information in one sitting, and then uses that to formulate their diagnosis of the client at a time when they still have only a limited amount of experience of their client. Working in a fluid, conversational manner means the therapist can gather information while still allowing the client to tell their story in their own way. The therapist can provide ongoing empathic responses to provide the client with the needed emotional support in the early stages of therapy that will help build the therapeutic alliance.

I suggest here an alternative approach to gaining information required for script analysis that has the net effect of gaining the same information, but done in a more 'attuned manner' which is in keeping with a natural, conversational flow. First the therapist needs to think about what information they are seeking to obtain. TA therapists are generally interested in developing some hypotheses about a client's injunctions, the kind of counterscript slogans they have internalized, their script themes in relationships, their overall script themes regarding their life course, their life position, the modelling and attributions they picked up from their environment while they were growing up. Take some time to think about which aspects of the script apparatus you are most interested in exploring with your client, and think about what such information will give you. What questions could you ask to find out this information? What information could the client volunteer for you to begin to formulate tentative hypotheses about these aspects of their script? What might you observe or experience in response to your client that might potentially shed some light on aspects of the client's script?

When you have started to formulate your own ideas about the above, then you can take some time to review established script questionnaires. Notice the questions that are asked, and what information the questions are designed to elicit, or what inferences might be drawn from the different answers. How might you adapt these questions to suit your own personal style of therapy and to find out the particular information you are interested in gathering?

My recommendation is that, rather than use these questions in a formal interview format, you embed them, or better still, embed your own versions of these questions into your work with your clients, and ask them as and when the therapeutic conversation naturally turns to that topic. For instance, a client discussing how they struggle with receiving praise might be asked how both their parents praised them, and for what. What is their internal process when they do get praised? Do they avoid praise? If so, how? The process of enquiry and of expansion, clarification and obtaining detail of the emotional and cognitive content in situations provides the therapist with adequate information to develop their script analysis and diagnosis for each client without the need for formal interview methods.

36

Being thorough in structural analysis

A transactional analysis diagnosis begins with structural analysis (Berne, 1961). In formulating a transactional analysis diagnosis of their client, the TA therapist makes observations and starts to make inferences about the content and process of the client's ego state structure. These inferences are checked using the four methods of ego state diagnosis for verification (see Point 33).

You may find it helpful to make some notes about the relative and apparent strength or predominance of each ego state, including different Child ego states with their different ages and also including different Parent introjects in your structural analysis. Which ego states are used most? How are these ego states used? Which are underused? Which Parental introjects seem most powerful or most virulent and toxic? What is notable by its absence? What is your subjective sense of the most commonly presenting Child ego state that manifests in the therapy room?

The content, affect and disturbances of each ego state category need to be accounted for. Second- and third-order structural models allow for refinement in developing a comprehensive structural analysis of each client (see Figure 36.1). I describe the process here primarily in terms of the second-order structural model; however, the therapist can use the same principles to refine the diagnosis into third-order structural levels. In the second-order Parent ego state, we analyse each Parent introject by dividing the introject into Parent, Adult and Child ego states. When we introject our Parent figures, we introject all of their ego states. If introjection is complete, then the parent is introjected with their structural conflicts (Clarkson, 1992). Thorough structural analysis accounts for the introjected pathology of each Parent ego state. The activation of a particular Parent introject can account for sudden, seemingly out of

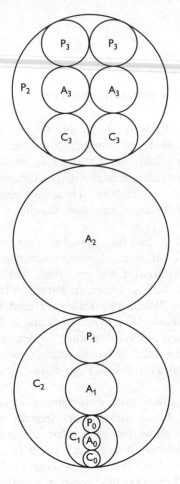

Figure 36.1 The third-order structural model (based on Berne, 1961)

character, changes that can take place sometimes within the therapy room. It is important that the therapist has a basic diagnosis of each Parent introject before working directly with the introject. This diagnosis can only ever be inferential and pure hypothesis (unless the therapist has the opportunity to meet and interview that client's parents directly). Such diagnosis needs to determine the depth and level of any pathology, plus potential risk factors in working directly with that ego state. For example, deliberately cathecting an abusive, violent or psychotic Parent ego state is generally not wise.

Note that Parent and Child both contain other ego states in a structural sense. What appears to be Child may be Child in the Parent, or what appears to be Adult ego state may be Adult in the Parent. Again, thorough diagnosis using all four of Berne's methods will reveal the likely ego state presented in the moment.

Thorough structural diagnosis needs to include different Child ego states according to age. Your client will experience and present qualitatively different Child ego states according to the age and developmental stage of the ego state cathected. This diagnostic process is often largely subjective, using social and phenomenological diagnosis primarily although it will also include historical diagnosis where the client has particular memories which are associated with the presenting ego state. Behavioural diagnosis is not entirely reliable here, as the client may be exhibiting ego states which did not use age-appropriate behaviours so social, historical and phenomenological diagnosis needs to be utilized to determine the age and developmental state of each presenting ego state.

The therapist may be aware of, or suspect that the client has excluded, or sequestered certain ego states. The exclusion or sequestering of ego states most commonly occurs within the Child ego state. These hidden ego states also need to be accounted for. This process of repression or dissociation may be so powerful within the client's structure that it is advised that the therapist be willing to consider the presence of such sequestered ego states, even if their presence is not immediately apparent.

37

Adding in ego state dialogue to develop dynamic structural analysis

When doing structural analysis it is helpful to consider what is the content and process of the client's internal dialogue. Adding such dialogue in the structural analysis will add a dynamic element that illustrates the script in action. Berne invited transactional analysts to account for this dialogue, which he described as 'voices in the head'.

> This dialogue between Parent, Adult and Child is not 'unconscious', but preconscious, which means that it can be easily brought into consciousness. . . . Once he understands what is going on, his next task is to give the patient permission to listen, and to teach her how to hear the voices which are still there in their pristine force from childhood. Here he may have to overcome several kinds of resistance. She may be forbidden to listen by Parental directives, such as: 'If you hear voices, you're crazy'. Her Child may be afraid of what she will hear. Or her Adult may prefer not to listen to the people governing her behaviour in order to maintain her illusion of autonomy . . . As a general rule, phrases in the second person ('You should have', etc.) come from the Parent, while those in the first person ('I must,' 'Why did I?' etc.) come from the Adult or Child. With some sort of encouragement, the patient soon becomes aware of his most important script directives as spoken in his head, and can report them to the therapist.
>
> (Berne, 1972: 369–70)

It is possible that a 'you' voice may originate from the Parent in the Child (P1 ego state) as a chastisement to an early (C1) Child ego state.

To facilitate awareness of the internal dialogue invite clients to notice their internal dialogue, over a period of a week or more, and to simply note it. This can be done by inviting clients to jot down in a note-pad examples of the mental dialogue they 'hear'. At this point, the client is not being asked to consciously change or challenge the nature of the dialogue, but simply to become aware of it. From the therapist's point of view, obtaining a fuller picture of the dialogue is helpful for diagnosis purposes. Some therapists are reluctant to invite such attention to the negative dialogue for fear of intensifying it. In my experience, this does not happen – the 'voices' are there already, and the content is already running through the client's head. Many subtle aspects of the dialogue from a variety of situations, and in interaction with a range of people, can be lost if not captured at the time. Inviting clients to keep a note-pad handy and write down the nature of the dialogue over a period of a few weeks will assist with increasing awareness of the dialogue in a range of situations. Analysis of the dialogue in terms of its historical origin ('Did anyone actually say this to you? If so, who?' or 'How did you come to such conclusions about yourself?') can also suggest possible sites within the client's ego structure where the particular part of the dialogue may be coming from. For example, is the critical dialogue coming from the Parent ego state (P2), or a more primitive, earlier Parent, such as the Parent in the Child (P1)? Becoming aware of such dialogue will allow the client's process to open up, move into awareness, and as such, become amenable to later intervention.

The therapist has several choices of how to intervene, largely dependent upon their own interests and approach. Cognitive-behavioural methods can be used, by directly challenging or questioning the dialogue, similar to the way cognitive therapists challenge negative automatic thoughts (NATS) (Beck and Beck, 1995). A more psychodynamic approach is to direct the client's attention to the nature of the dialogue and to experience the conflict consciously. The dialogue can be explored in terms of its historical origins and the relational wishes, responses of self and expected responses of others encoded within it. This dialogue can also be brought into the relationship by repeatedly inviting the client to become aware of the internal dialogue they experience in sessions and in relation to the therapist.

An additional refinement that can be useful is to make a note of the quality of interactions and means of interacting each of the client's parents used in relation to your client. These can then be included in the dialogue in your structural analysis diagram. For example, perhaps one parent ignored your client, whereas the other was often angry with them and blaming. This interaction will probably be repeated either intrapsychically or interpersonally in your client's current life, and your client may also anticipate such responses from you in therapy (Benjamin, 2003). Awareness of such interactions and inclusion of them in the diagnosis facilitates using any enactments therapeutically. Bary and Hufford (1990) highlight indicators for a client's readiness for ending psychotherapy. One indicator relevant here is that the client is ready for ending psychotherapy when 'She has an internal dialogue that nurtures and guides versus one that excuses or condemns' (Bary and Hufford, 1990: 220).

38

Accounting for cultural and religious parent

All development and all behaviour is culturally embedded and needs to be considered in relation to the culture in which the individual grows and lives.

(Tudor and Widdowson, 2008: 222)

In doing structural analysis of the Parent ego state and script analysis it is easy to focus exclusively on the client's parents, and the influence they had in the formation of the client's script, and to ignore the impact of cultural and religious Parent ego states. It is even easier to ignore these influences when they are identical to our own. Yet our environmental, social and cultural context plays a significant role in our script. Our cultural (and religious) introjects play an important part in our internal experience, and are mostly reinforced daily (certainly for those who are of the majority culture) in an implicit manner by dint of our being within a society and through our interactions with others. 'The dominant culture's wishes, demands, behaviour, and love are introjected through parental, family and community relationships and become part of the client's sense of self and personality' (Shadbolt, 2004: 120–1). All therapists can appreciate the powerful impact that having a quietly disapproving, or even an outright condemnatory parent would have on the self-esteem of a developing person, and yet it is all too easy to overlook the experiential fact that similar processes take place intrapsychically on an implicit and unconscious level. These processes are influenced by an introjected cultural Parent, and the interaction between this cultural Parent and our sense of self, our Child ego state. The feminist movement first drew our attention to gender scripting and the related gender-stereotyped cultural Parent, and the powerful but hidden impact that patriarchy has in shaping the self-esteem, the way of thinking and the expectations and behaviour of both women and men. The intrapsychic interaction between our cultural Parent and our own sense of self undoubtedly shapes our behaviour, our expectations, our way of thinking and our self-esteem. The components that interact include and go beyond our gender into our culture, our race, our sexuality and other factors which shape who we are.

Shivanath and Hiremath (2003) extend the concept of cultural scripting and develop a script matrix that accounts for cultural scripting factors. In their model they develop three layers of scripting: the scripting that occurs within the family; the individual's religious and cultural script; and the wider (predominantly white and heterosexual) cultural scripting. Cultural scripting is indirect, and insidious. It is the implicit messages and values all around us, that are constantly present and which inform the workings and values of institutions such as society, government, religious institutions and, of course, the media. For an example of this, recently the fashion industry has been criticized for using very underweight models in an attempt to raise awareness of the subtle influence such images have on young women regarding what is attractive, acceptable and desirable. This is taking place within a backdrop of media, which includes magazines which seem to focus on weight fluctuations among celebrities, and where weight gain is criticized and weight loss is envied. The socialization of the child also takes place in a wider social context, and in thinking about the individual we need to account for the powerful impact of peers, schooling, socialization and again the media they are exposed to. Peer relationships are enormously important to children and it is important to consider their contribution to the shaping of an individual's sense of self and self-esteem.

Religious aspects of a person's life also form part of an individual's Parent ego state, as religious figures, such as priests and ministers, as well as the religious institution, together with its own rules, code of conduct and beliefs all become powerful introjects. Many clients who have religious belief will 'need first for the therapist to demonstrate respect for his or her depth of conviction' (McWilliams, 1994: 18). Even people who have rejected religion are not exempt from its forces, and it is not unusual for people who had religious upbringings to be heavily influenced by them in adult life. Our sense of morality, our internal valuing processes, our ways of judging ourselves and our sense of personal ethics may all be deeply impacted by our own religious upbringing.

> As psychotherapists working with different cultures and communities, we need to work on both an intrapsychic level and at a level which addresses their cultural scripts. To ignore a person's cultural script, and the scripting from the wider white society, would be to deny the impact of culture, race and racism on their everyday lives.
>
> (Shivanath and Hiremath, 2003: 173)

Our cultural Parent also plays a part in how we feel about and experience our sexuality. As part of our socialization, we internalize messages about our gender, sexuality in general, and our own sexual orientation. Non-heterosexual people will have to deal with the impact of carrying a cultural Parent which is not affirming of their very being, and will need to deal with the oppressive introjects as part of their own movement towards greater self-acceptance. For people who are not part of the dominant culture (white, heterosexual, able-bodied, etc.), then it is highly probable that the person has in effect two cultural Parents: one of the dominant culture; and one from their own (sub)culture. Inevitably, the sub-cultural Parent will be hugely influenced by, and shaped in relation to the dominant one, but will nevertheless be different. Individuals who do not conform to either cultural Parent's expectation are likely to feel disaffected and alienated; an experience which needs to be attended to in the diagnostic process and not misdiagnosed as being an indicator of psychopathology. One example of this is how many women who choose not to have children are often made to feel that they are somehow strange or worse that there is something 'wrong' with them for their choice not to have children. There is a dominant cultural expectation that one should want to have children. Anyone who varies from this cultural expectation lives with the spectre of non-acceptance on a day-to-day level.

39

Accounting for oppression

In working with clients on issues related to belonging, the therapist needs to account for the very real ways in which the client may not belong. This process of accounting needs to begin with the therapist's own process. Stop reading right now and take a few moments to reflect upon the relative importance of issues of difference for clients, and the significance of your own cultural, ethnic and class background, your gender, sexuality, physical and intellectual ability, your economic status and how these factors shape your identity, your relationships and interactions and your sense of self.

It is important also to account for poverty and economic factors in the client's experience. Oppression related to poverty has a direct effect upon the resources available for change for a large number of people, and again, needs to be accounted for in the therapy. It is very difficult to think about deep personality change if you are hungry and have no heating or hot water at home.

Language patterns can also be symbols of oppression, which can be very relevant to clients from non-educated backgrounds who may be particularly sensitive to the therapist's (perceived) higher status and educated position. The use of overly complicated, wordy or formal language can be a subtle seduction for therapists who are keen to emphasize their credibility with the client or in the interests of presenting a professional persona or for therapists who feel the need to 'prove' themselves, perhaps driven by script issues related to not being taken seriously. A therapist who accounts for oppression will be mindful of the powerful impact their words can have on the client, and will sensitively, but not patronizingly, adapt their language to suit the client's own language style.

Oppression can also take subtle forms, particularly in relation to 'hidden' disabilities, including dyslexia (Lynch, 2007).

Undiagnosed or misunderstood dyslexia can result in the therapist attributing a 'don't think' injunction to their client who is very capable of thinking, but who needs a modified approach to access their thinking effectively. Incorrectly attributing non-completion of behavioural contracts as evidence of client resistance when in actual fact the instructions were presented in a manner that was not attuned to the dyslexic client's needs is oppressive. It is advisable for therapists working with clients who have dyslexia to engage their clients in a brief discussion about what the client may need from the therapist to help them process information optimally. There is considerable evidence now to suggest that those with dyslexia process information differently and finding ways of communicating effectively may require slight shifts on the part of the therapist. This may include pacing sessions differently, avoiding long and complex explanations (I would advocate avoiding long and overly complex explanations with all clients), use of visualization or multi-sensory approaches, utilizing 'active' methods such as two-chair techniques and so on. A similar approach, that is, asking the client for what they need is also appropriate with people with sensory impairments and disabilities (Lynch, 2007).

Sexual orientation is another arena where oppression operates. There is an implicit assumption within society that the 'normal' way of being is heterosexual, and that to be anything other than heterosexual is at best unfortunate, and at worst, sinful and profoundly evil. Shadbolt (2004) describes the toxic effects of introjected homophobia on gay people:

> It is not hard to understand how a core sense of self, however confident, will be conflicted and possibly eroded as it dawns on the individual that he or she is not a member of the majority heterosexual culture, not conventional and outside the norm intrapsychically. The person may have introjected . . . the sense that homosexuality is wrong, abnormal and culturally unacceptable.
>
> (Shadbolt, 2004: 116)

Certainly gay people have to live with the reality of daily prejudice and very real threats to their physical safety. Some feel that this threat can only be dealt with by living in a way that hides their true nature and so remain closeted. In this context, any acceptance or strokes can only ever be conditional and conditional on the basis of a continued collusion with this falsely portrayed image. Even what is presented as acceptance from heterosexual people who are aware of the individual's homosexuality is often only tolerance, and again, is sadly also often conditional. The pervasive messages the gay person internalizes from the wider society include 'don't exist', 'don't be you', and 'don't belong'.

In *What Do You Say After You Say Hello* Berne expanded on the concept of life positions to include 'three-handed positions' (Berne, 1972). In this lamentably short piece, he described how life positions move beyond the 'I'm OK (or not)' and 'you're OK (or not)' to include the extra position of 'they're OK (or not)'. Analysis of three-handed life positions can be useful in exploring an individual's experience and response to oppression, and can be used for wider social analysis of oppressive systems, and the different responses of oppressed groups of people to the oppression. Many marginalized groups, for example, develop an 'I'm OK – you're OK (because you're 'in') and they're not OK' position as a way of legitimizing their struggle and developing a sense of community and belonging in response to hostility from the outside world. This can also be true for members of the dominant majority, and is a position often seen in tabloid newspapers who take the political position of the newspaper and its readers as being 'OK', but whoever is considered to be the threat (immigrants, European government, gay people, etc.) as 'not OK'. This position effectively socially encourages the use of splitting mechanisms and the use of moralization as a defence mechanism (Gomez, 1997; Hargaden and Sills, 2002; McWilliams, 1994).

40

Levels of script: protocol and script proper

In transactional analysis we identify two main levels of script organization: the protocol and the script proper (Berne, 1972). These levels of script correspond to different orders of ego state structure (see Figure 36.1, page 136).

The word protocol in everyday language refers to a set of rules about how people interact. In transactional analysis terms, protocol refers to the implicit set of rules about how we interact with others, and how we expect them to respond to us that has been developed in infancy (Berne, 1972). The protocol includes our implicit memory systems. Protocol is the earliest level of script, and operates at an unconscious level. The hippocampus, a brain structure intrinsically related to our explicit, conscious memory, is not fully formed until around the age of three years, hence our inability to remember at a conscious level events prior to this neurological maturation. In these early, formative years, our brain is still developing. All stimuli are processed by the amygdala, a small almond-shaped structure, which is almost fully formed at birth, which processes all sensory stimuli adding an affective valence to the stimuli. The amygdala lays down critical emotional memories that operate beyond our conscious awareness. The orbito-frontal cortex, a part of the brain responsible for affective regulation, is also not fully formed until around the age of three. Stimuli experienced before the ability to regulate our emotional responses and self-soothe are all-consuming, and form overwhelming and unpleasant emotions, likely to be experienced by the developing infant as terrifying. In this early, pre-verbal stage of development key affective and relational patterns are being encoded and stored by the developing brain. Stern describes this process of development as the establishment of internal patterns known as *representations of interactions which are generalized* (RIGS) (Stern, 1985). Implicit and primary experiences of self and other coalesce into our life positions

(Berne, 1972) and our protocol – our most basic relational aspect of our script. The protocol can be considered to be script held at the third order of ego state structure.

After the age of around three, with the maturation of the hippocampus and memory centres in the brain and the development of capacity for language, the nature of scripting changes to develop the *script proper* (Berne, 1972). Script at this level is often pre-conscious, as opposed to the unconscious protocol and is held at the second-order level of ego state structure (Hargaden and Sills, 2002). Conceptually we can also think of a third level of script, which I call narrative script. This refers to the aspects of script that are entirely available to conscious thought, including our self-concept. I use the phrase narrative script to relate to script held at the first-order level of ego state structure. Narrative script is related to declarative and episodic memory whereby the individual has clear memories of experiences, interactions, emotions, decisions and beliefs.

41

Identifying structural level

The ego state model is just a theory – a metaphor which is clinically useful. Although there are numerous sub-divisions of ego states, for ease of use the model is divided into three levels (orders) of structure (Berne, 1961) (see Figure 36.1, page 136). The three structural levels are arbitrary divisions of personality categorized according to developmental epochs. Third-order structure relates to very early infancy. Second-order structure relates to early, pre-school childhood and first-order structure to later verbal stages of development. Sometimes beginning trans-actional analysts struggle to identify which level (order) of structure a particular experience of the client is located within. As the ego state model is just a visual and conceptual metaphor, identifying which structural level a particular experience is 'in' is an imprecise science. Diagnosing the most appropriate level of structure is largely determined by what is clinically most useful. Working with each level of structure requires a slight modifi-cation in therapeutic approach although there are degrees of overlap and in practice issues are rarely located within only one part of an individual's structure.

So, how does the transactional analyst approach structural analysis? In terms of identifying which ego state something 'belongs' to, we enquire into the nature of the belief/experience/emotion and so on and if it is historically something which is self-generated by the client, it is Child ego state. If it is intro-jected or taken in from an external source it is Parent ego state. If it is a here-and-now experience, it is Adult ego state. Some-times a belief may be held in more than one ego state, for example someone may hold a Child belief 'I am stupid' which is also a Parent introject if the person was told they were stupid by a parent or parent figure (such as a schoolteacher). If we take the example of someone who cannot speak French, an Adult belief would simply be 'I can't speak French'. A Child belief may be 'I am useless at languages'. The Parent content may match the Child content: for example the person may have had a teacher at school who told them they were 'hopeless' or maybe the individual had parents who believed learning languages was a waste of time.

The earlier ego state structures form the prototype for later structures (Widdowson, 2005), and are linked, according to their category. P0, P1 and P2 are all linked and represent an internalized 'other'. P0 and P1 are the very earliest introjects. P0, and to some extent P1, can be thought of as representing the 'affect regulating other' (Schore, 1999), or the emotionally containing parent who through the processes of neurological development became internalized and experienced as part of the self. C0, C1 and C2 are all linked and are the historically experienced self. A0, A1 and A2 are all linked and each is age appropriate for the chronological age of the cathected ego state (Hargaden and Sills, 2002).

Sometimes at second and third levels of structure distinguishing between Parent, Adult and Child ego states can be difficult. Fortunately effective TA therapy is not dependent on such precision or pedantry in structural analysis. As linked Parent and Child ego states (experience of other, experience of self and the subjective, qualitative relationship between the two) are largely simultaneously cathected, it is to some extent impossible to impact upon one without impacting the other (Little, 2006).

42

Building up the script system

If you decide to draw up a script (racket) system (Erskine and Zalcman, 1979; Erskine *et al.*, 1999) with your client, or to share with your client a script system diagram which you have compiled from information they have previously given you, it is important to broach the subject sensitively and carefully. In describing the script system to clients, I often use the phrase 'circuit boards'. This is language that most people can understand, and is a way of viewing the problematic experience which brought the client to therapy in a way which is often particularly appealing to men, or 'technically minded' clients. Compiling a script system gives a quick snapshot of the dynamics of a person's symptoms (including somatic experiences), contaminations and core script beliefs together with their associated memory bank.

Script beliefs

It is very helpful to identify script beliefs under the three headings of beliefs about self, beliefs about others and beliefs about the nature of the world/life in general. Taking time to think about your client and developing hypotheses about their script beliefs in these three areas is useful in understanding the different dimensions of script beliefs of your client and how they interact.

This can be refined further by considering these beliefs as operating in a 'layered' way. Cognitive-behavioural therapy has focused on the categorization of different levels of beliefs that individuals have which are limiting and unhelpful. A cognitive-behavioural therapist will look for the negative automatic thoughts (NATS) (Beck and Beck, 1995) that their client experiences in relation to a particular stimulus. Underneath these are a series of assumptions, and underneath these are core beliefs. The NATS, assumptions and core beliefs seem to correspond to contaminations and discounts, counterscript and core script beliefs respectively.

Questions to elicit script beliefs include: 'So when you feel really terrible, what are you saying inside your head about yourself? What kind of person are you?'; 'When you feel like that, what are your views about other people?'; 'When you're feeling bad, how do you view life in general?'

In inferring your client's script beliefs in compiling the script system you may wish to adapt the cognitive-behavioural classification and identify the 'layers' of script beliefs and the core, underlying script beliefs which lie at the heart of your client's script. Often these will be something such as 'I am unlovable', 'I am worthless', 'I am inherently bad'.

Erskine and Zalcman (1979) consider these beliefs as being contaminations, usually mutually reinforcing ones. It is my view that, while some script beliefs are contaminations, some of the 'deeper' ones (such as 'I am inherently bad') are more properly script decisions, which will be reinforced by contaminations.

Scripty displays

The scripty displays include the client's reporting of their subjective internal experience and externally observable behaviours in times of distress. From enquiry into the client's internal experiences when they 'feel bad', the therapist facilitates greater awareness of the experience of the emotional state and the subtle physiological changes which accompany the identified feeling state. This process of awareness is often useful to clients who may be relatively unaware of the physical cues that accompany their flow of feelings. The process of enhancing awareness of the physical aspects of feeling states frequently has the result of clients feeling more empowered in relation to their feelings. In the case of feelings such as anger or fear, which can often feel overwhelming, this can sensitize the client to their onset, development and possibly even associated cognitive processes and as such give the client some opportunity to tackle the problematic emotion directly as it emerges, or to prevent escalation of feelings to problematic levels by use of various behavioural strategies or by deliberately changing internal dialogue. Internal experience can also include psychosomatic symptoms and disorders or disorders exacerbated by stress, such as migraine, irritable bowel and so on.

Information regarding observable displays can be gathered by asking the client 'If I had a video camera, or were a "fly on the wall", what would I see you actually doing when you feel this way?' Again, such information gathering enhances the client's awareness regarding how their emotions operate, particularly on a behavioural, observable level, and can also lead the client into exploration regarding how others experience them and how the client's emotional behaviour impacts upon others (this may in turn provide further reinforcement of the script beliefs depending on the response of others). The client may, if you think it would be helpful, ask people such as family and friends for specific feedback on what they notice to gain more information on observable scripty displays.

In analysis of the scripty fantasies, the therapist will usually discover what the client's fantasy of their script payoff will be. These fantasies are often doom-laden and contain themes of abandonment, rejection or annihilation. Alternatively, these fantasies may be idealized, and contain elements of some unidentified rescuer coming along and dramatically changing the client's situation, or magically providing the client with the idealized childhood they never had.

Reinforcing memories

Reinforcing memories or memories of occasions that provided 'evidence' of the client's script beliefs are often remarkably easy for the client to access. It is probable that these memories are accessible through the process of state-dependent memory. State-dependent memory means that when we are in one 'state' we can access memories more readily that match that state; if you have ever spent time with an old friend recalling ever-increasingly hilarious events and situations for hours on end, you have experienced state-dependent memory. Similarly, people who feel depressed or hurt can at the time access what can seem like an unending stream of emotional memories that are linked. It is important to note that reinforcing memories will not include ones from very early childhood due to the 'childhood amnesia' relating to specific, episodic and verbal memories that exists around events roughly prior to the age of three. This is due to lack of neurological development in areas of the brain associated with memory (although the events will still be encoded and represented unconsciously, and held in the implicit memory systems).

In determining whether something is a racket or not, we can refer to the fact that rackets are considered to be substitutions (English, 1971), and that substitution is considered a later, neurotic defence (Klein, 1957; Terlato, 2001) and clients with severe, early stage pathology (for example, disorders of the self such as borderline disorder) rely on earlier, more primitive defences so are less likely to use substitution as a defence. It is possible also that, with some people, the repressed feeling is the same as the racket feeling. In this instance it is as if the repressed feeling became fixated somehow and the client has the feeling 'on repeat' in a failed attempt to resolve the feeling. All clients will have an intrapsychic script system and so taking time to compile a script system will provide the therapist with a detailed snapshot of the client's intrapsychic process.

43

Exploring counterscript

Supervisor: 'So, what is your diagnosis of your client's counterscript?'
Supervisee: 'Well, Definitely Be Perfect, and Be Strong, and some Please Others.'

This kind of interchange will be familiar to most transactional analysts, either as supervisors or as supervisees. Yet the supervisee's response is incomplete, and doesn't actually answer the question. A driver is a functional, behavioural manifestation of a counterscript (Stewart and Joines, 1987). To list a driver as the counterscript is therefore providing only a partial, behavioural diagnosis. Drivers are also more or less culturally embedded in that they are all behaviours which are present and stroked to some degree in most (western) cultures, and as such, each driver will be more or less present for everyone. '[A]nalysis of a person's counterscript can give some important information regarding the client's scripting process, to reduce this to a cluster of five behaviour patterns is reductive and restrictive' (Tudor and Widdowson, 2008: 222).

Attention to counterscript messages will reveal all kinds of 'rules for living' that the client introjected from their parents or parent figures and wider society. Analysis of the counterscript messages may reveal that the client is still heavily influenced by the counterscript. These messages may contain the ubiquitous 'shoulds' and 'oughts' that we are all familiar with. As part of the dynamic whole of someone's script, counterscript messages may also support and maintain contaminations. Counterscript messages include family slogans that may suggest wider script themes for an entire family, such as 'We never have any good luck. Only bad things happen to us'. Clearly a counterscript slogan such as this would influence the individual towards a pessimistic outlook, and would support the development and maintenance of a 'non-winning' or 'losing' script (Berne, 1972). Counterscript messages with explicit expectations of misery may also influence someone to engage in destructive games that would act as reinforcing evidence for the validity of the counter-script belief. It is possible that our clients may continue to move in social, familial and cultural circles that reinforce their counterscript. Although counterscript messages may also be useful to some extent, such as messages inviting caring for others, or the benefits of hard work, an individual is script bound if they do not have the freedom to choose whether they follow the counterscript message or not. The counterscript in some respects acts as a defence, and protects the client from feeling the impact of their injunctions. This tension is graphically depicted in Adrienne Lee's 'drowning man' diagram (Lee, 1998) whereby the counterscript (although in her diagram Lee uses drivers) is used as a buoyancy aid to keep the man afloat while his injunctions are weights which attempt to drag him down into the water. Analysis of counterscript may well suggest what rules for living the client is using to defend against the destructive pull of potentially lethal, restrictive injunctions. By exploring the client's counterscript, the therapist enhances therapeutic protection by not confronting the client's counterscript and counterscript behaviours until the underlying injunctions have been addressed.

Sometimes clients who present for psychotherapy have following a counterscript message as their initial therapy goal. An example of this is the client with counterscript messages around being valued for working hard and earning a high salary and gaining social status who describes their therapy goal as wanting to be more productive at work and obtain promotion. Careful analysis of a client's counterscript incorporating the counterscript slogans provides the therapist and client with insight into how the client's script is manifested. Clarkson discusses how sometimes 'the psychotherapist's directives, permission, values and example are substituted for the original counterscript messages of one or both parents' (Clarkson, 1992: 35–6). Recognizing this may well be an important part of the change process, she goes on to say:

It is not that it *happens* (that is problematic), but that psychotherapist and client may mistake it for the goalpost. If people get stuck here and terminate therapy without changing at a more fundamental 'script level', such contractual changes are unstable under stress and unreliable over time.

(Clarkson, 1992: 36)

Analysis of the client's counterscript provides the therapist and client with more information regarding a client's script and as such provides extra signposts along the journey to autonomy.

44

Analysing games

First, in discussing game analysis with clients, it is generally unhelpful to use the term 'games'. The word 'game' has a pejorative connotation (Woods, 2000), and tends to be received by clients as the therapist implying they are being manipulative, or are on the receiving end of conscious manipulation. I find using the phrase 'unhelpful relationship patterns' to be generally acceptable, as well as more accurate in conveying the nature of games as an unconscious interpersonal enactment which reinforces the script.

Game analysis has changed dramatically over the years within TA. It seems that during the 1970s and 1980s TA therapists watched for and confronted the opening con in a game (Berne, 1964). Following Berne's formula G (Berne, 1972) a number of methods of game analysis were regularly used, such as the James Game Plan (James, 1973). These methods assume games to be relatively predictable sequences that can be brought into conscious awareness. Although this is often the case, my clinical experience suggests that some games are so unconscious that analysis using such methods yields poor results. Furthermore, as games are so inextricably linked with an individual's script, unless the underlying script issues are dealt with, the game will manifest again in another, possibly even more covert form if confronted without first fully accounting for the significance of the game.

When exploring the client's relationship patterns, the therapist is listening for the patterns of the games the client gets caught up in, together with indicators that might suggest the underlying script issues which the game reinforces. Full game analysis therefore requires an appreciation of the underlying motivations for the game, and a sense of the original scenario the game symbolically represents. 'To understand the deep motivations of a game, it is necessary to identify the unconscious conflict from which the game develops . . . the switch in a game is designed to manage an unconscious conflict' (Terlato, 2001: 106).

If considered as a symbolic re-enactment of the past, or of some troubling interaction (often between the client and their parents), the game can be understood as a form of communication: '[I]n the context of therapy, externalizing or playing out one's internal scenario with others may serve as an unconscious attempt by the patient to communicate to the therapist the exact nature of the patient's internal conflict' (Woods, 2000: 96). 'The game is the externalization or projection of this internal scenario onto the external world in the form of an interpersonal interaction' (Woods, 2000: 94). A thorough game analysis therefore requires consideration of the nature of the unconscious communications the game contains.

Game enactments allow an individual to externalize their internal conflicts, and thus may temporarily stop the internal attack and conflict between Child and Parent ego states. This reduction in internal attack and externalizing of the conflict makes the original game scenario more receptive to deconfusion or, equally, reinforcement. When operating in the therapy room, the client's games therefore should be partially allowed, but contained (Bateman and Fonagy, 2006). This is consistent with Berne's concept of 'game dosage' (Berne, 1972).

In the ongoing and unfolding diagnosis of a client's games, here are some questions for the therapist to reflect upon:

• What was the original scenario that the game is seeking to replicate?
• What beliefs about the self does the game reinforce?
• What beliefs about, or expectation about how others relate to the client does the game reinforce?
• What were the original relational needs that were not met? What would be the intrapsychic and interpersonal impact of meeting these needs?
• What is the nature of the central conflicts that the game seeks to manage?
• What is the client trying to communicate to me through this game?

- What is my part in this? What is my vulnerability to this game? What aspects of my script does this game reinforce?
- How can I best manage my feelings so I remain therapeutically available for my client?
- What can be healed, both for my client and for myself, in understanding this game?

45

Escape hatches as a framework for understanding client safety

Escape hatch closure is a controversial piece of TA theory. It was developed by Drye *et al.* (1973), Holloway (1973), Boyd and Cowles-Boyd (1980), and more recently, Stewart (2007). The central premise of escape hatch closure is that individuals, as part of a tragic script, may incorporate an 'escape hatch'. The escape hatch is not the positive thing we might ordinarily assume it to be, but is one whereby the individual escapes from their situation. The three traditional escape hatches referred to within TA are: *kill or harm self*, *kill or harm others* and *go crazy*. Some TA therapists add a fourth escape hatch of *run away*. If an individual has an escape hatch 'open' within their script, the idea is that the individual believes at some level that 'if things get really bad around here, I will kill or harm myself or others, or go crazy, or run away'. These are seen to be manifestations of a tragic script, and may be the culmination of a third-degree game.

Regardless of whether you use escape hatch closure procedures, the concept of escape hatches is useful in conceptualizing risk and client safety. Certainly transactional analysis places great emphasis on client protection (Crossman, 1966). However, protection goes much further than inviting a client to close escape hatches. To consider whether a particular client, at any particular point in time, may be potentially moving along a trajectory of kill/harm self, kill/harm others, go crazy, or run away is a helpful shorthand framework.

Drye (2006) invites therapists to use 'no-harm contracts' as an assessment tool:

> Whenever I believe suicidal risk may exist – other than an actual attempt or thought and including self-destructive behavior, high risk-taking, gallows humor, and so on – I ask the patient to take a test to clarify the situation. I say,

'Please say out loud "No matter what happens . . . I won't kill myself . . . accidentally or on purpose" and tell me how you feel about what you just said.' If the patient states, 'It's true,' the risk evaluation is complete and treatment planning can continue.

(Drye, 2006: 1)

Drye goes on to invite therapists to pay particular attention to any qualifying statements or clauses clients may give for reasons why they wouldn't feel able to maintain the contract. He then suggests that the client be invited to repeat the statement with increasing time-spans included to get a sense over what period of time the client is prepared to keep themselves safe. Interestingly Drye states that this tool is only effective in monitoring suicidal risk and has not been effective at monitoring or containing clients who self-harm.

'In closing escape hatches, the client makes a commitment *from Adult* to renounce all three tragic options. Thus she accepts she is responsible for her own situation. She acknowledges she has power to alter that situation' (Stewart, 2007: 102). Escape hatch closure is a procedure undertaken by the client from their Adult ego state that invites the client to make a decision that they will not under any circumstances kill or harm themselves, anyone else or go crazy. 'The escape-hatch procedure is not intended to address any Child issues she may still have around the tragic options' (Stewart, 2007: 102). Escape hatch closure, and in particular 'no harm contracts', must not be viewed as a replacement for ongoing and thorough risk assessment of your clients. Indeed, a client closing escape hatches, no matter how congruent that appears to be, is no guarantee that they will not subsequently engage in harmful or third-degree behaviour. That notwithstanding, a significant number of transactional analysts have used such procedures over the past thirty years with relative success (Drye, 2006). Stewart (2007: 110) makes clear the important distinction between the decisional nature of escape hatch closure and a no-harm contract. 'A contract can be reviewed, renegotiated and changed if client and counsellor so agree. By contrast, the essence of closing escape hatches is that the client's decision is irrevocable and non-negotiable.'

In thinking about escape hatches it is possible to consider them as possibly operating on a continuum of behaviours that may link to each of the possible escape hatches. With the kill/ harm self or others escape hatches it is easy to see that a range of behaviours on a continuum can operate. This may also conceivably incorporate psychological, emotional harm. In the case of harm self, this could possibly also include a wide range of behaviours which the individual knows to be damaging, but yet they still engage with them. Boliston-Mardula (2001) discusses escape hatches in relation to the human hungers (Berne, 1970), and how harmful behaviours often represent script-driven ways of meeting these hungers. Boliston-Mardula invites therapists to account for these hungers in their work with clients who present with harmful behaviours and to promote healthier replacements for the destructive paths.

Many transactional analysts view a range of behaviours which are self-harmful, such as smoking, excessive drinking, overeating leading to obesity and so forth as being symptomatic of a strong 'don't exist' injunction and the presence of an open 'kill/harm self' escape hatch. There are indeed a wide range of behaviours that many people engage in that are to a greater or lesser extent harmful. However, to claim that they are all indicative of open escape hatches and a don't exist injunction may oversimplify matters, and may not fully or accurately account for the complexity and significance of the harmful behaviour(s). It is certainly true that a don't exist injunction is indeed an important causative factor for harmful behaviours and is useful shorthand for describing part of the internal process that surrounds such issues, although a thorough diagnosis of the components of the harmful behaviour and the motivating factors driving it are essential to effective and thorough therapy.

46

Suicidal ideation: a brief introduction

Transactional analysts have for many years worked with clients with suicidal ideation, and have tended to understand their client's urges as indicative of the presence of a don't exist injunction (Goulding and Goulding, 1979; Stewart, 2007) and related to their script payoff (Berne, 1972). Understanding suicidal ideation only as a manifestation of a don't exist injunction and an indication of a third-degree script payoff (Berne, 1964) is insufficient in understanding what is a complex phenomenon.

For the therapist, being with a client who is in such profound pain that they seriously wish to end their life is a disturbing experience, and some therapists, out of fear, react to such expressions of intent with rapidly introducing time-limited no-harm contracts, or introduce escape hatch closure procedures. Rather, the first task of the therapist is attempting to understand the client's frame of reference and the meaning for the client of the suicidal wishes.

Suicidal ideation needs to be understood for what it is, and what it represents to the individual. Invariably any suicidal ideation will include as a central feature a wish for the individual's profound pain to stop. Effective therapy with clients who experience suicidal ideation needs to account for this wish, and the therapist needs to repeatedly and empathically communicate their understanding of the extent and depth of the client's pain, and the desire expressed in the suicidal ideation for the pain to stop. When considered in this light, suicidal ideation can also be viewed as a contextually adaptive (albeit distorted) expression of the client's physis (Berne, 1972; Goulding and Goulding, 1979). Although the 'final solution' of pain is ultimately what is sought in suicidal ideation, this is only part of the picture, and each client's experience needs to be explored and accounted for fully. The urges to destroy can generally be structurally modelled to originate in the P1 (Parent in the Child) ego state, although the pain or 'psycheache' (McLaughlin, 2007) and internal conflict are generally central contributing factors in suicidal ideation. The most effective and therapeutically useful approach for the therapist to take is to enquire directly, and without euphemism or ambiguity, into the client's experience of suicidal thoughts and feelings. Each aspect of the client's experience needs to be carefully and empathically attended to (McLaughlin, 2007). Many people who harbour suicidal thoughts feel shame and guilt about these feelings, and often feel profoundly isolated. Such an empathic stance on the part of the therapist is therapeutic in itself as it minimizes the shame and guilt, and the sharing of the client's deepest experiences here reduces the sense of isolation associated with the suicidality.

Suicidal ideation also often includes an aspect of wishing to destroy some aspect of the self. Commonly the parts to be destroyed are aspects of either the Child (C1 or even third-order Child), or the Parent in the Child – P1, and possibly even both. Occasionally the part the client would like to destroy is some aspect of themselves that they recognize as an aspect of one of their parents (and so represents destroying an identification with a P2 introject). In my experience, directly asking the client to describe which parts of their self they would like to destroy is effective, as clients will have some sense of this that they will be able to articulate fairly readily. You may need to return to this question, as the parts can be 'layered' and the aspects of self which are most disturbing to the client at any one time may change (see Goulding and Goulding, 1979: 181–204 for examples of working therapeutically with such 'layering').

Sometimes one purpose of suicidal ideation can be the desire to punish, particularly punishing the self. This desire to punish the self is particularly prevalent in clients who hold deep guilt and shame. The desire to punish may also extend to others, who the client is wishing to punish for how they have treated the client (Goulding and Goulding, 1979). In considering the communicative aspects of the suicidal urge the therapist is invited to explore with their client what the ideation represents in terms of a communication, and what acting upon the urges would communicate to others. Injunctions, as aspects of an individual's script that was formed relationally by the infant in response to their environment, also may be useful to consider in helping to understand the client's process. When considered from the perspective of injunctions, suicidal ideation can be perhaps considered as an obeying of a don't exist injunction that the individual took from their environment – either directly, or indirectly and inferentially.

In working with suicidal thoughts and urges, the therapist is advised to account for the existential aspects that these thoughts represent. Paradoxically, suicidal ideation can be a manifestation of death anxiety (Yalom, 1980), or can be considered as an alternative to 'taking responsibility' for the client who feels desperately anxious and overwhelmed at the prospect of taking full responsibility for their life, with all the implications therein. Suicide can also seem to some people to be a means of taking charge of their own lives or pain and for reinstating some control over a life that can seem to be spiralling out of control, with hopelessness around regaining control. For further exploration of these themes, see Yalom's (1980) *Existential Psychotherapy*. As TA is an existential therapy, transactional analysts will find much rich material in his book.

Returning to a 'pure' TA perspective, script theory offers some explanations of suicidal wishes. Although it is certainly true that many people who experience suicidal ideation have suicide as a script payoff, to reduce a suicidal urge only to a manifestation of a single script issue could be an oversimplification that does not account for the complexity of the associated dynamics and issues connected with, and fuelling the suicidal ideation. Therapists working with clients who experience suicidal ideation, in any degree, are advised to take considerable time thinking about and discussing in supervision their client's ideation, and the different components of it and how they structurally and dynamically interact within their client's internal world and experience. Certainly, understanding any identified script outcome is a key task for transactional analysts. However, there are often multiple outcomes specified in an individual's script and a complex interaction of script issues associated with them, and as many of these as possible need to be accounted for and understood in their context and in relation to what circumstances would call for each potential outcome.

Finally, this point is not designed to provide the therapist with a full account or methodology for working with suicidal clients. There is no substitute for undertaking full training, including reading on risk assessment, treatment approaches and referral procedures. This material is to be viewed rather as an adjunct, or perhaps even a preparation to such training, and a beginning approach for therapists to consider suicidal ideation.

47

Diagnosis checklist

The simplest way to proceed with diagnosis in TA is to systematically go through the basic concepts of TA and determine how your client may experience their particular pathology. It can be useful to print out a list of TA concepts and, when writing your notes for each client, go through your diagnosis checklist making relevant notes along the way for each client. Your notes will gradually build up over a number of sessions into a comprehensive diagnosis using TA. You may choose to use the sample list below or devise your own according to your own way of working.

1   Ego states
    Remember Berne's four methods of ego state diagnosis: behavioural, social, historical, phenomenological.
    Parent ego state: general comments and strength
    Adult ego state: general comments and strength
    Child ego state: general comments and strength
    Contaminations
    Other structural pathology
    Main introjected significant caregivers/siblings
    Internal dialogue

2   Transactional style
    Common transactions (Which ego state does this client transact from? Which ego state responses do they elicit? What is their predominant functional style? Which transactional patterns do they report?)

3   Relational patterns
    What is the client's expected response to self and others?

4   Stroke economy
    Which stroke economy rules does the client exhibit?

5   Games
    Which games does this client frequently get into?
    What game do I think the client and I might get into?
    What is this client's familiar drama triangle pattern?
    What drama triangle pattern do they report that they elicit from others?
    What is my countertransference drama triangle urge with this client?

6   Racket analysis
    What are the racket feelings this client reports?
    What racket beliefs does this client report that they have about:
    a   themselves?
    b   others?
    c   the world and nature of life?
    What physical reactions do they experience when they feel bad?
    What observable behaviours do they get into when feeling bad?
    What is the scary fantasy that they envisage as the outcome?
    What is/are the feeling(s) that is/are repressed under the racket?
    What are the missing pieces of emotional literacy work this client needs?

7 Defence mechanisms
(For a description of the defence mechanisms listed here, see Nancy McWilliams' book *Psychoanalytic Diagnosis*, 1994.) In your diagnosis, highlight which defences you notice in your client, as and when you see them. Notice in what situation they occurred, and what you had been discussing in sessions prior to their emergence. Also notice when your client reports events from their life outside the therapy room, and which defences you suspect they may have used in certain situations.

Primary (primitive) defences
Tick those that apply and make brief notes about what evidence you are basing your diagnosis on.
primitive withdrawal
denial
omnipotent control
primitive idealization (and devaluation)
projection
introjection
projective identification
splitting
dissociation.

Secondary defences
repression
regression
isolation
intellectualization
rationalization
moralization
compartmentalization
undoing
turning against the self
displacement
reaction formation
reversal
acting out
sexualization
sublimation.

8 Personality traits
   Indicate whether these are present in the therapeutic relationship, the client's reported behaviours and approach to life, or both.

9 Personality type/character style
   (see Benjamin, 2003; Johnson, 1994; McWilliams, 1994)

10 Injunctions
    Tick those that apply and make brief notes about what evidence you are basing your diagnosis on.
    Don't exist
    Don't be you
    Don't be close
    Don't belong
    Don't be important
    Don't succeed
    Don't be a child
    Don't grow up
    Don't be well
    Don't think
    Don't feel
    Don't do anything

11 Passivity
    Tick those that apply and make brief notes about what evidence you are basing your diagnosis on.
    Usual reported or observed passive behaviour (include general comments about manifestations of passivity)
    Doing nothing
    Overadaptation
    Agitation
    Incapacitation/violence

12 Impasses
   Type one (include key dialogue forming the conflict)
   Type two (include key dialogue forming the conflict)
   Type three (include key dialogue or central theme of conflict)

13 Life position
   I'm OK – you're OK
   I'm OK – you're not OK
   I'm not OK – you're OK
   I'm not OK – you're not OK

14 Main script beliefs

15 Notes on deconfusion needed

Part 4

CONTRACTING

48

Contracting for the tasks and goals of therapy

Early agreement (within the first few sessions) between therapist and client on the tasks and goals of therapy is likely to be facilitative of the development of the working alliance, and as such may be indicative of a positive outcome of the therapy. Clients presenting for psychotherapy generally have an idea of their overall goals for therapy, which commonly relate to symptomatic relief. Many of these clients are also aware that considerable intrapsychic and interpersonal restructuring work may well be required for the resolution of their presenting problems. The problem for transactional analysts in contracting is in how to negotiate a clear contract that leaves room for flexibility and for potentials to emerge in the work. One difficulty we have is that if we assume that the client is entering therapy in a relatively script-bound position, then any articulated goals are potentially constrained by the client's capacity to envisage an autonomous state. The client's stated goals may also be script-driven and may relate to a furthering of the individual's script. The humanistic value base of TA assumes that at some level clients do indeed have this knowledge, although it may well be rather hidden at the outset. Hargaden and Sills (2002) suggest that a good therapeutic contract should ideally relate to increased options, rather than committing oneself to a set outcome or course of action from the start of therapy. This more relational approach to contracting is in contrast with TA approaches that value specificity in contracting (Stewart, 1996, 2007).

Contracting for the tasks of therapy

As part of the process of engaging in therapy, the client may well need information regarding how therapy works and what kind of activities they will be involved in both in the therapy room and also outside as part of the therapy (such as behavioural 'homework' contracts). Clients may need instruction in how to engage with self-reflective processes. This may also involve exploring expectations and preconceptions the client may have regarding the nature of the goals and tasks of therapy, as these may differ quite considerably from the therapist's. Contracting for tasks also includes the specific and ongoing seeking of the client's consent to work on a particular issue in the therapy. 'It sounds like this is important. Do you want to discuss this now?' or 'OK, I've heard that you feel X, can we come back to that later?' which marks issues that arise naturally as points for further exploration at another time.

Contracting for tasks related to the therapeutic bond

It is wise to specifically contract with the client that they will discuss feelings related to therapy and the therapist in sessions. This creates a contract that accounts for the tasks of using the therapeutic relationship and working with transference. A suggested wording for such a contract would be:

> The feelings people have about therapy and their therapist are often of vital importance. I have found that by paying attention to these feelings, and exploring them together, we can learn a great deal about people's problems, their ways of viewing things, their thinking patterns and, of course, how they relate to people. Therapy provides a unique environment to do precisely this. For example, sometimes people feel a little anxious, or inexplicably ashamed, or sometimes they even start worrying that I might be judging them. All of these feelings are important. Even though it will feel a little strange at first, I'd encourage you to share whatever is on your mind, particularly relating to coming here, or to me, no matter how strange or irrational it might seem. Would you be willing to do that?

Contracting for the goals of therapy

Clients presenting for therapy often have some idea about what they want to get out of therapy. There are many TA sources the therapist can draw upon in helping their client form clear contracts related to their goals. As Berne pointed out, a contract is 'bilateral' (Berne, 1966). The therapist will also have their own set of implicit goals, their concept of the 'ideal' or 'cure'. These goals will subtly influence the therapy and inform the therapist's interventions. It is important that the therapist has a clear construction of their 'goals of therapy' and is open with clients about these goals from the start. This reduces the potential for the therapy being influenced by covert intentions and operating on a non-contractual basis. In determining the therapist's own implicit ideal goals the therapist can reflect upon several questions: what is important to them about being a therapist? What do they consider to be the most important changes a client can make as a result of psychotherapy? For example it may be increased options and resources for living, or it may be increasing capacity for relationship. The therapist who is aware of their own overall goals of therapy can then engage the client in a discussion about these goals, and therefore the client can enter therapy (or decide not to) from a greater position of informed consent.

49

Contracting: developing 'lightness of touch'

A heavy focus on behavioural contracting and looking for solutions – the 'fix it' approach – is a common mistake of novice therapists.

> If the counsellor comes in too quickly into an outcome contracting process there is a real possibility that the unconscious processes of the client may 'go into hiding' or that the client will become over-adapted to the perceived Parent of the counsellor.
>
> (Lee, 1997: 101)

A guiding slogan for transactional analysts in approaching contracting could be 'Contact precedes contract' (Lee, 1997: 101). Contracting for change certainly needs to wait until the client has experienced at least some degree of the therapist's empathy and the therapist and client have engaged in some contracting regarding the tasks of therapy. It is best if contracting for overall goals of the therapy and developing a fuller treatment contract takes a second place in the therapy while the therapist spends several sessions compiling basic diagnostic information.

> A therapist who feels pressure to begin *doing therapy* before having come to a good provisional understanding of the patient's dynamics and character structure is, like a driver with some sense of direction but no road map, going to suffer needless anxiety.
>
> (McWilliams, 1994: 15)

Lee suggests the therapist use what she refers to as process contracts (Lee, 1997), which invite the client into a here-and-now process of engagement, exploration and experimentation.

Process contracting begins with therapeutic enquiry and then uses the response of the enquiry to determine the next movement. Process contracting involves a 'lightness of touch' to contracting that avoids some of the difficulties associated with hard, outcome-focused contracts that newcomers to TA believe they need to develop in order to be 'doing TA properly'. Woollams and Brown's treatment plan (Woollams and Brown, 1978) has developing the treatment contract as a specific stage of therapy; however, there are two preliminary stages prior to the contracting stage: motivation and awareness. Their approach suggests the therapist take a 'lightness of touch' approach to contracting in these first two preliminary stages of the therapy. Of course, the client will generally present with some wants or goals for the therapy, which the therapist can accept, and rework at a later stage in the therapy.

In promoting lightness of touch in contracting, I would also advise against the common therapy practice of suggesting six sessions and then a review of the work. I am of the view that such agreements plant the idea in the client that the work should be done within six sessions. A client who has not achieved their contract within six sessions may well feel angry that they haven't achieved the desired-for change, or feel disheartened and blame themselves for the lack of change. Realistically, for most clients only preliminary change will have taken place within the first six sessions as well as the exploration and deepening awareness of client patterns. Clients (and therapists) may mistake awareness for change and thus terminate therapy prematurely. A 'light touch' approach to contracting for this initial phase would be 'Let's meet for a few weeks, and keep checking out throughout those sessions how we're doing and how we're working together'. You can continue to use a session-by-session checking-out process throughout the entire therapy as part of your ongoing contracting and discussion about the therapeutic relationship.

50

Using a standard written business contract

Writing up a standard business contract (Berne, 1966; Steiner, 1971) that you can give to all clients in their initial meeting ensures clarity around arrangements, administrative matters and the terms and conditions of the therapy. A written contract is useful in that many clients are often highly tense or emotional during their initial meeting with their new therapist, and may well forget important information relating to the business contract. Providing a written contract not only minimizes potential for confusion, but it is also good ethical practice. All of the professional organizations governing the practice of psychotherapy, and the transactional analysis organizations advise members to be as clear in their contracting as possible. Ethical contracting requires the practitioner to attend to a range of areas where lack of clarity could cause potential problems in the therapy. Contracting usually takes place at the very outset of the therapy process, and so some details such as length of the work may not yet be determined. However, the practitioner can give an indication as to the expected format of the work, such as short term or long term. In relation to some of the above issues, as well as some additional points, I recommend making the following items explicit in a written business contract.

Fees

What are the fees per session and any arrangement around payment of fees?

Cancellation policy

What is your policy around notice period for cancellation of sessions and payment of fees for missed sessions?

Confidentiality

What are the boundaries and limitations of confidentiality? An acceptable clause is: 'I will not maintain confidentiality if I think that you or someone else is at risk of harm. In this instance, I will discuss my reasons and plans for disclosure with you before proceeding.' This clause covers a range of possibilities and does not tie the therapist down to specifics, but is clear about the boundary of confidentiality with regard to the management of risk. Special clauses regarding confidentiality and protection for clients on medication or where there is psychiatric history might include: 'If you are on medication, it will be useful for me to have some contact with your medical practitioner. Generally I do this in letter form, and would discuss the contents of that letter with you, and would not divulge the content of our sessions, but make general comments.' This allows for professional discussion with medical practitioners around the management of clients on medication.

It is important to be clear around case discussion in clinical supervision. A suggested clause is: 'In accordance with codes of ethics and professional practice I regularly discuss my case load with my clinical supervisor. Any discussion about you would be anonymized in such a way that you could not be identified from the material discussed.'

Trainees also need to provide a clear statement regarding using client material in essays and case studies. A suggested wording might be: 'From time to time I may refer to our work in assignments connected with my ongoing professional training. All case material will be anonymized and presented in such a way that you could not be identified from the material presented.' It is not ethical to include client material in assignments without prior consent from the client. If this clause is included in the general business contract, the therapist is advised to request that the client sign a copy of the document for the therapist to retain. Trainees are also advised to seek specific consent from clients who they intend to write extended case studies about.

Trainers and supervisors also need to account for disclosure of client material in teaching. The clause I use in my contract is: 'I may refer to our work in teaching psychotherapists and counsellors, or for the purposes of publication in professional journals and textbooks. Again, any identifying details will be obscured to ensure you could not be identified from any material.'

Recording of sessions

If you make audio or video recordings of your work, you will need to include a clear statement regarding how the recordings are used ('five-minute segments selected for the purposes of supervision, monitoring and evaluation of my work'), how they will be kept and procedure for destroying recordings. Therapists in the UK are advised that the keeping of digital voice recordings constitutes an electronic record of the work, and therefore will require the therapist to register with the Data Protection Agency.

Supervisors are also advised to put together a written business contract that covers the above as adapted to suit the supervisory situation but also addresses details such as emergency telephone supervision arrangements, approval of supervisees' advertising materials, provision of supervisor's reports, contact with training establishment/trainer, arrangements for frequency of supervision, ethics codes which impact upon the work and any special arrangements for group supervision.

51

Contracting with the unsure client

> Often the only contractual request that can be communicated, at least in the long beginning phase of treatment, is to share an intolerable load of suffering.
>
> (Terlato, 2001: 103)

Many clients who present for therapy arrive confused, uncertain as to the cause of their problems, and bewildered about what to do about their problems. They want to feel understood and accepted first and foremost. A therapist who ignores this and pursues a contract without first providing an adequate attuned 'play space' (Winnicott, 1971) for their client may well be experienced as unlikely to be able to provide a sufficient 'holding environment' (Winnicott, 1960, 1965). Furthermore, the goals clients initially set at the beginning of therapy may well be determined by their script. For example: a client states clearly that a life goal is to find a partner and get married. During the course of therapy it emerges that the client has a strong sense that they *should* be married, on the basis of the cultural importance of marriage and the sense of not being a valid person if you aren't married, as held by parental and societal Parent introjects. It may well transpire that this client then amends their goal to having the freedom to choose whether they want to actually get married at all.

Identifying clear goals for contracting can be especially problematic for clients with an undeveloped sense of self, and disorders of the self (Masterson and Lieberman, 2004). Indeed, for clients such as these, like a number of other clients, the initial working contract becomes 'finding a contract' (Steiner, 1974).

Another problematic situation is the client who may reluctantly be attending therapy, perhaps at someone else's suggestion. This can include the client who has been referred to therapy, for example by their family doctor, rather than purposely seeking out therapy independently. In these cases it is impossible to begin ethical change work until the client has identified specific areas of change for themselves. The contract with such a client would be a broad exploration contract for a few sessions.

A suggested opening contract for use with an unsure client is:

> Therapy begins with awareness. The first thing I propose we do is explore how things are for you and learn more about your patterns. Patterns of how you think, how you act, how you feel and patterns within your relationships. Once we recognize the patterns, we need to find out more about their origins and their purpose. We can then explore whether you want to change. Throughout all of this, we will of course be doing some therapy, although the focus will be more on exploration. For my part I'll provide you with support, but also challenge. Does this sound like the sort of thing you are looking for?
>
> (Benjamin, 2006)

This contract can be adapted easily for use with all clients, and also leaves space for the emergence of unexpected material.

Often a certain amount of change needs to occur before clear, non-scripty contracting can take place. In these instances, regular, session-by-session contracting, and contracting throughout the sessions, combined with checking on the client's experience of the therapy in each session provide a good backdrop for ethical, contractual therapy. It is possible to do good, contractual TA therapy without having a highly specific fixed outcome in mind.

52

Behavioural contracts

The design and introduction of behavioural contracts for specific out-of-session behaviours or courses of action ('homework') is a common strategy used in TA therapy. As a treatment strategy it has much in common with cognitive-behavioural therapy. Clients have different reactions to it – some actively seek (and complete) homework, others ask for it, but don't complete it, and others very clearly say that they do not want homework. There is some research, mostly conducted by cognitive-behavioural therapists, that strongly suggests that homework and its completion is of great benefit to therapy.

'[M]eta-analysis . . . showed that both homework assignments and homework compliance are positively related to psychotherapy outcome' (Tryon and Winograd, 2001: 387). They go on to say:

> Therapists who give patients homework assignments and who check on completion of these assignments achieve better outcomes than therapists who do not ask patients to apply what they learned in therapy in their daily lives. A recent study (Schmidt and Woolaway-Bickel, 2000) indicated that it is not necessarily the quantity of homework assigned, but the quality of the completed homework that leads to better therapy outcomes.
>
> (Tryon and Winograd, 2001: 388)

Despite this, it is important not to get overly focused on the necessity of homework, as many clients achieve great personal change without ever doing specific therapy homework. Indeed, 'behavioural contracts are (not) appropriate for all clients at all times' (Stummer, 2002: 121). It is of course entirely possible that the setting and completion of the behavioural contract and any benefit from completion is related to the therapeutic relationship, rather than the homework itself. In treatment planning for introduction of behavioural contracts, the therapist needs to reflect upon the client's diagnosis, and the implications of their diagnosis before proceeding with inviting behavioural contracts. The client's diagnosis may suggest potential contraindications whereby behavioural contracting would be a form of script reinforcement, for example clients with a schizoid structure who have a core relational pattern of control and domination may well experience behavioural contracting as a means of control, and so any such contracting would possibly reinforce the client's script beliefs about others, the motives of others and what is expected of them in relationships. Wherever possible the therapist should seek a collaborative interaction. All behavioural contracts that are set should relate in some way to the client's case formulation or key script issues and need to be integrated into a coherent treatment plan. At the very least, the therapist needs a clear idea as to why they are recommending a particular behavioural strategy.

Homework can be set for clients through a process of negotiation in the session. The nature of the homework, however, is often for some kind of awareness-building exercise, although it can be for specific courses of action. As a general rule of thumb, it is fine for the therapist to suggest awareness contracts, although behavioural action contracts are perhaps best self-generated by the client with the therapist facilitating, to prevent the client feeling pushed into something, and also to minimize the possibility of the therapist unhelpfully getting into a control game with the client. I recommend that the therapist keep some index cards, or slips of paper available, so that any homework contracts can be written down and the client can take them away to reduce the possibility that they will forget the contract. I also recommend that the therapist keep a copy of the contract in their notes, so that they can follow up on the contract with the client in the following sessions. In the follow-up discussion of homework in subsequent sessions it is advisable for the therapist to actively avoid taking a Parental position, or one which is excessively stroking. Exploration of the homework and the client's reactions to it is usually sufficient.

53

Dealing with resistance or non-compliance with behavioural contracts

Sometimes, even when 'homework' contracts have been carefully planned and negotiated, the client does not complete them, or finds the homework to have been counterproductive in some way. In this instance, firstly review and check the assignment – did it reinforce something for the client? Did it implicitly 'rubberband' the client in any way? What are the transferential implications of the original homework task, and also of the client's non-compliance? Sometimes analysis of the transference can suggest why a particular contract was not successful. It is as if the client's unconscious wisdom guided them away from completing an assignment that would reinforce their script in some way.

The use of the word 'homework' alone can evoke quite strong reactions in our Child ego state, which can result in triggering a rebellious response associated with a range of experiences the individual may have had in relation to parents and teachers in childhood. Although exploration of such reactions can be fruitful, it may well be prudent to avoid this kind of reaction by finding some alternative word to homework. 'Experiment' or 'development exercise' might be more acceptable and avoid the triggering of such resistance.

The most common reason given for non-completion is the client reporting that they 'didn't have the time'. How the therapist deals with this is important, in that we need to account for how busy our clients are and for their need to rest and relax. In doing so we need to support any movements towards change and also confront any sign that they not taking good care of themselves. In the case of a client who repeatedly reports that they didn't have the time to complete agreed-on homework, the therapist can deal with this by suggesting the following contract to the client 'to make a note of how much time I'm spending on different activities'. The therapist suggests this new contract with something along the lines of: 'I'm concerned that you weren't able to set fifteen minutes aside over the past week to do this. Perhaps we might look at how you work out your time, and how you prioritize what you do with the time you have to make sure we are both using our energies effectively.'

It is certainly true that for most people there is a part of the self that wants to change and another part that strenuously resists any change and complies with the script. Such ambivalence to change can be puzzling for both client and therapist, although, once understood, it can be worked with and addressed. If we take the view that all our script was developed in a relational context, and that our script represents some kind of internal link with our early relationships, then we have one way of understanding the ambivalence to change more clearly. In this instance, our client fears change at some unconscious level as it threatens to destroy the link with the internal objects/ relationships (our attachment to our parents) and resistance can be seen as a 'loyalty battle'. The Child logic is something like 'If I hold onto this script belief, truly believe it, and act out my script, I can be sure to be loved and accepted'. Understood in this context, change would generate deep anxiety and fear of abandonment. This is just one possible explanation for resistance to change, and it is likely there are many different reasons people are ambivalent to change (others, for example, include the emergence of impasses). The therapist is advised to maintain a spirit of enquiry and curiosity and acceptance towards the client's ambivalence and to invite the client into exploration of their ambivalence. It is unlikely that ambivalence or resistance will be resolved in one session, and will often need revisiting many times throughout the course of the therapy. This is particularly true for clients with complex problems or those with personality disorders or problems of a characterological nature.

In approaching behavioural contracts, it is important that the therapist does not get seduced into thinking that behavioural contracts are essential to the change process. Simple behavioural change does not in itself generate complete internal change and results from behavioural change may be short lived. The therapist is also advised to be open to considering behavioural change as being a result of overadaptation (Schiff and Schiff, 1971) rather than a script-free change. Cathexis theory would suggest that overadaptation is fine if it gives the client a temporary relief from a more damaging script pattern but that eventually the overadaptation will need to be addressed for the client to move on to autonomous ways of being (Schiff *et al.*, 1975). It is also worth remembering that the existential approach to therapy teaches that taking responsibility for our lives, claiming our freedom, results in some anxiety (Yalom, 1980). There is no blueprint or map for autonomous living and this can feel profoundly unsettling while being simultaneously liberating.

54

The 'good enough' contract

Sometimes our contracts with our clients are not as 'tight' or clearly defined as we would like them to be. It is worth periodically revisiting the overall therapy contract(s) with your clients to see how they are progressing towards their stated aim(s) of therapy, and whether they want to change direction, or develop a more specific contract where the existing contract is more general.

In relation to contracting, do not get into contracts or set up promises that you cannot deliver on. If a therapist says they are willing to do something for a client, or sets up special arrangements, even on a temporary basis, they have to be prepared to do it for the long haul. This includes, but is not limited to, telephone contact between sessions, increasing session frequency, extending session length and so on. It is far better not to offer such extensions than to offer them and then later have to withdraw them (Benjamin, 2006).

The approach and process of contracting can be reparative in itself. Seeking collaboration and clarification of wants, inviting the client to think for him or herself and set their own priorities all demonstrate a respect for your client that may in turn invite them into self-valuing.

In forming a contract, there is no need to get caught up in 'doing it right' or attempting to create the perfect contract. Developing a treatment contract with a client generally progresses through several stages of specificity. Each stage of contracting is revisited and developed through the course of the therapy. For example a client may present with severe, long-standing depression. At the beginning of therapy the client may state their treatment goal as 'not to feel depressed'. To suggest a contract such as 'I will feel happy in myself' may seem unrealistic and far-fetched at this stage as it so dramatically contrasts with the client's existing self-image that the client will not consider such a contract as possible. Furthermore, without spending some time building a diagnosis, the therapist may not have a clear sense of the client's prognosis so to offer such a contract may be unethical. The therapist is advised in instances such as this to suggest a contract that the therapy will begin with exploring the client's patterns and the structure of their problems. This contract, after a period of therapy focusing on the development of awareness, may then change to 'not to give myself such a hard time'. Once a further period of therapy has taken place, focusing on the client not internally beating themselves up, the contract can be renegotiated to 'accept myself', which in turn may eventually be revised to 'self-love'. In this example the contract is related to the client's diagnosis (severity of depression and loss of hope) and refining the contract becomes part of the therapist's ongoing treatment plan. At each stage the contract was 'good enough'. Each of these contracts may also be successively refined to include specificity and observable changes or actions (Stewart, 2007) as the work progresses and the client gains in awareness and vision. Working with progressive contracts such as these also allows for earlier termination of the therapy. For example, a client may decide they want to finish therapy once they reach symptomatic relief, rather than progressing through to script cure. I suspect that a large number of clients will actually stay in therapy that is broken down into smaller chunks and where success seems possible, rather than leave with limited gains. In the case of a therapist establishing a loose contract (such as the depression example given above) with the intention of progression and refinement later in the therapy, it is important that the therapist regularly checks the existing contract and discusses any suggested amendments to the contract with their client.

Contracting: preparing for conflict and negative transference

Contracting can pave the way for what is to come in therapy, and the changes the client is likely to experience along the way. From an ethical perspective we have a responsibility to facilitate our clients making as informed a choice as possible about whether to enter therapy or not. Part of this negotiation and preparation needs to include reference to the turbulence that may occur as part of the change process. It is doubtful we can ever totally prepare clients for the reality of the disruption, both internally and interpersonally, that can occur throughout the therapy process. It is, however, possible to forewarn our clients of the turbulent, and sometimes conflictual nature of change. I suggest that such warning is both ethical and also provides a foundation for dealing with such issues as and when they arise. In my experience, contracting for this at the outset provides a clear frame for dealing with problems as they arise. The contract provides a guide for what to do when the client is experiencing intense transference or conflict with their therapist and is something the client will hold in mind when they are uncomfortable about aspects of the therapy. This preparatory work is often remembered by clients at difficult times and can prevent premature termination by a client who simply got upset and didn't realize that conflict was not only to be expected, but a potential source of healing.

Sometimes clients can present for therapy with rather unrealistic expectations that once 'cured' they will lead completely harmonious lives and will never encounter conflict again. 'Pain, ambiguity, paradox and conflict are inevitable in life. They are necessary in a deeply searching psychotherapy and, most importantly, can become vitalizing resources in living one's life' (Cornell and Bonds-White, 2001: 81). It is also wise to be honest about how the process of therapy can have an unexpected impact on other relationships in the client's life. It is not unusual for clients to end friendships or for close relationships to become tense for a period while everyone adjusts to the client's changes. Sometimes these changes are precisely what the client wants, but sometimes they are frightening and take the client by surprise.

Just as it is prudent and ethical to forewarn clients that the therapy process can disturb their extra-therapy relationships, it is also wise to discuss the potential for the emergence of distress and negative transference in the therapy. My own method is to say something like the following at an appropriate time during the first few sessions:

> As the therapy progresses, and the work deepens, your feelings will also very likely intensify. This can feel very strange, and sometimes even a little frightening. What is important is that whatever you are feeling in and about our relationship is important, and it is important to be honest about those feelings and bring them out into the open where we can look at them and understand them. As part of this, it may well be that you might feel very angry with me or even in some way hurt by me. I believe that these feelings are very important, and that although you might not feel like it, it will be important that you find a way to express them to me. I can give you my word I will take your feelings seriously, but to do that, I'll need you to tell me about them. How does that sound to you?

Generally, clients respond positively to such statements, although they will commonly demonstrate some discomfort or unease at the thought of being so honest and dealing with conflict so directly. It is also very hard to imagine someone who you have experienced as being supportive as being someone you might be angry with. In the case of such incongruity, it is useful to explore the client's feelings about their discomfort. My experience is that in such situations clients will express a general unease around conflict and managing unpleasant interpersonal feelings. Expressing difficult feelings and learning to manage conflict can then be brought into the therapeutic arena by the therapist, suggesting this as a potential area for change for the client through further contracting.

Part 5

TREATMENT PLANNING

Comparative treatment sequences

Treatment sequence models are widely used in TA practice, as a conceptual framework to understand the types of stages and associated tasks that a client and therapist are likely to move through on the therapeutic journey. In practice, many transactional analysts develop their own synthesis of two or more of these sequences to understand the different stages of the therapeutic work. Although these models appear on the surface to be rather different from each other, they contain a number of similarities in that they all identify the beginning stages of therapy to comprise building a working alliance and then move to deeper, restructuring levels of work later in the therapy. Mostly they assume that decontamination precedes deconfusion, although this view of therapy has recently been challenged by a number of TA authors, primarily those from the relational approach, who consider deconfusion to be occurring from the very outset of therapy (Hargaden and Sills, 2002). These models can be helpful in giving the therapist a sense of the progression of therapy, and develop their patience in waiting for a client to be ready to move onto another stage of the therapeutic process. However, they can be unhelpful, and even limiting in that they can give the impression that therapy is a linear process and that clients move through stages sequentially, when in reality therapy is more circular, or perhaps more accurately, spiral in its unfolding. If therapy is conceptualized as a fluid and an unfolding process, then these models can be helpful for providing a 'roadmap' of where one is in the therapy, and what might need to come next. Table 56.1 below aligns four sequences. TA therapists can choose from, or combine these sequences to create their own 'therapy roadmap'.

Table 56.1 Therapy road map

Berne (1961, 1966)	Woollams and Brown (1978)	Clarkson (1992)	Tudor and Widdowson (2001)
Establish working alliance	Motivation	Establish working alliance	Establish working alliance
		Initial contracting	Initial contracting
Decontamination	Awareness	Decontamination	Decontamination
	Treatment contract	(Treatment contract)	(Treatment contract)
Deconfusion	Deconfusion	Deconfusion	Emotional literacy
		Internal nurturing parent	Internal nurturing parent
		Emotional literacy	Deconfusion
	Redecision	Redecision	Parent ego state work
		Parent ego state work	Redecision
		Rechilding	
		Reorientation	Reorientation
Relearning	Relearning	Relearning	
			Recycling
Termination	Termination	Termination	Termination

57

Formulating individualized treatment plans

Effective treatment planning is a key skill for transactional analysts, and yet the TA literature has so far not provided trainee transactional analysts with a framework for developing individual treatment plans. An individual treatment plan is usually devised in supervision, or on the basis of reflection about a client and their presenting issues. The method presented here is the one I teach to trainees and supervisees and has proven to be effective and simple to use.

Step One

The therapist begins with reflecting upon the following two questions: '*What do I think this client needs to do? What changes do they need to make?*' Answer your questions intuitively and write your answers using any wording you like. At this stage, you do not need to be precise. Your responses may be for global, large changes or for small changes. Include both in your list. If you are working with clients, I would encourage you to go through this process with your current clients now and discover for yourself how simple and effective this method of treatment planning can be. It is absolutely fine at this stage that these target changes are generated solely by the therapist. You may at a later stage share your ideas with your client for verification if you feel that to do so would be therapeutic for your client. Below is an example of possible responses to these questions. These are fairly common themes and you may be able to identify these in your clients.

- Internalize a sense of self-worth.
- Learn to be assertive with their family.
- Stop trying to please everyone all the time.
- Stop feeling guilty about not being perfect.

- Stop giving themselves such a hard time about their real and imagined shortcomings.
- Learn to relax and let their hair down.

The lists you generate for your clients might possibly be much longer.

Step Two

Take each item on the list and see how we can understand that particular change using TA concepts. To take the above example:

- to redecide script beliefs about 'being no good' to 'being good enough';
- to be able to accept, ask for and give self positive strokes (self-worth);
- to redecide the 'don't be important' injunction;
- to use positive controlling Parent transactions to set limits when appropriate;
- to stop grandiosity about pleasing others and associated discounting of own needs and feelings;
- to stop overadapting;
- to interrupt and stop critical internal dialogue between Parent and Child;
- to start accounting for successes and stroking self in celebration of personal strengths;
- to develop a realistic appraisal of self rather than seeking 'evidence' of script beliefs;
- to stop setting up situations and games whereby the script beliefs are 'confirmed';
- to use Adult resources for recognizing when it is time to stop and relax.

You now have the basis of your treatment plan for this client.

Step Three

Now, take the list of target changes, and compare this with the client's expressed wants and presenting problem. Indicate if any items do not correspond with the problem or wants your client originally told you about. These target changes that are not part of your client's reason for coming to therapy need to be contracted for if they are to become part of the therapy. This can be done at any stage you feel it is appropriate to raise the issue with your client. The remainder of the issues are already covered by your existing contract and so can become part of your treatment plan.

Step Four

Taking the list you compiled, highlight which are the three most important, or priority target changes. Often certain changes will bring about other changes in an intrapsychic catalytic reaction. Using the example above, the three most important target changes might be:

- to redecide script beliefs about 'being no good' to 'being good enough';
- to redecide the 'don't be important' injunction;
- to interrupt and stop critical internal dialogue between Parent and Child.

With these three changes, the other changes would be easier, or may take place spontaneously. It may be, however, that other changes can happen sooner, for instance in this example, the script belief of not being good enough is likely to be a very deep issue and only redecided after much therapy. Taking Adult control, evaluating situations and actively avoiding situations whereby the script beliefs are confirmed or even recognizing and changing these situations when they are taking place would weaken the strength of the underlying script beliefs and so may be a more realistic change to go for first. Take some time to work out which changes can happen first, or are 'live' in the therapy at the moment with your client. Explore in supervision which interventions you might make to help facilitate each of these target changes.

Step Five

Indicate on your list which of the target changes are short term and can be addressed soon, which will require ongoing attention and those which are long-range target changes, that would be more appropriate to introduce later on in the therapy process. You now have an individualized treatment plan for your client.

58

Monitoring and revising treatment planning

Once you have identified a client's target changes and developed an individualized treatment plan you will need to regularly revisit and revise your treatment plan. Ideally your treatment plan would be checked and revised after each session, but I would recommend that you review your treatment plan at least once a month for each client. It is important to continually monitor, review and track your client's changes over time.

An effective way to monitor changes in the process and client progress is by drawing up a table relating to your client's individualized treatment plan. In the process of change, often such central changes take place gradually with incremental change taking place over a period of time. One way of doing this is to write the list of 'target changes' on a single sheet of paper, and then, in columns corresponding to sessions, make a note of which changes were addressed. Do bear in mind that most changes will require repeated revisiting before the issue is finally resolved.

Using the examples given in Point 57, we can develop the treatment plan 'tracker' in Table 58.1.

Take time to read your treatment plan before each session with your client, to refresh your memory of its contents. Keep your treatment plan in the above format with your client notes and make a note when each was tackled during a session. At the end of each session, simply marking which items from the treatment plan were addressed will enable you to keep a close track on the client's changes over time. Cross any changes off the list as they take place, indicating that the particular change has been fully made and add new items as relevant or as they emerge. Keep the three priority target changes under review and make notes on their current status.

Table 58.1 Treatment plan 'tracker'

Target Change	Date:	Date:	Date:	Date:	Date:	Date:	Date:
Redecide script beliefs about 'being no good' to 'being good enough'							
Stroke economy – to be able to accept, ask for and give self positive strokes (self-worth)							
Redecide the 'don't be important' injunction							
Support use of positive controlling Parent transactions to set limits when appropriate							
Confront grandiosity about pleasing others and associated discounting of own needs and feelings							
Confront overadapting							
Interrupt and stop critical internal dialogue between Parent and Child							
Accounting for successes and stroking self in celebration of personal strengths							
Promote realistic appraisal of self rather than seeking 'evidence' of script beliefs (decontamination)							
Game analysis of setting up situations and games whereby the script beliefs are 'confirmed'							
Stroke Adult resources for recognizing when it is time to stop and relax							

59

Psychotherapy as a grieving process

Some of the most important tasks of psychotherapy are grieving processes. The grieving is not just grieving for people who have died (although that is part of it), but grieving for, and eventually letting go of the past. Of course, this is easier said than done, and the process of grieving is often long and painful. What is often grieved over is the loss of relationship, the loss of opportunities gone forever. A number of psychotherapy models assume that the inability, or unwillingness to grieve forms a core part of a range of psychopathology, or that symptoms or dynamics in the therapy relationship can be understood as attempts to avoid the pain of grieving (Stark, 2000).

Your client may have, at some unconscious level, a wish that if they are sick for long enough, or comply or rebel for long enough, then some kind of magical transformation will take place, or that they will be magically granted a new childhood, or their parents will change or some such magical thinking (Davies and Frawley, 1994; Goulding and Goulding, 1979). Part of the work of psychotherapy is helping your client to become aware of this wish, and to gradually give up and grieve for the longed-for restitution, which will not take place. This process is what coming to terms with the past is really all about. Once this grieving has taken place, your client will often experience significant reduction in intrapsychic tension, as there is a degree of 'peace' between Parent and Child ego states.

It is important that clinicians understand the stages of mourning and see therapy as a way to help clients mourn their relational losses. Failure on the part of the clinician to understand the mourning process can lead to arrested mourning that leaves losses unresolved. Such losses will continue to impact a client's life.

(Clark, 2001: 160)

The grieving process cannot be rushed, but can be facilitated. Understanding grieving processes and accounting for them in treatment planning ensures that important tasks of psychotherapy are not missed. Much has been written about grieving processes that will help you integrate grief work into your treatment plans (see Kubler-Ross, 1969; Erskine *et al.*, 1999; Clark, 2001). The grieving process often follows common stages. An understanding of these stages helps the therapist assess where they and the client are in the therapeutic journey and can help with treatment planning in relation to completion of tasks needed in moving through to the next stages. These stages are adapted from Kubler-Ross's (1969) model and the work of Clark (2001). Like all stage models of psychotherapy, the stages are somewhat arbitrary and generally overlap.

Denial

Denial is an unconscious wish that something not be so . . . when one seeks psychotherapy, it is often long after the original experiences of abuse and neglect. However, the use of denial continues as a defence against re-experiencing the pain of loss.

(Clark, 2001: 157)

It is possible that some of our clients who come to therapy unsure about why they are actually in therapy, other than a growing sense of 'something not being right', are in this denial stage but have some awareness that all is not what it might be. The first stage of most psychotherapies is the development of awareness. This process, although illuminating, is generally very painful and some clients can feel that the therapy is making them worse, rather than better. This is true to the extent that the client is feeling their feelings, rather than repressing them. Denial is overcome once the client realizes that they have indeed experienced a loss. It is a loss of what never was, and now never can be. On moving from denial, there is often an intense experiencing of pain. Clients may feel rage or anger towards their parents and also towards themselves for years of lost opportunities, and situations that are irreversible.

Anger

When we are angry, it is often because we want something to change. Our clients may want their parents to change, their past to change, their destructive behaviours and patterns to change, and they can be very angry about it. The therapist can also be the recipient of the client's anger, particularly for those clients who feel that therapy has 'made them worse'. Clients can feel a sense of having been cheated or badly treated and feel understandably furious about this. The therapist needs to acknowledge and affirm this anger. For those who were not allowed to be angry as children, this phase may need to be somewhat prolonged.

Bargaining

'One of the most common plea bargaining beliefs is, "If I fix whatever is wrong with me, then my parents will love me"' (Clark, 2001: 158). This bargaining generally takes place out of awareness, or at an unconscious level and so can be very difficult for the therapist to see. The client may appear to be rather cheerful or accepting, which can give the therapist the impression the client has moved to the acceptance stage before they actually have. Bargaining is essentially an attempt to avoid a total acceptance of the loss, and the associated despair which goes with that. It can be seen as a creative strategy of the Child ego state.

Despair

Entering despair is a profoundly painful and disturbing experience. This is true for the therapist also, who is accompanying their client on this journey. Clients presenting with symptoms of depression will often report a significant worsening at this stage, although on questioning there is a qualitatively different subjective experience between despair which is part of a normal grieving process and the despair which is part of the experience of depression. Full acceptance of the loss comes from feeling and working through the pain, finally mourning the loss of relationship, the relational trauma and truly accepting that it *is* too late to have a happy childhood. In relation to grieving the loss of opportunities from adult life, the client may well be feeling guilty and regretful, blaming themselves for a multitude of errors. Despair can also include the grieving over future loss; the loss that the restitution will not take place and that it is perhaps too late to repair certain relationships, giving up the illusion that things will turn out in a particular way. Despair follows on the extinguishing of hope. Again, the therapist's task is to support, remain empathic and validating and not try to soothe or comfort the client out of their despair. The work here is much quieter and requires a potent presence rather than fancy interventions.

Acceptance

Finally, the loss is accepted. This does not mean that what has happened in the past becomes OK, or that with acceptance comes serenity or inner peace or even happiness. What it does mean is that the energy that was tied up in the blocked grieving, the bound cathexis (Berne, 1961), is finally freed up for the client to use elsewhere.

60

Treatment sequence: a relational view

There are a number of treatment stage sequences described within the TA literature (see Point 56). The therapist needs a conceptual framework for understanding the process of psychotherapy, to understand where they are right now with their client, and where the therapy might go. Although there has been much written in recent years regarding the relational approach to TA, little has been written on treatment sequence in relational therapy. In some respects this is congruent with a relational approach, which would generally avoid a prescriptive or linear approach to therapy, but nevertheless I think it is important for therapists (particularly trainees) who practise relationally to have a framework for thinking about the evolution of the therapy.

In some respects, the stages in this treatment sequence, like those in all treatment sequences, are arbitrary, in that they overlap and in reality operate on a multiple cycle and in a multiply layered fashion. Clients will often move from one stage to another and back, and this process can be working on different stages simultaneously, on different issues or different aspects of the same thing. People are complex beings and the process of change is complex.

Stage one: the basic working alliance

This phase of the therapy includes a preliminary period of therapy that involves developing a basic orientation to therapy, the processes of therapy and the business contract (Cornell, 1986). In parallel with this the working alliance (Greenson, 1967) is also developing. Enquiry, empathic attunement (Erskine, 1993) and contracting are the main therapeutic interventions for this phase. Information gathering using the conversational method and Berne's four methods of diagnosis is also used during this stage of therapy (see Points 33–35). Here we begin to develop a sense of the client's relational patterns, mostly through our experience of them, but also through what the client reports regarding his or her past and the state of their current relationships. Through these processes we form tentative diagnostic hypotheses. This stage can take time to complete, and in some respects it could be argued that it is never complete and requires constant revision. This stage involves the development of 'good enough' trust, and an alliance between the Adult of the therapist and the Adult of the client to work together collaboratively. From the first moments, there is some initial deconfusion taking place (Hargaden and Sills, 2002). In this stage, our personalities begin to emerge, and our clients notice. They unconsciously find 'hooks' to hang their transference onto in the person of the therapist. Total abstinence whereby the person of the therapist is obscured is impossible, as clients notice all kinds of cues about us and our personalities.

Stage two: transference testing

This stage continues the deconfusion, but in a 'deeper' manner. The unconscious re-enactment of the primary situation with caregivers begins to take place within the therapy. The client can be seen to be unconsciously testing to see whether the therapist will reinforce their script, or be potent enough for the necessary therapy to take place (see Point 76). How the therapist deals with these transference tests is of prime importance to the eventual success of the therapy. Unsurprisingly, this stage can be turbulent and conflictual. This process allows for emergence of the 'negative', the toxic introjections and the feared (but anticipated) responses and the turbulence creates opportunities for change and internal and interpersonal re-working. In this the therapist is not just seen as 'the good object' but as being potent and able to provide a secure base and a source of tolerance and containment of the client's pain, anger and rage. Game invitations will emerge at this stage. A relational TA therapist does not block them, but watches for them to become apparent in order to learn from them and work with them and also reflects upon their own game invitations and their contribution to the enactments. Cycles of relational rupture and repair are taking place throughout this stage and so some essential reparative work is taking place.

Stage three: working through

This can be seen as 'deconfusion proper' and includes significant implicit redecision. The therapy will involve the development of the transference and transference analysis to enable the re-working of the protocol. This stage is often profoundly painful as the client works through her internal and relational conflicts and eventually moves through various stages of grief – grieving the past and 'what was not'. The therapy will involve more and more cycles of rupture and repair, but this time, different material surfaces for resolution in the process. This stage takes varying amounts of time, but is generally a very lengthy process.

Stage four: practising and consolidation

This stage can take a substantial amount of time to go through. As cycles of rupture and repair are integrated, and the protocol is changed, the client needs to find new ways of being-in-the-world. Existential issues may be more to the forefront here and the client is exploring the day-to-day realities of making meaning in relationships. To some extent this is akin to the consolidation and reinforcement of the redecisions made throughout the therapy. There may be some recycling of previous issues or symptoms as old patterns are revisited.

Stage five: termination

The client begins to dis-invest in the relationship. It is possible that this is the first consciously planned positive ending of any relationship they have ever had. It can also be painful for the therapist, and the client being dismissive of the process of therapy can leave a therapist feeling hurt and devalued. This can be considered to be a normal process whereby the client is dis-investing energy from the relationship, and possibly not accounting for the full extent of their loss. The therapist's own approach to the ending is important. The therapist's emotions can, if not carefully explored and discussed (perhaps in supervision), get in the way and block a positive ending. Issues related to separation and individuation (Mahler *et al.*, 2000) are likely to be present, and the client needs a positive affirming experience to consolidate the therapy and ensure the ending is an optimally therapeutic experience.

61

Awareness, spontaneity, intimacy and autonomy

Berne defined autonomy as being characterized by the release of three capacities: awareness, spontaneity and intimacy (Berne, 1964). Stewart (2007: 34) has summarized the transactional analysts' role in the slogan 'confront script – invite autonomy'. In addition to addressing the client's script issues, the TA therapist proactively utilizes methods that will promote the development of awareness, spontaneity and intimacy. The movement towards enhanced awareness, spontaneity and intimacy can be used as an alternative treatment planning method that focuses on health rather than pathology (Cox, 2000).

Awareness

In Berne's descriptions, awareness is similar to the method of phenomenology which involves: bracketing, or the putting aside of one's assumptions, biases and prejudices; description, in staying with the most initial, simple descriptions rather than digression into speculative and theoretical explanations (Occam's razor); and equalization, that is the giving equal value and significance to each descriptive component. Phenomenology, like true awareness, is concerned with *what* is experienced and *how* it is experienced (Nuttall, 2006). Awareness requires an uncensored openness to and noticing of new experiences (Cox, 2000). Awareness can be promoted in a range of ways, including mindfulness techniques which invite a flow of present-centred awareness.

Spontaneity

Spontaneity involves an attitude of curiosity and adventurousness and experiencing the world as a continual new moment (Cox, 2000). It requires an openness to experience and trying out new things, and new ways of being. Creative experiments designed and used in the therapy room promote spontaneity. Clients in therapy are seeking to rid themselves of the constrictive, limiting nature of their script so invitations to respond differently can be exciting and liberating. For therapists, spontaneity in the therapy room is difficult in that we have to maintain a continual reflexive stance in relation to our impulses rather than acting them out. Being open to our experience and our full range of awareness and judiciously experimenting with our awareness and different ways of responding to transactional stimulus may enhance the client's experience of spontaneity in the therapy. It is likely that the unpredictability of spontaneity can be unsettling and anxiety provoking for some of our clients. Inviting an acceptance of this lack of predictability and an attitude of experimenting may result in increased and welcomed spontaneity.

Intimacy

Intimacy permeates the therapeutic relationship. The depth of intimacy is characterized by the level of honesty, trust within the relationship and a willingness to be open to our (own) vulnerability in relation to another (Cox, 2000). Considered, frank disclosure of countertransference that does not burden our clients with the therapist's experiences or personal issues deepens intimacy.

> For a client to adventure into this level of relationship, both with another and with himself, he must be with someone who is also willing to be in relationship in this way at this depth. So the therapist must face her own unintegrated-ness, and consequent vulnerability, rather than remain the cloaked professional.
>
> (Cox, 2000: 84)

As the therapeutic relationship develops, the level of intimacy between client and therapist increases, with the aim that the experience of intimacy in therapy can be taken by the client into their everyday life as they find new, more resourceful ways of relating to others.

Part 6

AVOIDING COMMON PITFALLS

62

Being realistic about treatment length

Berne admonished therapists to attempt to 'cure their clients in one session' (Berne, 1972). This position is emphasized in subsequent TA literature sources such as Stewart (1996). In my view, an overemphasis on briefer therapies does not bear much relationship to therapy as it is practised. It is also possible that an emphasis on briefer therapies and the expectation of change in relatively short periods of time can contribute to disillusionment on the part of both therapist and client. One potential result of disillusionment could be that it is a contributing factor to eventual therapist burnout.

In the current political climate, short-term therapies are encouraged and are often seen as 'the norm'. Although many organizations (including employee assistance programmes and NHS primary care-based services) now offer some counselling or psychotherapy input, sessions are frequently limited to a maximum of eight sessions. Many therapists enter an initial contract with a client for six sessions, and a review of the work. Although there is no doubt that significant benefit can indeed arise from short-term brief therapies, there are many variables that need to be considered.

Expectations of recovery within a few sessions can be unhelpful to clients, who can experience taking longer than eight sessions as shaming, or evidence which supports negative script beliefs such as 'I am useless'. The therapist is advised to be clear with clients that full recovery from symptoms can take quite some time, and that longer-term therapies are the norm. Explicit discussion regarding treatment length is also good contracting practice, as clients who are aware that therapy commonly takes longer than this 'eight session standard' are in a better position to enter into therapy with a degree of informed consent (Steiner, 1971). I now routinely pre-warn all clients that therapy will take longer than the 'eight session standard', and have found that these prospective clients have generally been appreciative of my honesty. Clients with greater levels of disturbance tend to be relieved, which I suspect is connected with their awareness that their problems are deep and unlikely to ease quickly, and also that they feel that the therapist has appropriately grasped the complexity and depth of their problems. Where longer-term therapy is impossible, for example in working with agencies which only allow for short-term therapy, the therapist needs to be realistic with the client about what can be achieved within the permitted time frame. Taking a realistic approach to the possible outcome of the therapy again puts the client in a stronger position to begin the therapy from a position of informed consent, and also addresses the shaming potential from the outset.

Issues of prognosis and length of treatment are also dependent upon the client's stated goals and the interaction of these with the client's diagnosis. It perhaps goes without saying that more disturbed clients will need longer therapy to attain their goals than clients who are relatively highly functioning. Information regarding a client's level of disturbance cannot be reliably gathered in the first few sessions, as clients who are relatively well organized internally sometimes present as being 'in a mess' due to the intensity of the stress they are experiencing, and conversely, clients who have extensive and deep pathology may present initially as highly functioning with their level of disturbance only emerging gradually.

Although there is no doubt that significant benefit can indeed arise from short-term brief therapies, there are many variables which need to be considered and accounted for in making an estimate regarding treatment length. One such variable is comorbidity: the presence of more than one disorder. There is now a wide range of research that suggests that comorbidity is more common in clients presenting for psychotherapy than single-issue/disorder presentations (Morrison et al., 2003).

Efficacy trials of psychotherapies are often time-limited to around sixteen sessions and treatment is manualized to provide a degree of consistency in terms of methods used. Efficacy trials, however, use strict inclusion criteria, and generally exclude between 35% and 75% of all presenting clients (Morrison et al.,

2003). Such high rates of exclusion call into question assumptions about generalizability of such treatments, and clearly do not accurately reflect the 'average' client who presents for psychotherapy. Furthermore, some efficacy studies of short-term therapy indicate that 78–88% of clients treated either relapse or seek further therapy within eighteen months of termination of short-term therapy (Shea *et al.*, 1992).

Inexperienced therapists can also in their eagerness to 'do it right' get seduced by a pressure to speed things along unnaturally, inviting clients to make changes they are not yet ready to make, or going with a superficial approach to change, equating some intellectual knowledge with resolution. This presupposes that change is always simply a matter of some conscious effort and a little knowledge. This approach generally does nothing to effect real, lasting positive change for clients, and can be potentially damaging for the profession or put clients off engaging in therapy in future in its naivety in relation to change. Often great repetition is needed for change to take place, and for change to be permanent. Sometimes therapists and clients assume that because they have already discussed an issue, or even done some therapy (used techniques, or made an interpretation, etc.) on a particular issue, that the issue is finished with. It is unwise to make this kind of assumption, or to collude with such unhelpful expectations as the client may lose faith in the therapy when the inevitable happens and the issue returns, or internal change is not felt or experienced in the long term. Psychopathology, personality traits and established patterns of thinking, feeling, relating and behaviour are not as malleable and amenable to change as the short-term emphasis literature would have us believe (Westen *et al.*, 2004).

I also wonder if the urge to 'get well quick' is representative of some deeper social malaise which is in itself pathogenic. Perhaps something similar to the gestalt theory of paradoxical change exists in relation to time, in that it is when we let go of our need to rush and to change quickly that we free our resources and potential to do so?

63

Avoiding premature contracting

Those new to TA therapy are often of the impression that all TA therapists manage to obtain a fully formed, behavioural outcome-focused contract within the first session. This is an enormous misconception that can lead trainee therapists to feel bad (because they aren't getting the clear contracts with their clients they think they 'should' be getting). It is my view that pursuing a 'hard contract' (Stewart, 1996) too early in the therapy is a common cause of clients terminating therapy after one or two sessions. Clients can feel 'bullied' or coerced into a contract that is clumsily approached, or one which is introduced prematurely in the therapy. This can be particularly traumatic for clients who have been on the receiving end of bullying in the past. Contracting in too hard a manner can result in clients experiencing the therapist as at best misattuned, and at worst, as punitive. Such heavy-handed contracting can result in some clients taking either an oppositional or a compliant stance (functional Adapted Child) in relation to the contract – neither of which allows space for an Adult–Adult contractual process.

Excessive and premature focus on establishing clearly defined behavioural contracts can also be interpreted by clients as meaning that they are only going to be accepted for their performance. This has obvious implications for clients who have experienced being accepted only on the basis of what they do, rather than for who they are. An additional factor that needs to be accounted for is that clients often do not have a clear sense of their goals (especially clients who are extremely disconnected from their needs and wants) at the early stages of therapy, or their goals may be script-driven, so excessive focus here can be a therapeutic mistake. Pursuing a contract early on can also be a seductive pull for therapists who personally struggle with experiencing uncertainty and need a sense of control.

Woollams and Brown offer some interesting and useful suggestions as to when the therapist should refrain from focusing on the contract in their 'four rules of therapy' (Woollams and Brown, 1978: 265–7). I list these below in italics, with my comments following each principle.

1 *'The therapist should remain in an OK position both during and after therapy.'* It is difficult to feel OK as a therapist when you feel incompetent, or that you are not 'doing therapy properly'. By relaxing about contracting and focusing on relational contact, the therapist is better placed to remain in an OK position. This extends to the client – by not seeking to drag a contract out of a confused client, who doesn't know what they want, but does know they have a great need to offload their feelings and feel understood, the client is more able to feel OK.

2 *'Deal with the structure of the relationship between the therapist and the client before dealing with the content of the contract.'* The therapeutic relationship is positively strengthened by a focus on empathic attunement: 'contact before contract'. Allowing the contract to emerge over time gives room for the structure of the therapeutic relationship to 'cement', which provides the necessary foundation for the contract to emerge and the therapy to proceed within a strong working alliance.

3 *'Deal with transference or countertransference issues before dealing with the content of the contract.'* This tends to be more relevant in later stages of therapy. However, transference issues run throughout the course of the therapy from the outset. When apparent, these need to be attended to as generally transference dynamics *are* the work that needs to be done at that time.

4 *'Deal with here-and-now problems that exist between the participants (including the therapist) and other major life events before dealing with the content of the contract.'* Rigidly sticking to a contract, or pursuing contracting can be (mis)used by a therapist who is uncomfortable in dealing with direct discussion of how the client experiences them and the therapeutic relationship, or one who is uncomfor-

table in handling conflictual aspects of the therapy relationship. Clients commonly bring the events of the week, or what is going on in their life at the moment, as the focus of each session. Refusing to discuss this as it is 'not part of the contract' does not respect the client's needs for processing. At times of crisis, the contract in some respects might be temporarily suspended, or replaced with a 'debrief contract'. Sometimes a more intuitive and moment-to-moment approach is needed to provide the maximal therapeutic support to a client in distress.

64

Avoiding the pitfall of 'certainty'

Many therapists (particularly trainees) want to develop a sense of certainty in their work, and in relation to their clients. Sometimes this need for certainty can manifest as wanting to know what to do next, of wanting recipes or formulae to guide the therapist step-by-step through the therapy process. Novice therapists can find the absence of clear, detailed and long-range instructions unsettling, frustrating and a source of anxiety.

> However, for a therapist to be certain is, in our view, problematic. Certainty may reduce therapist anxiety, perhaps especially amongst trainees, by giving them a sense of what's happening. However, it does not help to develop their capacity to hold the anxiety of not knowing and, indeed, the unknown. Many people, including experienced therapists, report that the more they learn, the more they realise what they don't know. The capacity to tolerate uncertainty and to contain the existential anxiety this brings both for oneself and for another is, in our view a significant skill for therapists.
>
> (Tudor and Widdowson, 2008: 221)

This position is supported by Stark, who says 'The most effective therapists will be those who . . . manage to somehow tolerate – perhaps even for extended periods of time – the experience of not knowing or, in Bollas's (1987) words, the experience of necessary uncertainty' (Stark, 2000: 148).

Given that we can never truly know all of what is going on, for both oneself and others, and that no analysis is ever fully complete, a search for certainty is mistaken. All psychological processes can have multiple meanings. Certainty can limit the extent to which one can see hidden meanings. Mentalization requires an attitude of curiosity and an absence of certainty, and indeed once one is certain, mentalization has stopped. An approach that seeks to enhance mentalizing is one which embraces uncertainty (see Point 92).

A strong emphasis on diagnosis and finding the right intervention or combination of interventions can seduce the therapist into taking a mechanical approach to therapy and not honouring or seeking the client's uniqueness (Clark, 1996). This mechanical approach can be a defence against entering into the anxiety of uncertainty. For some therapists, uncertainty is too overwhelming as an experience; it takes them back to times in their childhood where they were powerless and uncertain. It is possible that therapists who grew up in such situations developed a script of caring for others and solving problems as a way of managing the anxiety that the uncertainty and lack of relational contact generated (Barnett, 2007).

Embrace uncertainty, and make peace with the anxiety this generates.

65

Reducing the risk of iatrogenic shaming

Iatrogenic illness is illness that is caused by medical treatment. Wordnet gives the definition 'induced by a physician's words or therapy' (http://dictionary.reference.com/browse/iatrogenic). This definition is closer to what I am referring to here.

Many clients present with core issues related to shame and shame-based identity (Nathanson, 1994; Cornell, 1994; Erksine, 1994). One goal of the therapy for such clients is the reduction and resolution of shame issues. Unfortunately, therapists can induce or exacerbate shame in their clients by not paying attention to their use of methods. Other ways in which a transactional analyst can inadvertently induce shame in their client is through their use of language, their demeanour, and their attitude, all of which can subtly, yet powerfully, convey an 'I'm OK – you're not OK' position to their client. This can be true, despite the best of intentions on the part of the therapist, and a client may nevertheless experience the transactions as being 'not OK' (regardless of how they are delivered by the therapist), according to the script and internal process of the client. Iatrogenic shaming can inadvertently be activated through the poor application of a great number of therapeutic concepts, but within TA, the potential for iatrogenic shaming seems to occur most frequently through lack of skilful application of the following concepts or tools.

Contracting

Contracting can be used excessively, particularly in the early sessions when clients are often still uncertain of the potential of therapy, the scope of what will happen in sessions and uncertain of their goals (see also Part 4, Contracting). An excessive focus on generating specific goals can leave clients feeling bad for not knowing exactly what they want, that they know what needs to happen, but they can't manage to make the changes, or that they don't know how to get what they want. Coming on too strong with behavioural contracts can back clients into a metaphorical corner, and if for whatever reason the behavioural contract was not completed, the client can feel shame. Indeed, 'sometimes the process of contracting may itself suggest that the person is not OK' (Lee, 1997: 99). Managing this tension is not easy, as clients (ostensibly) come to therapy to change, yet enthusiastically embracing the idea 'you must change' can reinforce the message that the client needs to experience some kind of transformation to be OK. The Gestalt therapists describe the *paradoxical theory of change* (Beisser, 1970) whereby in accepting ourselves and who we truly are we liberate the capacity for change.

Decontamination

Attempting to do decontamination through exhortation (Berne, 1966) or an excessively 'educational' approach to the therapy can be experienced by the client as being Parental (although the therapists using this approach would quite possibly swear they were 'offering Adult information'). Exhortation occasionally works as a therapeutic approach but does not promote the client's autonomy and freedom. It can leave the client feeling small and stupid, or patronized, particularly when they intellectually grasp the exhortation, but cannot yet make the internal change needed, or change their behaviour to fit.

Game analysis

Games are by definition an *unconscious process*. Games may be very obvious to outsiders, but not to those who are mired in the experience of the game. Pointing out a client's games can be very shaming. Indeed, the word 'game' is often taken to imply a degree of conscious manipulation (which will of course usually be strenuously denied!). There is no virtue in feeling satisfied and clever after pointing out a client's games while they sit and feel bad about themselves for their 'stupidity' or 'manipulativeness'. Raising the idea of secondary gain can also be profoundly shaming, and needs to be done sensitively, and gradually over time. Do not use game analysis for 'blame storming' – an exercise whereby the participants shift and assign blame for a situation.

Discounting

Once more, discounting is by definition an *unconscious process* (Schiff *et al.*, 1975), and therefore is not immediately amenable to direct, conscious thought. The phrase 'you are discounting' may well be met with a denial, or with a shame response which may in turn reinforce the client's script messages such as 'I am so stupid'. The areas in which a client is discounting can be enormously illuminating, and indeed not confronting the discount can reveal a lot of information regarding the client's patterns of defence. Confrontation of discounting needs to be done carefully to prevent the client from hearing the message 'You are wrong to think how you think, think how I think instead'.

'Pollyanna-ing'

A desire to soothe, to hurry the client into feeling better, to 'do something useful' and fear over the potential of exploring profoundly painful feelings can seduce therapists into defensively focusing on the positive or providing simplistic answers for the client. It is often very difficult to 'be with' and contain the depth and extent of our client's pain. Ignoring the profundity of the 'psycheache' of a client who feels very down is experienced by the client as an empathic failure. The resultant cognitive dissonance the client experiences, while feeling alone due to the empathic failure, can reinforce script beliefs and result in shame.

This list is not exhaustive but is meant to give the practitioner some examples of how unskilful and insensitive application of TA tools can be damaging rather than healing and as such runs counter to the therapeutic principle of 'do no harm'.

Analysis of transactions can be helpful in minimizing iatrogenic shaming. The stimulus that triggers shame can come from the therapist and can be extremely subtle, and may be out of the therapist's awareness. It is also possible that the stimulus can be partially internally generated in that there is something about how the therapist has responded (or initiated) with the client that has some kind of resonance for the client, in terms of their implicit memory. The wise TA therapist is prepared to examine, non-defensively, their transactions with their client, and to accept their own contribution to this stimulus (and consequent shift). Refusal on the part of the therapist to see their part in the sequence can give the psychological-level message to the client that the client is somehow 'wrong' and that the source of the interpersonal problems is located solely in the client. Such a process would be likely to reinforce the negative script beliefs the client may have regarding how 'self' and 'other' operate in relationships.

In summary, the therapist needs to be attentive to their way of relating to their client, and to account for the impact of their communication upon the client to minimize the potential for reinforcing script through iatrogenic shaming.

66

Avoiding racket 'OK-ness'

It is not unusual for people newly introduced to TA to embrace the philosophical principle of 'people are OK' enthusiastically. They go around 'being OK' with others, adopt a positive view of people and challenge others who they experience as behaving or viewing others in ways which might be considered 'not OK'. Although this can certainly make for a more pleasant world and is the beginning of developing an accepting therapeutic stance, congruent with a humanistic model, it can also develop into a deeply problematic position.

What can happen that turns this into a problematic position is a seductive pull to ignore the less than pleasant aspects of our emotions and emotional responses to others. That is, the pull to disavow or discount our 'shadow side' in the pursuit of 'OKness'. In the service of this desire to 'maintain OKness at all costs', a racket of OKness develops. If we take the definition of a racket to mean the adopting of a substitute, permitted feeling covering a forbidden feeling (English, 1971), then certainly 'OKness' can be seen at times to be a racket.

In the case of the development of an 'OKness racket' the neophyte transactional analyst in their zeal to 'be OK' may begin to significantly discount the existence (Mellor and Schiff, 1975) of emotional data that feel unpleasant or uncomfortable in some way, or emotional reactions towards their clients which are not one hundred per cent positive. Of course, this discounting process becomes problematic because shutting out these emotions means shutting out a resource that can be of profound use to both therapist and client. Our understanding of the development of rackets is that the individual buries disavowed and disallowed emotions, and covers them with an inauthentic emotion. The conventional view of rackets is that this process somehow links to the individual's script and the racket reinforces important aspects of the individual's script. If this is the case, how can 'OKness' be rackety? Clarkson (1992) described 'counterscript cure', the 'flight into health' as one potential means of transformation, whereby the client (in this case, the TA trainee) adopts a position which on the surface appears to run against their script, but in some ways is actually a modified version of their script, and is an adaptation to another intro-jection. It could be for example that in burying their 'not OK' feelings, the individual is seeking belonging – belonging to the TA community – and is actually adapting to an external source in a similar way to how they adapted to their parent's frame of reference. I suspect this is a particular threat to those who come to TA with an 'I'm not OK – you're OK' life position, in that it is relatively easy for them to see others as OK, and they want to believe that by repeating the mantra they can truly believe that *they* really might be OK, thus fulfilling a magical transformation fantasy. Adapting to the racket 'OKness' position would also, using Hargaden and Sills' (2002) conception of the self, allow the individual to identify with the A1+ self-identity system, and in doing so disavow and repress their 'not OK' feelings towards self or others. By maintaining a positive identification with the 'OKness', the individual can maintain a fragile identity of being 'one of the good guys'.

I am proposing that as transactional analysts we develop a more realistic position in the teaching and practising of the concept of 'OKness', and one which accounts for the existence of negative, unpleasant feelings. In his seminal paper 'Hate in the countertransference' Winnicott (1946) paves the way for the therapist to allow themselves to experience the 'unpleasant' and 'unkind' thoughts and feelings they have towards their client, and to see them as a normal and possibly even central aspect of the therapy. Maroda (1994) takes this position further by urging therapists to utilize their affective responses towards their client as a potent therapeutic tool. Maroda advocates regular, but carefully timed and carefully worded, disclosure of the ther-apists' affective countertransference towards their client, even when the feelings are 'unpleasant'.

Projective identification is a particular transferential phenom-enon that can induce a range of unpleasant feelings and thoughts within the therapist. In projective identification the client is thought to be projecting certain intolerable feelings into the therapist, so the therapist can process, metabolize, detoxify and transform these feelings for the client who can then in turn re-own them. Ogden (1982) identifies four primary functions of projective identification: a defence against experiencing unwanted, disavowed aspects of the self; a means of communicating – if one's feelings are experienced by another this creates a profound sense of being understood; a way of relating to the other person, and maintaining relationship; and a method of psychological change – the feelings are changed by the other, and we also learn new, more productive ways of transforming and containing our own intolerable feelings. Considered in this light, projective identification can be viewed as having great potential for therapeutic change, and as being a creative means for the client to communicate their feelings and their needs.

> Where the patient has need, the therapist must have capacity. In other words, where the patient has need to defend herself against all sorts of unacceptable feelings, the therapist must be able to tolerate the presence of such feelings within herself – or, at the very least her own potential to have such feelings. The therapist must be able to do (for the patient) what the patient cannot yet do (for herself) – that is, the therapist must have the capacity to sit with bad feelings without needing to disavow them.
>
> (Stark, 2000: 274)

Not acknowledging the unpleasant feelings that might be projected does not mean that they don't exist for the client, or indeed within the therapist, but what it does mean is that the feelings are not available for re-working in the therapeutic relationship. By adopting a stance of racket 'OKness' and refusing to see ourselves as anything other than infinitely patient, tolerant and understanding we can rob the client of this powerful opportunity to reintegrate previously intolerable emotions. Indeed, disavowal of these feelings by the therapist is likely to reinforce on an unconscious level for the client that such feelings are inherently dangerous and therefore should be disowned, discounted and projected out. For clients who experience themselves as being inherently bad, being with a therapist who is in a racket OKness position can feel profoundly lonely and isolating, and can reinforce on an unconscious level the client's script beliefs of being intrinsically bad or unworthy. Maroda (1994) also warns against the tendency of therapists to adopt a racket OK position, making the observation that it is when bad feelings are disavowed that they can exert intense unconscious pressure upon the therapist (and consequently their client) and can get acted out destructively, despite all wishes to maintain the 'good' position.

Berne recognized the significance of these 'bad' feelings, and the importance of acknowledging their existence: 'He who pretends that these forces do not exist becomes their victim. His whole script may be a project to demonstrate that he is free of them. But since he is most likely not, this is a denial of himself and therefore of his right to a self-chosen destiny' (Berne, 1972: 270). The transactional analyst is invited to make space for their own unpleasant feelings to emerge; to give themselves permission to feel all of their feelings – no matter how unpleasant. Accepting negative feelings and welcoming them as a source of useful information is both a challenge and an important developmental step in the process of becoming an effective transactional analyst.

67

Avoiding marshmallowing

Many clients presenting for psychotherapy experience strong internal 'stroke filters' (Woollams and Brown, 1978); discounting positive strokes, disbelieving them or redefining them in some way to neutralize them. The tenacity of these stroke filters and their imperviousness to simple stroking and contradiction can be quite startling. Positive stroking can hit up against the client's resistances, especially when the client believes only bad things about themselves and has an extensive negative self-belief system in their script.

There can be a tendency among some inexperienced transactional analysts to excessively stroke their clients, as if stroking will somehow magically transform them. This heavy use of strokes can appear to clients to be disingenuous, partly as a result of its being a culturally dystonic way of interacting (Steiner, 1974). An overly stroking approach can also appear patronizing, and can have a tone of infantilizing the client, or can be experienced as such by the client. This is in contradiction to an approach that seeks to strengthen and promote Adult ego state functioning. Furthermore, heavy use of stroking can also promote symbiosis (Schiff *et al.*, 1975). I have had a number of clients who stopped seeing previous therapists because they felt the therapist was 'too nice' and overly permissive. In almost all of these cases the client reported that they experienced the therapist's use of stroking to be false or unrealistic and left the client feeling that the therapist was reluctant to confront them. There is also the possibility that for clients with dependent or avoidant personality traits that a 'stroke heavy' approach keeps the client stuck in script, and dependent on the therapist to provide them with their quota of strokes, rather than challenging the underlying neediness. Such a collusive relationship is not one that is conducive to therapeutic change.

Clients occasionally solicit their therapist's reassurance, either directly or indirectly. Eager to demonstrate their understanding and acceptance, and fuelled by the desire to 'be useful', inexperienced therapists can succumb to this pull and offer the client their sought-after reassurance (i.e. accept the game invitation). Not providing a stroke to a client can sometimes facilitate the client in becoming aware of their neediness or desire for approval. By not giving a stroke, the client's need is brought to the surface, where it is amenable to change, rather than lying buried, but motivating the client's behaviour and way of interacting with others.

Example

A client was discussing a problem with a male colleague in her small team who often acts dismissively and who the client feels does not appreciate how she helps him out. This then moved into discussion of the client's fear of her (male) boss and lack of confidence around men in positions of authority. The atmosphere of the session was becoming tense, and the client went on to say: 'I think he thinks I am stupid. In fact sometimes I wonder about that, and I think I'm stupid.' The tension in the room was almost palpable. Her (male) therapist felt that the psychological-level message in the client's last transaction was 'and you think I'm stupid – tell me I'm not'. After a long pause, the client said, slowly and carefully, 'I sometimes think that you think I'm stupid'. At this point, it would have been easy to stroke the client and refute this belief. However, her therapist responded with an empathic interpretation – 'It must be very difficult spending all your time looking for approval and reassurance.' This hit the spot and the client nodded agreement and wept for several minutes. The therapist sat silently, witnessing the client's distress, eventually saying, 'It seems like what I said hit upon some truth for you. How was it for you to hear that?' The client nodded and recognizing the psychological-level message said, 'I was wanting you to say that you approve of me, and that you think I'm smart.' Her therapist replied 'Would you have believed me, even if I'd said so?' to which the client responded, 'No, I wouldn't have. Not deep down.'

By not providing the initially sought-for strokes, the therapist created an atmosphere where the client's neediness for reassurance was brought to the surface. In doing so, the mechanisms that lead the client to seek for, but not believe positive strokes were delivered directly into the therapy.

Certainly there is a place for stroking in therapy. We all need strokes to some degree or another. Clients, supervisees, trainees and colleagues all need strokes, and we certainly should offer strokes. However, sometimes, 'less really is more'.

68

Teaching TA concepts sparingly

Teaching TA concepts to clients is often irresistible to TA therapists. We know how useful the concepts can be in understanding the world, and in helping us make sense of and change our behaviour. We know that language does not always need to be complex to understand important internal processes and that some knowledge and common language demystifies the therapy process for our clients. Because of all this, sometimes TA therapists teach TA concepts to their clients with an almost missionary zeal. This can indeed be very helpful, and can help clients to make sense of their experiences. I am sure all of us who came to TA had many rapid insights and implemented behavioural change almost immediately on learning some of the concepts, and yet, as all of us will attest, learning such concepts does not necessarily change how we feel inside, nor does it stop us from acting in self-destructive ways. The teaching of TA concepts therefore needs to be used sparingly, and needs to account for both the reasons we have for wanting to teach the concept to our client, and of the intrapsychic implications and the impact that such an approach will have on the therapeutic relationship.

Cognitively 'knowing' something in Adult does not necessarily change the affective charge of a particular experience. This is particularly true for clients who have a more disturbed, fractured and discontinuous experience of self. Explanation, one of Berne's eight therapeutic operations (Berne, 1966; Hargaden and Sills, 2002), is often cited as a rationale for teaching clients bits of theory, or providing dazzlingly complex explanations as to why they feel the way they do. As an intervention, explanation is best used sparingly, with your explanations ideally being short and concise; I would suggest no more than three sentences long. There is a real danger in providing explanation that the material becomes so complex that the client is unable to take it all in and make full use of it. Far better to provide a short piece of information, and then explore the significance of this for the client in discussion, than to overwhelm them. Beginning therapists of all approaches often make the mistake of using interventions that are too long or providing over-elaborate explanations for their clients. A useful analogy may be to think of a large, rich meal: if you try and eat too much, too quickly, you will soon experience indigestion and discomfort. It is best to take one's time and savour each mouthful and give time to fully chew and begin to digest the food before moving on to another dish.

It is also important for the therapist to bear in mind that, although explanation can be useful, it cannot replace client-generated insight, or the kind of emotional knowing that occurs when important connections emerge in the therapy and both therapist and client make meaning of them. The process in explanation is generally only cognitive and, as stated above, often does not change how one feels. Explanation can be useful, however, in helping the client prepare for difficult times, or to help them make sense of particularly distressing experiences, even while staying in Adult, and clients may therefore take a sense of hope from an explanation, despite the fact that deep emotional change is unlikely to come about from the explanation alone.

Teaching a client TA concepts can also have more subtly destructive effects, in that it can set the therapist up in a position of 'expert' ('I'm OK – I know the answers') and can leave the client in a one-down, 'not OK' position. Also, clients can feel embarrassed or ashamed when, after learning the concepts, they find it difficult to implement behavioural change, or change their internal experience and emotional states.

There are important transferential implications to teaching clients theory and providing explanations that will subtly change the dynamic of the work. How might clients experience being taught TA concepts? A client with some paranoid process might be suspicious of why they are being taught, and may fear brainwashing. Other clients, particularly those who are less sure of themselves and the validity of their own thinking, may feel criticized, or that they are somehow wrong, or stupid for not thinking like that originally, and in the process reinforce script beliefs. Some clients can overadapt (Schiff and Schiff, 1971) to the therapist's frame of reference, taking the therapist's explanations unquestioningly. In overadapting they may defer explanations to the therapist, or seek to please the therapist by making their own formulations of situations based on what they think the therapist wants to hear, generating a collusive dynamic in the therapy. On the reverse side of this, some clients may subtly rebel against the therapist, or may consider the explanations as superficial or banal (which could be a true perception). From the point of view of games, the client can be invited to play 'Psychiatry – transactional analysis' or 'Gee you're wonderful Professor' (Berne, 1964). Transferentially, the teaching of concepts can stimulate a teacher transference, or even a parental transference, which could be problematic if the client had one or more parents who were dogmatic, domineering and lecturing. At first glance such a transference may well appear to be benign, in that the client may use it for transference cure, or counterscript cure (Clarkson, 1992), but it will inevitably be problematic as moving beyond the dynamic or bringing it into awareness can be deeply threatening for the client. In considering the impact this may have on the client's relationships, teaching clients concepts can also be used by the client to enter an 'I'm OK, you're OK, they're not OK' position (see Point 39).

Therapists can also 'hide behind' the theory and can use the theory to attempt to contain their own anxiety and can use teaching theory to attempt to communicate to the client that they know what is going on for the client, where it might be more helpful to experience, tolerate and contain not knowing.

Although explanation can be useful, it needs to be used sparingly as an intervention, and needs to be carefully thought about and introduced into your treatment plan mindful of the potential implications.

Part 7

REFINING THERAPEUTIC SKILLS

69

Balancing challenge and support

It is easy for therapists to become over-reliant on a particular preference in relation to challenge or support, which often relates to their own personality and needs. This, however, may become rigid and consequently not be appropriate for a large number of clients. Challenge and support can be considered on two continua and the therapist needs to attune to the required level of challenge and support needed for each client at any given moment. High levels of support can be very important for clients who are feeling profoundly emotional, or who are experiencing painful transitions, or while dealing with emergence of repressed feelings. High levels of support can, however, be problematic when overdone or misattuned and can effectively impair the therapist's potency and render the therapeutic relationship a cosy, collusive space where little change takes place. Low levels of support can be helpful in promoting resilience in the client and inviting a client to take Adult responsibility, but can be experienced as persecutory or withholding by the client, who may well leave therapy if they feel their needs are not being sufficiently attended to and who may experience the therapy as an unsafe place to explore deeper levels of affect.

Challenge also needs to be carefully attuned. Again, low levels of challenge promote a climate of collusion, and do not contain the required leverage to facilitate change. If challenge levels are too high, clients will feel persecuted and the potential for iatrogenic shaming is high. This is particularly true in the early stages of therapy if the therapist makes extensive use of confrontation or discounting (Schiff *et al.*, 1975). Most clients presenting for therapy realize that a degree of challenge will be necessary for the work, and many welcome the therapist's challenge (at least at the social level) as a catalyst for change, provided it is sensitively balanced with sufficient levels of support: 'The therapist's task is to challenge habitual assumptions and relationship patterns and create sufficient turbulence for new structures to emerge' (Holmes, 2001: 17).

70

Optimizing therapy by assessment of where the client is open, and where they are defended

The Ware sequence (Ware, 1983) is a commonly taught piece of TA theory, and one which has immediate appeal in its simplicity, and also its sense of being systematic, and guiding the therapist in their interventions. Yet in practice it has limited usefulness as a model and in my view can be obstructive to the therapy process. For a critique of the Ware sequence and the personality adaptations model see Tudor and Widdowson (2008). Here I offer an alternative to the Ware sequence that uses the same therapeutic skills, but in a way which tracks the client's process on a moment-to-moment basis.

The division of a client's experience into thoughts, feelings and behaviours is in many respects a false 'trichotomising' (Tudor and Widdowson, 2008) which does not account for the complex and multifaceted nature of a client's experience, which will at any given moment include thoughts, feeling and behaviour as a whole. Focusing on one aspect of the client's experiencing also does not pay sufficient attention to the client's unfolding phenomenological process in the moment.

Also, designing interventions according to a pre-determined sequence significantly limits the therapist's flexibility, creativity and affective resonance with the client. It could be argued that this in itself is not helpful in that following a sequence will by definition impair the therapist's capacity to utilize awareness, spontaneity and intimacy (Berne, 1964) in the therapeutic encounter – the very capacities which are characteristic of autonomy, and as such ones we need to promote in the therapy.

The three 'doors' of the Ware sequence are the *open door*, or where the client is most receptive, the *trap door* or where the client is most defended, and the *target door* or the area where the most change will take place. Following a set sequence in working with any client will significantly limit the therapist's capacity to attune to the client on a moment-to-moment basis. What I have found *is* helpful is to consider where *this* client is open and receptive, at *this* moment, and to consider where *this* client is most defended, at *this* moment. Analysis of the areas of receptivity and defence will reveal that it is only certain thoughts and feelings in relation to specific things that are limited. These configurations will change repeatedly throughout the progress of the therapy, and indeed throughout a single session.

In some respects, it could be argued that feeling is always the 'open door', in that all stimulus we receive is initially processed via the amygdala and the emotionally driven limbic system. We process on an emotional level before we engage cognition. However, affect and cognition are not easily separated as both operate simultaneously within the individual. All affective experiences are appraised using cognition, and all cognition is affect-laden and motivated by affect (Stern, 1985; O'Brien and Houston, 2007). At any one time an individual will be experiencing on an affective level, and even the most affective-defended person will at some level be experiencing emotionally. A key task for the therapist is to attune to this affect, regardless of how buried or repressed it is, and to incorporate that into the therapy either via empathic transactions or interpretation.

To be empathic and attuned (Erskine *et al.*, 1999) requires that we set aside any preconceptions about the client and their experience. In this respect it is crucial that to fully attune to our clients we set aside any notion of a preconceived, limited (and limiting) fixed sequence to their process.

71

Deepening affect

A large majority of clients presenting for therapy are seeking a means of regulating their emotional states. Often their feelings are intense and overwhelming, or they feel detached and confused by their emotions and the emotions of others. Leader (2008) argues that there is a culturally prevalent model whereby individuals avoid any intense or distressing emotion and that these unpleasant emotions are 'medicated away'. He discusses how individuals, rather than learning key emotional skills, seek to live in a sanitized, non-distressing world. This avoidance of distress risks the loss of the vitality and richness of experience that these emotions bring. Part of the task of the therapist can then be seen to be to enliven and revitalize; promoting healthy acceptance and expression of emotions.

Deepening affect is not the same as catharsis or cathartic methods, although such deepening may well have a positive cathartic result for the client. By facilitating the deepening of affect, the emotional intensity may stimulate the emergence of an impasse. The redecision school of TA employs heighteners for this purpose (McNeel, 1976). The heightener deepens the affective charge of the piece of work and facilitates the triggering of a redecision.

Deepening affect in therapy sessions can be used to promote emotional literacy (Steiner and Perry, 1999). For clients who have very low levels of emotional literacy, the therapist can assist by helping the client verbalize their internal experience, and decode it into the language of feelings. This process develops emotional differentiation (Steiner and Perry, 1999). In some respects this process of identifying and decoding emotional experience parallels the developmental processes parents engage in with their children (Stern, 1985). This may be particularly important for clients who did not have parents who were able to decode effectively. The subsequent containment (Bion, 1970) and affect regulation role the therapist engages with here can be an important part of the therapeutic process. It is possible that this process may even stimulate change in neural pathways, particularly within the orbito-frontal cortex, the area of the brain concerned with affective regulation.

Swede raises the distinction between discussion of feelings and expression of emotion:

> Discussion is concerned with events that are removed from the present in time and place, including discussions of what happened at earlier therapeutic sessions. This is usually an evasive maneuver. Description is an intellectual way of handling feelings. The Adult tells the therapist what the Child is feeling, but the Child himself does not show in the description. This is often an evasive maneuver into pastimes. Expression is the direct expression of affect concerning the here and now at the time the affect is felt. This may be gamy or it may be intimate. The therapeutic goal is the expression of intimacy.
>
> (Swede, 1977: 23)

Deepening affect has many potential therapeutic outcomes. Any therapy that promotes greater experiential awareness and phenomenological exploration and processing may well generate insight and promote Adult awareness. It is possible that in deepening the emotional charge of an issue that physis is mobilized, and the client experiences a sense of organismic disgust, and spontaneously seeks redecision, such as may happen with the use of heighteners. Systematically deepening affect in sessions, facilitating its effective and appropriate expression and then following this with analysis and processing of the emotional experience may well also contribute to increasing affective tolerance. This is particularly so with an open, accepting and mindful stance in relation to the emotions, rather than seeking catharsis for its own sake. It is wise to avoid 'over-nurturing' in relation to feelings, or rushing in too early to resolve the feeling which does not promote affective tolerance, but can infantilize and promote dependence. The Child ego state of the client may well need to experientially learn that they can experience intense emotions, express them appropriately and that they and others around them will survive the experience.

Some authors advise 'striking while the iron is hot' (Luborsky, 1984), that is, selecting the most affectively charged aspect of a client's communication (particularly ones which may highlight parallels in the therapeutic relationship) and intensifying them to make affective links between different feeling states (ego states) and the client's present experience. The advantage of this approach is that highlighting such links in an affectively charged way minimizes the possibility that the client may intellectualize the experience. This approach should not however be used in a blanket manner, and several authors also advise 'striking while the iron is cold' (McWilliams, 1994; Pine, 1985; Yalom 2001); that is, raising such discussions at a time when the client is calm and in a different feeling state. This second approach is more appropriate for clients who have a greater degree of disturbance, such as clients with personality disorder, or clients who may experience the therapist's intervention in the midst of an intense emotional experience as shaming or as criticism.

Contraindications

Interventions that deepen affect should not be used where the therapist is not able to provide sufficient containment and protection for the client. Clients who have poor tolerance of affect need any work on expression of emotions to be done gradually. Rapid or intense deepening of emotions can be experienced as profoundly overwhelming and does not provide sufficient protection for such clients. This is particularly true for clients who struggle with affective regulation, such as clients with borderline personality disorder, who, rather than increasing the affect, need a therapeutic approach which promotes regulation and containment of emotions and one which helps them develop appropriate means of expressing them.

Sometimes deepening affect or facilitating the expression of emotion can result in 'script backlash' in that the client may experience a worsening of symptoms or some kind of internal attack, following the breaking of some unconscious rule. The intrapsychic repercussions and unconscious significance of deepening affect need to be considered, before, during and after interventions that seek to deepen the affective charge in order to maintain client protection.

Interventions that deepen affect include empathic responding and enquiry into the affect the client is expressing, or those which focus on the affective aspect of a client's experience, even in reporting on or discussing prior events. A well-timed interpretation can also deepen affect, particularly hidden feelings or those being defended against. An example of this is 'I understand that you feel sad. I wonder if a part of you also feels angry'.

72

Promoting healthy expression of emotions

Traditionally, transactional analysts have either not stroked (acknowledged) racket feelings, or have confronted them (Stewart, 2007). This presupposes that the 'therapist knows best' and can accurately identify a feeling as a racket or not. In practice this ability to detect in the moment is not so easy, nor is it necessarily helpful to either ignore a feeling or to confront a particular feeling a client may be experiencing. When clients arrive for therapy, they are seeking a safe space where they can explore. When clients are disclosing their feelings, they initially need all of their feelings to be accepted, and for the therapist to understand them – to understand the client's frame of reference and to begin to see why the client feels the way they do. Once these initial presenting feelings have been empathically accepted, then the client may feel safe enough to explore the underlying feelings.

> The client . . . needs to feel heard at this 'racket' level of communication before feeling safe enough to go deeper. It is important initially to respond to the client's felt meaning. . . . Eventually the empathic bond makes it possible for the client to feel secure enough at an 'unthought' level to revive unmet needs and suppressed developmental needs. For her to feel safe enough to do this she has to inherently trust that the therapist is capable of understanding her most profound emotional states (Clark, 1991).
>
> (Hargaden and Sills, 2002: 33–4)

Facilitating the healthy expression of emotion in terms of Steiner's emotional awareness scale (Steiner and Perry, 1999) promotes the movement from numbness, physical sensations and primal experience by moving across the verbal barrier to differentiation and causality, where the individual can recognize emotional states and identify their origin. Clinical experience would suggest that a great number of clients are afraid of emotional expression, conflating it with being 'out of control', which may be reflective of the internal chaos the client feels at some level in response to their early life experiences and their awareness of the oceanic feel of their repressed emotions which may emerge through the process of deconfusion. A common example of this is the fear many people experience in relation to anger that is often confused with aggression. Sensitive and gradual re-educational work that invites an awareness of the difference between the two states and which emphasizes personal responsibility for the expression of emotions can be relieving for such clients.

The expression of emotion is to some extent culturally determined. Some cultures emphasize and encourage emotional restraint, and the minimizing of emotional reactions. Other cultures emphasize strong, exaggerated emotional expressiveness. When working with clients we need to be conscious of the impact of the client's cultural background and context on their level of emotional expressiveness.

Thomson (1983) emphasizes the problem-solving function of emotions that are located within the appropriate time frame, and that, although often uncomfortable, such feelings should be welcomed and allowed space to be worked through to their natural resolution. Moiso (1984) invites analysis of the emotion in terms of its message: fear tells us of present danger, anger of damage being done, and sadness speaks of loss. Joy obviously speaks of pleasure. Each emotion has an instinctive action and a social request: fear requires escape from the danger, and help or reassurance from others. The action of anger is to attack or protect and it requires a change in the environment. Sadness requires a withdrawal of energy into one's self, and consolation and compassion from others. Joy impels us towards others to connect and share our joy (Moiso, 1984). Basic analysis of transactions can be tremendously helpful in promoting healthy expression and the subsequent resolution of emotions, as it is not unusual for people to unwittingly communicate in unclear ways that do not invite a positive response from the environment. By facilitating positive, appropriate, and clear communication and using their own affective responses to the client (social diagnosis), the therapist can help the client relate to others in more growthful and intimate ways.

73

Promoting emotional literacy with 'homework' assignments

Often clients want homework exercises to do in between sessions. I have used this particular method with many clients, who consistently report back that they have found it to be useful. There are a range of uses for this exercise and I invite you to explore and experiment and find your own uses and creative variations on this. The exercise implicitly invites clients to account for a full range of emotions, and the complex and mixed emotions we may feel about any given situation, and how at any time we have a range of emotions connected to different things which we may not be immediately aware of. The process invites a degree of receptivity to a range of emotions. Although material may remain unconscious, by allowing oneself to *feel* a range of emotions, the emotions can be tracked, understood, and generally awareness of one's own process is increased. Identifying (differentiating) and naming emotions and thinking about their cause (causality) is often effective at promoting greater emotional literacy. The exercise is a sentence completion exercise that systematically focuses on different emotions in turn.

Contraindications

Clients who are easily overwhelmed by emotions may find this exercise too disruptive as they may get too 'caught up' in the feelings. It can be used later in the therapy with these clients if they have sufficient Adult ego state available to ensure that they will complete the exercise, and reflective capacity to observe their self in the process although the exercise will in itself help develop reflective capacity. Appropriateness can be assessed by inviting the client to perform the exercise in the therapy room, so the therapist can gauge the client's level of containment. In inviting any client to do this exercise the therapist needs to make an assessment as to the client's capacity to regulate and self-soothe, although many people find it easier to regulate differentiated emotion. Ability to remain focused throughout is also important, as finishing the exercise half-way through may leave someone in a heightened emotional state. It is often worth pre-empting difficult emotions surfacing and exploring what options the client might have for self-soothing after doing this exercise.

Instructions

The exercise is a sentence completion exercise that focuses on primary emotions. It normally takes about fifteen minutes to complete, and is best done regularly, perhaps even daily for a few weeks to facilitate emotional processing. The list I use is:

- *I am angry that . . .*
- *I am scared that . . .*
- *I feel guilty or ashamed about . . .*
- *I am sad that . . .*
- *I am glad that . . .*

I suggest that the client starts with whichever emotion feels most prominent at the time of starting the exercise, but that they always end with the glad sentence, to encourage the ending of the exercise on a positive note. Each sentence is written at the top of a sheet of paper and basically the person doing this exercise completes the sentence in as many ways as they can think of. I normally suggest that, once the list feels complete for each heading, and before moving on to another emotion, they pause for a minute or so, to see whether anything else emerges.

What clients do with their awareness, and how you choose to use this exercise, is a matter for you and your client to discuss. Sometimes clients are surprised by material that emerges in this exercise, discovering that their emotions in relation to something are more richly textured and complex than they expected. Some clients find that in repeating the exercise over a number of days or weeks their emotional reactions to an experience change. It is possible that accounting for and expressing feelings in this way facilitates the process of resolution of held-in or discounted emotions. Systematic focus on deepening emotional awareness can enhance the deconfusion process, by facilitating the acknowledgement and expression of hitherto repressed affect. You and your client may experiment with this method or design and choose other similar exercises. In constructing exercises with your client, be mindful of your client's diagnosis, their therapy contract and your client's individual treatment plan. Don't use a technique when you feel stuck and don't know what else to do – only use techniques as part of an integrated treatment plan, with a clear outcome for a specific change in mind. Remember the 'treatment triangle' (Guichard, 1987; Stewart, 1996): 'How does this intervention link to my diagnosis, the contract and the direction the therapy needs to go?'

74

Encouraging journaling to promote self-reflection

Several processes take place in TA therapy that written methods can effectively enhance. Regular reflective time will develop the client's reflective capacity, enhance mentalizing and promote greater awareness of the client's own internal process. This can include greater awareness of the internal dialogue between ego states. Additionally, reflective writing promotes contained affect expression and affect analysis (Yalom, 2001). Written techniques can be used at any stage of the therapy and can clarify, deepen and accelerate various processes such as contracting (by focusing on the client's goals and wishes), decontamination (clients may recognize hitherto implicit contaminations and challenge them without therapist intervention), emotional literacy (emotional awareness, affect expression and analysis), deconfusion (recognition of repressed emotion), reinforcement of redecision, right through to helping process feelings on an approaching ending of the therapy.

Reflective journals

The simplest method of using writing in therapy is by inviting your clients to keep a journal. I often suggest to clients in their first session that they get a notebook for this purpose. The journal can serve many functions. Clients might use it to:

- record their feelings;
- monitor specific symptoms;
- explore particular feelings in greater depth;
- 'diary' specific events, the situation, people and feelings involved and reflections they trigger;
- record reflections after therapy sessions;
- make notes as reminders of material they want to bring to therapy sessions;
- monitor change.

Reflective learning journals are a key component of the course-work of most psychotherapy and counselling training pro-grammes – there is good reason for this. Regular, structured journaling will enhance your development as a therapist by promoting development of reflective capacity (for further infor-mation see *Reflective Journals as a Tool for Psychotherapists* (Widdowson and Ayres, 2006)).

75

Differences between decontamination and deconfusion

Decontamination and deconfusion are therapeutic processes frequently discussed by transactional analysts, which along with redecision form the 'backbone' or central tasks of TA therapy. Decontamination and deconfusion are two discrete, yet often interlinked and overlapping processes. Beginners to TA therapy sometimes struggle with understanding the difference between the two concepts and the processes involved in them. Structurally speaking, decontamination is a process involving the Adult ego state, and deconfusion is a process involving the Child ego state.

Berne developed his ideas around the Adult ego state independently, but parallel to discoveries in cognitive therapy (Schlegel, 1998). A contamination of the Adult ego state involves the individual mistakenly accepting some Child or Parent content for Adult ego state (Stewart and Joines, 1987). An example of this would be an unchallenged belief that has no rational basis, and one which falls apart under rational scrutiny and dialogue. As the formation of a contamination happens in the context of the whole individual, it is very likely that a double contamination will occur, that is contamination of the Adult by both Parent and Child. For example, a parent figure may repeatedly tell a child they are stupid, and the child unquestioningly accepts this and believes it to be the case (perhaps using their poor spelling as 'evidence' of their stupidity). These beliefs are often held at an implicit, pre-conscious level and TA therapists seek to uncover these implicit beliefs and engage the client in scrutiny and challenge of their here-and-now validity.

Much of what transactional analysts describe as decontamination has a great deal in common with the methods of cognitive therapy. Decontamination can be considered in many ways a cognitive therapy process, and indeed a number of cognitive-behavioural methods can be used successfully for decontamination. It is, however, important to recognize that the Adult ego state is not just a rational data processor: the Adult ego state is the ego state which is adapted to the reality of the here-and-now situation, therefore methods which invite full here-and-now awareness, such as many gestalt therapy techniques or methods drawn from mindfulness approaches (Kabat-Zinn, 2001, 2004) can be used successfully for decontamination.

Deconfusion on the other hand was clearly described by Berne as a psychoanalytic process (Berne, 1961). The process of deconfusion would therefore be more likely to be similar to processes normally used in psychodynamic therapy, and would include methods such as transference analysis (Hargaden and Sills, 2002; Moiso, 1985).

> Deconfusion is the process by which the therapist facilitates the patient to connect with her internal Child ego and bring experiences, feelings and sensations . . . into the therapeutic relationship. . . . The treatment plan involves the therapist's capacity and ability to be attentive, thoughtful and skilful in understanding her countertransference responses. . . .
> The methodology for deconfusion consists of an analysis of the domains of transference together with the therapist's use of empathic transactions (Hargaden and Sills, 2002). The aim of deconfusion is the transformation of unconscious processes such as archaic, dormant and conflicted aspects of self, into a more conscious, vibrant and mature dynamic.
>
> (Hargaden and Sills, 2003: 188)

Another way of thinking about the difference between decontamination and deconfusion relates to the process of development of script decisions. How we conceptualize script beliefs being formed in TA can be roughly summarized as follows: the child has an experience and he experiences feelings connected to his experience. He develops fantasies connected to these experiences and feelings in order to make sense of them, and these fantasies become 'fact'.

Experience → Feeling → Fantasy → Fact

If we are using Berne's principle that decontamination precedes deconfusion, the process of resolution (treatment direction) of associated script decisions can be considered to run parallel to this, but running in the opposite direction.

Experience → Feeling → Fantasy → Fact

Deconfusion ← Deconfusion ← Decontamination ← Decontamination

This diagram shows the connections between decontamination and deconfusion and different aspects of the process of the development of a script decision, but does so in a linear fashion which does not necessarily represent the process of decontamination and deconfusion. Some TA authors see the process as a progressive one, with decontamination being an earlier stage of treatment than deconfusion (Woollams and Brown, 1978; Clarkson, 1992). However, some authors have recently presented the idea that deconfusion can begin right from the moment of meeting between therapist and client (Hargaden and Sills, 2002). In many ways this matches my experiences, in that the formation of the therapeutic relationship requires a degree of containing of the client's affective state, and the emphasis is on empathic transactions (Clark, 1991). Using empathic transactions will inevitably involve a degree of deconfusion so to draw a distinction between the two as a linear process which follows a set sequence is in some ways not representative of the therapy process in practice. It is likely that the TA therapist will be working on multiple aspects of experiences, feelings, fantasies and cognitive construal in a fluid way.

What is important is for the therapist to have a clear sense as to which ego state they are predominantly working with at any given time, and to be clear about their intentions in terms of whether they are promoting decontamination or deconfusion, and their rationale behind their intervention choice.

76

How clients confirm script beliefs in therapy

Clients come to therapy with their established script (and protocol) regarding how they and others behave in relationships, and with the associated meanings and script beliefs about self and others. These aspects of script operate by and large out of awareness as part of the client's unconscious process, but the client will in accordance with script theory be seeking inadvertently, and usually unconsciously, information which will provide 'confirmation' of their script beliefs. The power imbalance inherent in the therapy situation makes the therapy a particularly ripe situation for the enactment of such issues. As the client is generally in a more vulnerable position than the therapist, the transferential similarity is clearly a parallel of early childhood, with the therapist representing (in terms of power) the client's parents. The emergence of patterns that the client could use as 'evidence' to confirm their script is an inevitable part of therapy and one which the therapist needs to be alert to, watching out for ways the client can subtly reinforce their old, unhelpful patterns.

The process of seeking script confirmation can be understood using game theory. Game enactments are a regular aspect of any therapy, as part of the unconscious processes which influence the way in which the therapist and client interact. As games operate out of awareness as unconscious process it is impossible and undesirable to avoid them completely (Guistolise, 1996). The therapist may fruitfully use the enactment in therapy to assist the client in uncovering their core script beliefs, and relational script in this process. The game invitations clients may issue in therapy can be extremely subtle, and so it can be easy to reinforce the client's script inadvertently. The therapist is advised to reflect upon, and discuss in supervision, how their client may indeed be confirming their script in therapy. Below are some possible ways in which a client may confirm their script in therapy. This list is not exhaustive, but is intended to give the therapist some suggestions regarding common means of script confirmation.

Confirmation one

Clients will act in ways that are driven by their script beliefs, and see whether the therapist strokes them, or colludes with them.

Example: Marie is a bright and attractive woman in her mid-twenties who is in therapy to deal with relationship issues and problems with assertiveness. Her therapist was left feeling deeply uncomfortable at the end of a session. In discussion in supervision she realized she had given Marie a lot of suggestions, and repeatedly offered different courses of action, in response to Marie's request to 'brainstorm ideas'. The therapist realized that she had re-enacted with Marie a familiar pattern – Marie would not trust her own judgement, and would phone several friends and family members to obtain their advice before deciding which course of action to take in accordance with script beliefs that she is not capable of making her own mind up and that others' wishes are more important than her own.

Confirmation two

Clients test out the prohibited behaviours to see whether the therapist disapproves.

Example: A client who is normally compliant may become rebellious, or disagree with the therapist to see whether the therapist becomes critical of him, or whether the therapist displays irritation or emotionally withdraws.

Confirmation three

Clients will project various prohibited behaviours or feelings onto the therapist (who may enact them via projective identification) and then the client may take the role of their parent to see how the therapist handles the situation (concordant transference).

Example: The therapist is aware of increasingly feeling inadequate in the session, and that the client is becoming more critical of his interventions. After some time of struggling with this, he recognizes a parallel with his client's experience of her super-critical father and says, 'It seems that today I can't do anything right for you. I keep wanting to get it right, and not managing to do so. It occurs to me that this might be how you felt as a child around your father. Does that make any sense to you?' This intervention moves out of the enactment, but would have 'confirmed' the client's script if the therapist had become more and more desperate to please and then moved into a victim position (Karpman, 1968).

Confirmation four

Clients will state the accuracy of their beliefs to see whether the therapist confirms them in any way.

Example: A client has misunderstood the therapist's intention in a statement the therapist made. The therapist goes back, apologizes for not being clear in their transaction, and clarifies their meaning. The client responds with 'Here I go again! I am just no good at relationships. I always get it wrong, and mess things up'. A reinforcing transaction from the therapist at this point might be 'You did misunderstand me'. A less confirming response might be 'Yes, you misunderstood my intention but also, I wasn't clear in the first place and I can see how you came to your point of view'.

Confirmation five

Clients may act in ways that provoke a particular response which would confirm their script beliefs.

Example: A client who believes they will be rejected may repeatedly provoke the therapist until the therapist refers the client on to a colleague or for psychiatric treatment. Or clients with a belief that they will be abandoned may 'disappear' by missing a session and not contacting the therapist, with the expectation that the therapist will not attempt to contact them.

77

Using alliance rupture and repair for deconfusion

The process of relational repair begins with identifying the relational rupture. Ruptures can be identified by the recognition of a rupture marker – some behaviour on the part of the client which the therapist notices and interprets as indicating a rupture (see Point 24). When ruptures occur, the client activates their protocol regarding their 'response of self' – a characteristic way of responding in anticipation of not having an underlying wish fulfilled, and the 'response of other' – the response the client expects from the projected, transferred Parent as part of their protocol. Safran and Muran (2003) identify two primary types of relational rupture markers: *withdrawal* and *confrontation*. The ultimate goal is for the client to express underlying repressed feelings – usually feelings that were repressed and forbidden during childhood. Thus rupture and repair form a potent method of deconfusion involving the expression of repressed emotions and the gradual healing of the relational wounds associated with the repression. Unfortunately, the way the client responds to ruptures can actually subtly invite the expected 'response of other' – particularly so with confrontation markers which can invite a defensive or rejecting response in the therapist and thus confirm for the client the need to protect their vulnerability with hostility (see Point 76). When withdrawal markers present the therapist needs to be attentive to any underlying repressed anger and hostility and subtly and sensitively invite its expression. With confrontation markers the aim is to invite the expression of any repressed feelings of vulnerability and hurt that lie underneath the overt hostility. Safran and Muran (2003) offer two different processes, one for each type of relational rupture. I have adapted their model here and synthesized the two processes into one. Please note that this is not a linear process with easily identifiable stages, but an overlapping and often cyclical process whereby different parts may be worked on simultaneously, or re-worked over and over in the process of repairing the rupture. Although this model uses two types of rupture markers, each with a particular underlying feeling, it is important to remember that there are in reality more than two types of rupture markers, and any rupture marker may have any underlying feeling. The ones presented here are, however, common markers and common repressed feelings.

The process of deconfusion is a slow and gradual one. The therapist is advised to utilize their countertransference responses to inform them as to what might be going on. Using meta-communicative transactions (Widdowson, 2008) (see Point 78) to bring an awareness of the relational enactment that is taking place into the here-and-now of the therapy deepens this process. In this process, the client will be contacting deep emotional pain and so the therapist must maintain an empathic stance throughout and keep an awareness of what is (potentially) going on for the client behind the apparent social level of the message to inform their responses. The therapist also needs to account for their part in the enactment and not respond from a position of blaming the client. Metacommunication can assist with staying present and in contact and also exploring the significance of any enactment.

To move forward, the therapist invites the client to say more about how they are experiencing the therapist. Particularly with confrontation ruptures, it is absolutely crucial that the therapist is willing to hear the client's feedback – no matter how hard it might be for them. The therapist needs to take seriously and empathically affirm the client's experience. The therapist needs also to seriously consider the 'grain of truth' in what the client is saying and make a serious attempt to acknowledge their part in any enactment. The rupture repair does not necessarily require disclosure from the therapist, nor does it require a position which takes full responsibility for the problem, but it does require the therapist to admit their oversights and errors. With both types of marker, the therapist's task is to invite the client into full expression of their underlying, repressed feelings. Safran and Muran (2003) note that clients who began with a withdrawal marker may begin to express feelings of anger or hostility here, but often 'pull their punches', by qualifying their statements, or by becoming hesitant.

Clients with a confrontation marker are invited to explore the underlying feelings of vulnerability their hostility is covering. Again, the client may well defend against the emerging vulnerability. The therapist can use metacommunicative transactions to highlight the process that is occurring when clients retreat from expression of underlying feelings. Another possibility here is to invite the client into an awareness experiment, whereby the therapist invites the client to state their feelings (which may be still partially repressed) more stridently – for example, 'As an experiment would you try saying "I feel a little worried about how I'll cope over the next few weeks" and see how it feels?' The client's response is then explored – if they take part in the experiment, the therapist explores the feelings; if the client refuses, their reluctant or anxious feelings are explored. Remember, the client's pattern of withdrawal or confrontation was developed as a defence against some kind of pain and so the relinquishing of the pattern is likely to be a slow process. The deconfusion takes place gradually as the client expresses their feelings and underlying needs. This may take a considerable amount of time, and will probably require repetitive cycles of rupture and repair before the deconfusion is complete (or at least partially resolved). The client's feelings here may well be clouded by rage or despair and terror of abandonment which reflects the underlying pain of the original affect. The therapist needs to remain potent, and stay empathically attuned to the client throughout this process, particularly in cases where the client expresses a request to their therapist that their therapist is unable or unwilling to gratify.

78

Using metacommunicative transactions

Metacommunications are based on the therapist's subjective sense of what is happening in the therapy in the here-and-now. The therapist relies upon direct observation of the client, continual observation of their own internal state and observation of their subjective sense of what is happening in the relationship on a moment-to-moment basis. The therapist then invites a dialogue with the client about their experience and the process of how therapist and client are relating. For example the therapist may notice the client looks uneasy, that they are feeling slightly tense and they have a vague sense of distancing between themselves and the client, and so the therapist uses these three experiences to construct a statement which is offered to the client for mutual analysis. 'I notice you're looking around the room, and I'm feeling a little tense. I get a sense of distance between us right now. Does that make any sense to you?'

> A metacommunication is an intervention that utilizes the therapist's countertransference in the here and now of the therapy together with exploration of the here-and-now process of the therapy in a collaborative engagement with the client so as to explore the relational significance for the client of what is occurring in the therapy . . . Metacommunicative transactions usually contain a process observation, that is, an observation about the unfolding process, or the many unfolding processes, that are happening between the therapist and client.
>
> (Widdowson, 2008: 58)

Metacommunicative transactions are in many respects direct interventions that incorporate the characteristics of autonomy: awareness, spontaneity and intimacy. As interventions they embody a spirit of enquiry, curiosity and collaboration. In exploring the therapeutic relationship in an ongoing fashion the therapist and client can gain significant information about the client's subjective ego state shifts, their transactions (and ulterior transactions), their games and their script.

Construction of metacommunicative transactions requires that the therapist pays close attention to directly observable events, such as shifts in the client's position, but also to less tangible shifts in the energetic quality of the connection between them, their sense of relative closeness or distance and their sense of the client being relationally open or closed and withdrawn at any given time. The therapist uses their observations and intuitive sense of the energetic flow within the session and comments on their experience, and invites the client into a dialogue about his or her experience, and the significance and meaning of the experience. Metacommunicative transactions can also name a relational dynamic that is happening between the therapist and client, such as a sense of being overly cautious, a competitive edge, a sense of longing, a cosy atmosphere of stroking. This requires that the therapist pays close attention to their feeling states and repeatedly checks their 'relational barometer'. To do so, the therapist will need to be striving to continually develop their self-awareness, particularly in relation to how they interact with others, and also to have done considerable personal therapy to give them a foundation that enables them to begin to disentangle their own issues and projections from the client's. All of this requires a profound honesty and openness, both to self and others (including sometimes hearing difficult feedback) that facilitates the therapist's use of self and the use of the therapeutic relationship as a vehicle for exploration, change and growth.

79

Therapy of games

Alliance ruptures can be conceptualized in relational TA terms to signify the possibility of a game enactment between the therapist and client. Therapists who work relationally with the transference and countertransference as a major therapeutic tool do not consider the enactment of a game to be intrinsically bad, but rather an inevitable process whereby the client's unconscious process or core conflictual relationship theme (Luborsky, 1984) surfaces in the transactions and relationship with the therapist. Such a relational approach sees that it is not the enactment of a game which is problematic, but rather that the emergence and enactment of the game provides the therapeutic dyad with an excellent opportunity to re-work the underlying script or protocol issues which the game originates from.

As therapists, we have two main options in dealing with games in the therapy room – watch for the game and confront (at the opening con), or be receptive to the game and allow ourselves to be engaged in the unfolding of the client's unconscious processes. Whereas confronting or interrupting the game may be useful in certain situations, and in other fields of application of TA, making space for the game to emerge can be a crucial feature of an in-depth TA therapy. There are proponents within the TA psychotherapy world who advocate the early confrontation of, or avoidance of games (Goulding and Goulding, 1979). A psychodynamic or relational approach views staying out of games as not an optimal therapeutic stance and that 'confronting or aborting a patient's game [is] not therapeutic' (Woods, 2000: 94). The exception to this is the therapist participating in a third-degree game, which therapists of all persuasions would agree is antitherapeutic. Indeed, the therapeutic stance is to become aware of the game and interrupt its flow, and work with the underlying conflicts before the game payoff is reached. In cases where first-degree games have reached their payoff, the therapist engages the client in an analysis of the interactions and seeks to understand and repair any rupture in the relationship. Stark says 'the optimal stance is one that involves semipermeability – the therapist allowing herself to be impacted upon but not completely taken over' (Stark, 2000: 109). She describes how the therapist needs to be receptive to the client's projections to give the client

> the experience of delivering all of herself into the room and discovering that both she and her therapist can survive. The therapist must allow herself to be responsive to the roles imposed on her by the patient, so that the patient can have the opportunity to master her internal demons.
>
> (Stark, 2000: 109)

Another relational psychoanalyst, Karen Maroda, also describes the therapeutic stance and the importance of the therapist's semi-permeability:

> I have learned that my role is not to refuse to be stimulated in this way. My role is to help the patient understand what he is doing and, toward this end, allow myself to be incorporated into his historical play by being responsive. The therapeutic objective is not necessarily for the therapist to feel differently from the others; it is for the therapist to handle his feelings more constructively than did the patient's significant others. Ultimately this enables the patient to be aware of his own feelings and behaviour and take responsibility for both.
>
> (Maroda, 1994/2004: 129)

For effective relational analysis of the game process the therapist needs to adopt a non-defensive position regarding their own contribution to the game enactment. In basic TA terms, a game is not possible without two players (Berne, 1964), therefore it is unhelpful and theoretically inaccurate to consider that one person (i.e. the client) is 'playing a game' with another (i.e. the therapist) in isolation and with no contribution to the situation from one party. The power differential in the therapeutic relationship is in many ways (at least on an emotional level) a direct parallel with the client's early relationships with their parents (being more emotionally powerful than their children). As such, the client is likely to take on the responsibility for the enactment of the game, thus reinforcing script beliefs, for instance beliefs about 'being bad'. Effective therapy and repair of such alliance ruptures requires the therapist to be self-aware regarding their own particular relational vulnerabilities (and engagement in therapy to resolve these issues).

Therapists also have an unconscious, and one which is not immune to proactively issuing game invitations. Clients can respond to the game invitations of their therapist, and in some respects will be particularly vulnerable and susceptible to responding to such invitations due to the nature of the power imbalance in the relationship. As therapists we need to be particularly vigilant for how our own issues are acted out in the therapeutic arena, and to commit to ongoing personal development and thorough personal therapy (see also Points 27, 44 and 96). Following Berne's recommendations, it is wiser for the therapist to reflect upon the question 'What game am I in?' rather than 'Am I in a game?' (Berne, 1966).

Games are an unavoidable aspect of human interactions, including psychotherapy. The role of the psychotherapist is not to avoid them completely, but to seek to understand what *this* game means for *this* client at *this* time as a manifestation of the client's unique unconscious. Similarly, the therapist can productively learn about what *this* game means for *them* as a manifestation of their own unconscious. Finally, the therapist's role is to reflect upon what the participation of both them and their client means *at this time*, and upon how the game was co-created (Summers and Tudor, 2000).

8**0**

Therapy of injunctions

Injunctions provide a summary of themes present in an individual's internalized prohibitions. Injunctions are considered pre-verbal, implicit aspects of a client's script: the child develops their injunctions in response to reactions and behaviours from primary caregivers. In this context, injunctions can be considered to be relational in origin in that they provide a set of rules that the individual needs to follow in order to preserve relationships and thus maintain a (script-bound) sense of 'being OK'. Holmes describes this process from the perspective of attachment theory:

> The key point about defences from an attachment perspective is that they are interpersonal strategies for dealing with suboptimal environment. Their aim is not so much to preserve the integrity of the individual when faced with conflicting inner drives, but to maintain attachments in the face of relational forces threatening to disrupt them.
>
> (Holmes, 2001: 25)

From this we see that injunctions serve a purpose in that the child develops their injunctions to make sense of their world, and to develop rules for living which will ensure that their attachments are preserved. They act as 'internal safety rules' that the individual can follow, and thus keep key caregivers around. Unfortunately, as we know, these injunctions are limiting in later life and can represent the essence of an individual's script that we are seeking to resolve in TA therapy.

The Gouldings' list of twelve injunctions provide a useful shorthand, but need to be considered carefully for each client, as using a defined list of twelve injunctions can miss both the subtleties and variations of an individual's child-hood experience and meaning. It seems both theoretically accurate and therapeutically useful to encourage clients to find their own words to express script conclusions, to articulate their own 'meaning-making'. It is also crucial *not* to restrict the analysis of script to negative, restrictive decisions.

(Cornell, 1988: 279)

That notwithstanding, the shorthand of the injunctions can be a useful tool for the therapist to begin their process of formulation of understanding the client's process and experience using a series of common themes.

Injunctions are tenacious aspects of an individual's script and need to be repeatedly addressed, implicitly and relationally for effective resolution. The Gouldings developed elaborate redecision therapy methods that tackled the injunctions directly. However, all TA sources on redecision methods emphasize the need for ongoing reinforcement of the redecision. It is important in seeking redecision of injunctions that the therapist is mindful of the attachment-preserving intention of the injunction and the desperate fear the client may feel in their Child ego state at the possibility of disobeying an injunction. Resolution of injunctions is a gradual and relational process and one that the therapist needs to pay attention to over time. Often the very processes of psychotherapy provide a direct challenge to our client's injunctions. With planning, the therapist can seek to repeatedly challenge their client's injunctions in an indirect fashion, in addition to any direct methods they may also utilize.

81

Interventions and approaches to therapy of injunctions

Don't exist

In many respects therapy in and of itself is a potent confrontation of this injunction. Clients are reminded through the empathic relationship that they exist, and their existence is validated. Acknowledge their pain, and their struggles with life.

Don't be you

Encourage self-definition and expressions of individuality. By promoting development of a 'coherent narrative' (Holmes, 2001) the client's sense of self is developed and validated.

Don't be close

Pay careful attention to level of 'felt closeness' with your client. Sensitively and gently enquire into their experience. Pay attention to how the client 'avoids' or fears closeness in sessions. Avoid repeated or long theoretical discussions or 'teaching TA' or extensive discussions about third parties.

Don't belong

Understand twinship transference (Kohut, 1984; Hargaden and Sills, 2002) as signifying the need to 'belong'. Invite the client to reflect on *how* they feel accepted in therapy, which cues they pick up on to let them know that they are OK with you. Explore the client's wider social relationships.

Don't be important

This is often a very difficult injunction to treat and will need repeated attention as subservience and the desire to 'not be selfish' is culturally reinforced. Gently confront the client 'talking about others' in their session and enquire as to how they feel receiving all of your attention in sessions.

Don't succeed

Cultivate a positive but realistic attitude in respect of goals. Show interest in the client's goals and interests. Recognize and take to supervision (and perhaps personal therapy) any envy that you may feel towards your client.

Don't grow up

A variation on this is 'don't be separate'. By consistently emphasizing the client's autonomy and capacity to change and individuate, the therapist challenges this injunction. The therapist can also address the client's fear of acting autonomously, and their fear of taking responsibility.

Don't be a child

A variation on this is 'don't be dependent'. In my clinical experience, 'don't grow up' and 'don't be a child' often occur together, creating a difficult double-bind for the individual. Validate the client's childhood experiences, their ways of making sense of the world and survival strategies, but not in a 'marshmallowing' or overly-enthusiastic way. Stroke playfulness and fun. Normalize relational needs of 'having the other initiate'. Also in therapy of this injunction, there may be need to develop a prolonged idealizing transference and work with the client's dependency needs. It is important the therapist has also begun examining their own dependency needs in their own therapy.

Don't be well/don't be sane

Stroke effective problem solving and emphasize health. Often the fear of being well or sane is the fear of the responsibility this brings, or the fear that if they are well, then they won't get looked after, so strategies which invite your client to identify that they want to be taken care of and then going about and getting age-appropriate ways of being taken care of can be supported.

Don't feel

Repeated attention to feelings, empathic transactions and promoting healthy expression of emotions are all effective methods of gently confronting this injunction.

Don't think

Invite expression of the client's own thoughts and reflections. Sometimes the client may need to disagree with the therapist, to develop their own independent thinking; in this case stroke the client for thinking for themselves. Stroke clarity of thinking and clarity of planning.

Don't (do anything)

Stroke positive action and movement out of procrastination. Celebrate spontaneity.

82

Escape-hatch closure revisited

There are two linked, but different procedures within the TA literature that directly address tragic script outcomes: escape-hatch closure and no-harm contracts. The key difference between escape-hatch closure (even time-limited closure) and no-harm contracts is that an escape-hatch closure is by definition a decisional process, and is 'taken by the client for him/herself, with the therapist as witness, and is inherently non-changeable (the unconditionality is part of the decision). A no-harm contract, like any other contract, is agreed between client and therapist and is changeable' (I. Stewart, 2008, personal communication). Escape-hatch closure is a process whereby the individual verbally makes a commitment to her/himself with the therapist acting as witness that no matter how bad things are, they will not kill or harm self, kill or harm others or go crazy (see Stewart 2007 for a full description of this process). Stewart asserts that escape-hatch closure has the potential to be therapeutic for all clients, although the process must be carried out at an *appropriate* time in the therapy, and not done 'for the sake of it' without sufficient preparation (Stewart, 2007).

Attachment theory offers some interesting perspectives for consideration of escape hatches. An attachment perspective would suggest that an individual keeps their own escape hatches as an internal secure base (Holmes, 2001). It would stand to reason from this position that an individual will not be ready to close their escape hatches until they have internalized a new secure base, which will normally be the therapy and the therapist. This emphasizes the need for the development of a good working alliance before escape-hatch closure is contemplated. Part of the function of a secure base is as a provider of internal self-soothing and as a means of tolerating intense affect. So in addition to ensuring that escape-hatch closure is not raised until there is a sufficient working alliance, the therapist needs to ensure that the client has begun to develop new, positive means of self-soothing and developed the capacity to tolerate intense affect. The primary means of learning to tolerate affect is widely accepted to be the experiencing of an empathic relationship. Raising escape hatches prematurely in therapy can provoke alarm and confusion in the client. Some clients interpret the therapist's questions as the therapist's way of subtly suggesting that they think the client is at imminent risk. Heavy-handed or premature focus on escape-hatch closure can lead clients into adapting to the therapist, and 'going through the motions' of closure, without intrapsychic closure or can raise the issue of harm in a client who is not yet ready to discuss or resolve these issues. Clients who have closed escape hatches need to be aware that, although they will not act upon ideation of harm, that they may well still experience the same feelings. Premature or insensitive closure of escape hatches can foreclose meaningful discussion of suicidal or harming ideation and can leave clients with the impression that these feelings are unacceptable, thus leading to shame experiences (Mothersole, 1996; Ayres, 2006).

A number of transactional analysts are opposed to the use of escape-hatch closure procedures with clients, on the basis that escape-hatch closure which is prematurely done, or done in response to the therapist's (intolerable) anxiety, will either be an overadaptation (Schiff and Schiff, 1971) or will foreclose discussion of the client's harmful ideation. This results in the client deducing that their suicidal (or harmful, or crazy) thoughts are not acceptable, and therefore will be repressed or not discussed in the therapy. A number of psychoanalytically orientated transactional analysts also feel that escape-hatch closure will prevent an opening and emergence of unconscious processes in the therapy. Interestingly, a number of psychoanalysts are now using procedures that are very similar to no-harm contracts (McLean and Nathan, 2006). In the psychoanalytic context, no-harm contracts are used with clients with personality disorders as a limit-setting method that acts as a reality confrontation and promotes the development of the client's sense of mastery and control over their world and their behaviours. McLean and Nathan also contest that the process of limit setting and the associated conflict this generates between therapist and client can be used fruitfully. They also posit that by not setting a limit on the client's destructive behaviour the client can experience the therapist as abandoning and not taking their pain seriously. The process used by McLean and Nathan has a flavour of being a Parental procedure for use with clients who have significant pathology. These are interesting perspectives, and ones which are worth considering by transactional analysts.

Drye says of no-harm contracts that 'I see the . . . procedure as designed for use not as a regular part of treatment (however valuable timely use may be) but as a rapid and reliable evaluation in emergency situations' (Drye, 2006: 6). It is essential that the therapist be alert to, and seriously consider the potential of, the client overadapting to the therapist (Schiff and Schiff, 1971), and 'going through the motions'. The subtlety of overadaptation can be missed on first sight, and it is worth the therapist keeping in mind the possibility that overadaptation has taken place in following no-harm contract or escape-hatch closure procedures (the same is true for any procedures for that matter).

There is no doubt that escape-hatch closure is indeed an incredibly powerful method. This needs to be balanced, however, with recognition that escape-hatch closure is not the 'be all and end all' and is certainly not a cure for suicidal ideation. Rather, escape-hatch closure, like most therapeutic techniques, is appropriate for some clients, some of the time. Approached carefully, sensitively, and with appropriate timing, exploration of a client's escape hatches can reveal a whole raft of hitherto unexplored existential issues underlying the client's difficulties.

Whatever the philosophical, cultural or social pressures, psychotic, suicidal or homicidal behaviours are experienced by the ill, confused or desperate individual as potential solutions to problems experienced as overwhelming, insoluble or intolerable. There are exceptions to this, particularly when people are choosing to kill or be killed, or if they are terminally and incurably ill or very old, or in situations where a child may be in danger, or where they may need to act in self-defence, or they may choose to sacrifice their lives in favour of other values such as religion or patriotism, or in order to defend themselves and/or others against oppression.

(Clarkson, 2003: 48)

Existential issues relating to the implications of taking responsibility for our own lives, and the state of being truly free, together with rescue fantasies, and the facing of the meaninglessness of life (Yalom, 1980) are all issues which can emerge in therapy following such a sensitive exploration of escape hatches.

It is possible that a number of transactional analysts who state that they do not use escape-hatch closure are in actual fact using other processes to determine that escape hatches are closed, rather than the formal procedure recommended by Stewart (2007). Escape-hatch closure can be approached using a range of methods other than the standard declarations. For example, a client might be invited to visualize the parents or persons with whom they had the experiences that led them to establish their 'don't exist' injunction (or use redecision-style two-chair work), and verbally make a statement to the projected parent(s) which affirms a decision not to kill or harm self or others, or go crazy. Although technically not escape-hatch closure (as the client may well be in Child ego state in this type of work), work of this nature is a piece of redecision therapy and may well lead to the client making a redecision to live. Following such a piece of work, it would be advisable for the therapist to invite the client back into Adult to go through the escape-hatch closure (even if already done once) to affirm this as an Adult decision.

Stewart (2007) states that one should not generally undertake script-change work until escape-hatch closure has been completed. I disagree. In my experience, clients who have open escape hatches as a serious option are very unlikely to congruently close their escape hatches *without* having done considerable script-change work. It is possible that clients who can readily close escape hatches did not in a real sense have them open in the first place. Stewart (2007) adds that, in the absence of the client having congruently closed escape hatches, the therapist needs to pay particular attention to the client's ongoing safety and protection. I agree with this position but feel that even when escape hatches have been congruently closed the therapist is wise to not become complacent or forget about ongoing client protection.

83

Client protection

There is a range of considerations the therapist needs to take into account in ensuring there is sufficient protection for their client and also for managing their own needs. Resourcing yourself as a therapist is a vital aspect of protection. Obtaining adequate and regular ongoing supervision is a key part of ensuring there is sufficient support and protection available for the therapist, but also for the client in terms of quality assurance and the ethical management of the therapist's caseload. Commitment to reading, attending workshops and other aspects of continual professional development form part of the resourcing of a therapist, and ensure that the therapist's skills and knowledge continue to develop.

TA therapists resource themselves through their own engagement in personal therapy, which seeks to resolve aspects of their own script which may get in the way of their work. Personal therapy for therapists also has a part to play in the therapist developing their capacity to experience, contain and deal effectively with intense and unpleasant emotions. A therapist who is not in touch with or is unable to handle their own anger, or profound grief, or be the recipient of the intense emotions of others is unlikely to be able to provide adequate protection or containment of a client who is experiencing similar intense emotions.

Obtaining a client history, particularly with regard to any previous suicide attempts or self-harming behaviour or violence is important. A previous history of acting destructively to self or others or of impulsivity provides a strong indicator that the client may not be able to contain the intense feelings that psychotherapy can unleash. In the case of a client presenting with such a history it is important that the therapist seeks supervisory advice on whether to work with the client or to refer on. All therapists have a responsibility to be familiar with at least basic risk assessment methods and strategies for dealing with increasing or imminent risk of suicide or violence. Alongside this, the therapist needs to determine how each client deals with acute distress and contains their impulses. Clients who do not handle strong feelings well may well need to develop social control (Berne, 1961) by learning key self-soothing strategies or impulse control strategies before the therapy work can progress safely.

The pacing and timing of the work is important also in providing protection. The pull to delve too deeply too quickly can be strong in early sessions. This is particularly the case with clients who have some insight, and who feel a huge pressure to 'offload' the intense emotions they are struggling with, or those with strong urges to tell their story. In my experience, when we rush things, we invariably have to go back and re-do them. The difficulty in therapy is that once an issue has been covered, particularly in the early sessions, it can be hard to go back and go through it once more later on. In the early sessions we have to strike a careful balance between getting to know the client and find out about their history, while also attending to the content and process and facilitating the integration of material as the client settles into the therapy (see also Point 18). Providing a degree of containment can be vital in instances of strong emotions that threaten to overwhelm the client, leaving them feeling disorganized or fragmented. Knowing when to slow down, or even stop a client is an important therapeutic skill, and is more an 'art' to master than a skill which is easy to develop. Rothschild makes a similar point in the context of describing working with trauma survivors. Her principle is that one should 'know where the brakes are, and how to use them, before one applies the accelerator' (Rothschild, 2000: 79).

Diagnosis is also a central aspect of determining client protection. The most fundamental question each transactional analyst has to answer about each client is 'How much available Adult ego state does this client have?' Different character styles (Johnson, 1994; McWilliams, 1994; Benjamin, 2003) each have different ways of presenting, and some are more prone to destructive acting out than others. Taking time to examine your diagnosis is important as the therapist can pre-empt issues and provide protection by way of things such as specific contracts according to the client's diagnosis. Stewart (1996) also cautions against using dramatic or cathartic techniques until a clear contract is in place, the therapist has completed their diagnosis and some preparatory work has taken place. Familiarity with psychiatric disorders, their features and manifestation is important here, as is the ability to recognize potential rapid escalations of feelings, for instance increased agitation moving towards incapacitation or violence (Schiff *et al.*, 1975).

84

Potency and permission

The 'Three Ps' of *potency* (Steiner, 1968), *protection* and *permission* (Crossman, 1966) are central to the practice of effective and ethical TA psychotherapy. Having discussed client protection in Point 83, I focus here on potency and permission.

Potency

The potency of the therapist lies in the capacity to contain despair, uncertainty, doubt, meaninglessness, hatred, rage, shame and anxiety, both within the therapist and their clients. Potency also includes the therapist's sense of emotional and psychological resilience. Potency relates to the therapist's ability to provide sufficient intensity and strength in the therapy for the client to disobey Parental injunctions and scripting (Berne, 1972). The therapist's potency is also increased by the use of the therapist's training, skills and knowledge in the service of the client, and by the therapist having a clear sense of why they are doing what they are doing (treatment planning) (Stewart, 2007). Ongoing personal and professional development work, recognizing and accepting the need to take regular breaks and holidays from work, and attending to personal needs all model good boundaries, self-care and, by extension, therapeutic potency. Our potency as therapists also involves an awareness of our own personal strengths and resources, and an acceptance of our personal limitations.

Permission

Permission is an interesting concept, and one which in my view needs careful consideration. Historically, a number of TA therapists took a parental stance and literally gave clients verbal permissions, often in the form of verbal affirmations in sessions. This approach has all kinds of inherent potential problems, not least the risk of infantilizing adult clients. It is also unclear to what extent a client will accept a positive verbal message from a therapist when their internal self-experience is highly negative and critical. In this instance it is possible that the direct giving of verbal permissions can exacerbate the client's sense of internal badness and isolation. I do, however, believe there is a place for the provision of encouragement, support, strokes and the replacement of negative, limiting script beliefs with more positive and resourceful beliefs in the therapy. However, the means by which this provision takes place needs careful thought and discussion in supervision, and not just automatically churning out positive statements for the client. The developmental and transferential implications of gratifying and providing permissions need to be considered carefully. Although some people have had dreadfully restrictive upbringings and are hungry for permission and may require encouragement and invitation to begin to live in more flexible and expansive ways, permission giving can serve the therapist's needs far more than the client's.

> When one of my supervisors commented that I see every-body as hungry, thus confronting my tendency to project my depressive issues on all my clients, I was able to start discriminating between those who needed to be emotion-ally fed and those who needed to be asked why they had not learned to cook.
>
> (McWilliams, 1994: 230)

In approaching clients who need to be asked why they have not learned to cook, TA therapists can use a more psycho-dynamic approach. This approach, rather than directly giving permissions, is one which affirms the client's autonomy in a way which is congruent with TA philosophy. The method involves noticing when the client is implicitly seeking permission, or whether the client appears to 'need' permission in some area and to attempt to amplify the client's desire for permission and facilitate the client's expression of their neediness. Once this desire is in conscious awareness, and the client has articulated it as a direct statement, the therapist can invite the client to explore the significance of asking for permission and how they stop themselves from taking permission independently.

85

Impasse theory revisited

An impasse is a stuck point, where there are equal and opposing forces present. The Gouldings first elaborated impasse theory following their work with Fritz Perls, the originator of gestalt therapy who understood internal conflict as being an internal battle between the 'topdog' and 'underdog' (Perls, 1969). The Gouldings took this understanding and applied TA structural theory to understand the conflict as a conflict between ego states (Goulding and Goulding, 1979). Ken Mellor (1980) later developed impasse theory to create a consistent model (the Gouldings' model mixed structural and functional ego state models) that incorporated some child development theory. It is Mellor's conceptualization of impasses which is most widely used amongst TA practitioners at present (Figure 85.1).

Students who are new to TA often confuse an impasse with the client feeling 'stuck'. Whereas an impasse will always involve a sense of stuckness, stuckness is not necessarily indicative of the presence of an impasse. For an impasse to be diagnosed there need to be equal and opposing forces in conflict. Impasse diagrams must also show the two sides of the conflict, as an impasse is often confused (diagrammatically) with internal dialogue between ego states. Describing the dialogue for type three impasses can be particularly problematic, as these are global, impressionistic and developmentally early conflicts which are often experienced on a somatic level. They have a timeless quality in that clients will often report having 'always felt that way'. Describing these impasses is usually done by way of describing the general themes of the impasse, for instance a type three impasse around existence may simply hold the words 'die' and 'I want to live', or may be connected to themes such as abandonment, engulfment (Gobes, 1985; Lee, 1997) and so forth.

Often the emergence of an impasse is indicative of a move towards greater health on the part of the client. The early stages

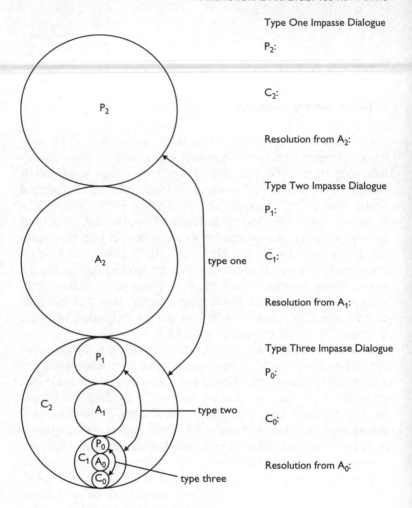

Type One Impasse Dialogue

P_2:

C_2:

Resolution from A_2:

Type Two Impasse Dialogue

P_1:

C_1:

Resolution from A_1:

Type Three Impasse Dialogue

P_0:

C_0:

Resolution from A_0:

Figure 85.1 Impasses (Mellor, 1980)

of therapy are often characterized by a Parent-led process in that the client's intrapsychic process is following the 'instructions' of the Parent ego state. When the client's Child ego states resist these Parental wishes and desires and their Child ego states have been activated then an impasse may emerge as the two opposing sides conflict with each other.

Recent TA authors have begun to explore the relational dimensions of impasse theory, and the role of impasses in explaining seemingly intractable stuck points in therapy. Petriglieri (2007) proposes impasses as necessary points of repose and reflection whereby the individual experiencing the impasse collects their thoughts and reconfigures them in a process of meaning making. Cornell and Landaiche (2006) consider the interpersonal aspects of the impasse and explore how therapy often works with the deepest, unconscious impasses – those at type three level (Mellor, 1980) – and how the very work of therapy pushes both the therapist and client to their relational edge.

Indeed, many transactional analysts now view the process of impasse resolution in very different terms from those of the Gouldings, who focused on the use of two-chair methods for impasse resolution (Goulding and Goulding, 1978). Current TA therapy tends to view the resolution of type three impasses as being a relational process, and linked to deconfusion. There is great interest in integrating body psychotherapy methods to work with such early and often somatically based processes.

Commonly practitioners seek a rapid resolution of an impasse once an impasse is identified. My experience would suggest that prematurely seeking resolution of an impasse results in a hollow and short-lived victory: the impasse will either return, intact, or the impasse will emerge in a different presentation. Impasses are complex intrapsychic processes with complex dynamics and are mostly not amenable to rapid resolution. Practitioners are advised to spend a great deal of time in the process of impasse clarification with clients, which will often lead to a spontaneous impasse resolution. The process of 'being with' the impasse can be incredibly frustrating for both therapist and client, but taking time to complete the process effectively will avoid the need to revisit material at a later date, and may well provide space for the integration needed for the impasse to be resolved.

86

Two-chair Parent ego state work: some guidelines

Projective two-chair techniques are widely used by transactional analysts, particularly in working with Parent ego states and in promoting resolution of difficulties between Parent and Child ego states. These methods were introduced into TA by the Gouldings (Goulding and Goulding, 1979), who were taught these methods by Fritz Perls. They have been subsequently developed by a number of TA authors, including John McNeel's Parent Interview method (McNeel, 1976) and more recently by Richard Erskine (Erskine *et al.*, 1999).

1   Establish a clear Adult contract for the piece of work. Explain carefully what you propose, what the method involves, and give the client a real opportunity to discuss this and to refuse if they are not comfortable with the suggestion.
2   The therapist needs to communicate, either explicitly or implicitly, that they are as potent as, or psychologically stronger than the client's introjected Parent. It is critical that the client's Child feels protected and feels that the therapist will not abandon him. Potency, protection and permission are all vital parts of this process while the client is resolving these issues (Crossman, 1966; Steiner, 1968).
3   Be mindful of the internal sense of loyalty a client will experience towards their parents, no matter how abusive their parents were. Inviting disagreement or 'fighting' with the Parent can be extremely destabilizing for a client and can set up strong intrapsychic resistance (Clarkson, 1988).
4   It is not always necessary to use an empty chair – slight modification of the method can have the same result and can feel substantially safer for many clients. Clients who are likely to feel silly talking to an empty chair can be asked to close their eyes and mentally imagine seeing the parent in

front of them. Clients who struggle visualizing can be invited to imagine hearing the dialogue instead.

5 If using this method 'in imagination' or by using visualization, invite the client to choose a neutral place as an imagined setting for the piece or somewhere they feel safe.

6 It is not always necessary to invite the client to physically shift chairs – and indeed it may not be desirable for them to 'become their parent'. Asking the client to allow the Parent ego state to respond, for the client to 'hear' the response and then to verbally relay this back is sufficient.

7 Clients who do shift chairs are recommended before continuing in dialogue to adopt a posture that would be typical of that particular parent. There is often a mental shift at this point as the client 'thinks themselves into their parent's skin'.

8 Be respectful to the Parent. Introduce yourself, and ask the Parent how they would like to be addressed by you. Be sensitive to the Parent's wishes and sense of what is appropriate.

9 Use sustained empathic enquiry with the Parent. It is important that the Parent ego state does not feel threatened but feels respected and has an opportunity for healing. Often the Parent will spontaneously move into strong affect or reveal information regarding their own personal history. This may pave the way for the Parent resolution process (Dashiell, 1978).

10 You may invite the Parent ego state to make a new, alternative decision. This may involve the resolution of type one or type two impasses (Dashiell, 1978; Mellor, 1980) within the Parent ego state.

11 Be prepared to coach and teach the 'Parent personality' in parenting methods, and also how to proceed. For example: 'OK, so you say you love your son, tell him that, he's sitting over there . . .'

12 Invite the client to ensure that they have cleared their projection, and move around or move the chairs slightly to signify the end of this piece of work.

13 Do not make a big deal about verb tense – let the client go with their own way of doing this method. It may be that

the client is defending against intense emotion for good reason. Also there is a risk that full phenomenological re-experiencing can be re-traumatizing so some distancing may be desirable and will enable the client to maintain sufficient cathexis in Adult.

14 Ensure that you spend plenty of time debriefing after using two-chair methods. The debriefing should also include some discussion of how the experience felt for the client, and the impact of the method on the therapeutic relationship. As part of this, the therapist needs to spend time thinking about the impact the method has had on the transference dynamics in the relationship.

(Acknowledgements to Adrienne Lee)

87

Two-chair Parent ego state work: contraindications

There is no doubt that two-chair methods are extremely powerful, but their use needs to be carefully thought out and introduced into the therapy sensitively and mindful of the intrapsychic implications. Furthermore, these methods are not appropriate for use with all clients or with all issues and so may need to be modified or adapted so that a similar outcome can arise from using an alternative method.

1   Do not do two-chair work if it is the only thing you can think of to do (for that matter, never use any 'technique' if it's all you can think of). All methods used need to be part of a clear rationale and a coherent treatment plan and chosen as one of many possibilities.
2   Do not use two-chair work too early in the therapy. There needs to have been a significant period of therapeutic alliance building for the client to experience the therapist as trustworthy and to avoid the client feeling shamed or overexposed in using methods that a client might experience as unusual or odd (talking to empty chairs is certainly an unusual thing to do). It is not appropriate to introduce two-chair methods within the first few sessions, and probably not within the first six sessions.
3   Do not use two-chair techniques until you have compiled a thorough diagnosis of the client.
4   Do not use two-chair techniques with clients who are presenting with problems with anger and rage until they have developed sufficient control of their anger. Premature introduction does not provide sufficient protection for clients who may be struggling to contain their emotions.
5   Do not use two-chair techniques to 'get at' a Parent ego state or to vicariously vent your anger towards a client's parents. Careful self-examination of the therapist's countertransference is required before introducing such methods.

6   Do not use two-chair work with Parent ego states that will involve a cathecting of a parent who was abusive, violent or psychotic (McNeel, 1976). You may develop other methods of inviting the client to dialogue from Adult or Child to such a parent, but do not cathect an unstable parent without the capacity to provide plenty of protection.

7   Do not use two-chair work with clients who use splitting mechanisms, such as clients with borderline personality structure, as such methods can effectively reinforce the intrapsychic split.

8   Do not use two-chair work with clients who are heavily overadapted or extremely compliant. It is highly likely that they will go through the motions of the two-chair work, but not actually make any significant intrapsychic change and may well at some level reinforce script beliefs. This also applies to clients who are 'performers'.

9   'Avoid two-chair methods with clients with Borderline, Narcissistic or Dependent personality structures. With clients with such structure, the Child ego-state interprets the entire therapy situation as an arena for working out transferential issues with the therapist. Thus such clients, even if ostensibly engaging in techniques like two-chair or early-scene work, usually do not in fact intrapsychically address the projected figure; the whole process then becomes a matter of play-acting by the client' (I. Stewart, 2008, personal communication).

10   Do not use two-chair work with clients who are passive and expecting someone else to change, or who attempt to manipulate the therapist into providing direction or who harbour fantasies of the therapist having a 'magic technique' which will solve their problems.

11   Do not use two-chair work until you have carefully considered what the intrapsychic implications (and possible repercussions) of the piece might be for the client, and also its impact upon the therapeutic relationship.

12   If, after a piece of two-chair work, you are left feeling exhilarated and powerful and are experiencing a sense of smugness and self-satisfaction, take your feelings and your motivations for using the method to supervision.

88

Confrontation

Confrontation is a loaded word; it carries such negative connotations of 'being told off', of angry conflicts and so on that a number of people, therapists included, shrink inside when even the word is mentioned. In spite of all of this, sensitive and well-timed confrontation remains a potent therapeutic method. In discussing the need for confrontation to be made from a position of empathy and care, Masterson recommends the following:

> Confrontation must be done intuitively and empathically and must 'fit' the clinical material the client presents. It requires the therapist confront from a neutral, objective, emotional stance because it is clinically indicated, not out of anger or from his or her own personal needs, that is, to be aggressive and assertive, to direct, control, or admonish the patient.
>
> (Masterson, 1981: 136)

Hahn, in using the Masterson approach, offers the following four areas as particular aspects of the client's process to attend to and confront problematic distortions in the treatment of clients with borderline personality disorder.

1   Limit setting.
2   Reality testing.
3   Clarifying the consequences of maladaptive thoughts, feelings or behaviours.
4   Questioning the motivation for maladaptive thoughts, feelings or behaviours (Hahn, 2004).

This approach is not incongruent with a TA approach, in that TA therapists should always confront third-degree script/game behaviours (Stewart, 1996) and effective confrontation strengthens reality testing and Adult ego state functioning (Schiff *et al.*, 1975). Strengthening Adult ego functioning would also include developing the capacity for reflexivity and thinking through the motivations and consequences of one's actions.

Confrontation can act as a strong invitation for the client to cathect Adult. One difficulty with confrontation is that even with the best will in the world a confrontation can be heard by the client as being Parental. In the case of confrontation that is (or is perceived as) Parental the intervention is likely to be ineffective. Berne (1966) identified confrontation as an intervention used for decontamination purposes. Berne also added that confrontation should not be used 'when it makes you feel smarter than the patient' (Berne, 1966: 236).

Berne suggested that confrontations should be followed up later in the therapy with confirmation. A confirmation is one of the therapeutic operations that is designed to 'reinforce the ego boundaries still further' (Berne, 1966: 240). The confirmation basically reinforces the original confrontation and prevents the client from slipping backwards, so to speak. Confirmation also strengthens decontamination: 'for the Adult, confirmation has a strengthening effect because of its logical force' (Berne, 1966: 240).

'In systems theory there is an acknowledgement of the importance of creating a crisis in order to find the necessary turbulence or disruption or destructuring from which new growth and healing can arise' (Clarkson, 2003: 53). Indeed, as Berne described, after confrontation 'the patient is stirred up and his psyche is thrown out of balance' (Berne, 1966: 235). Striking the right balance with the degree of confrontation is not easy. Confrontation can, with some clients, provoke extreme reactions, which may be as a result of the confrontation putting the client in touch with an internal vacuum (Bateman and Fonagy, 2006). It is perhaps wise for a therapist to bear this turbulence in mind and provide opportunity in the therapy for the confrontation to be processed and integrated by the client before moving on to something else.

89

Enhancing effectiveness with audio recordings

Transactional analysts commonly audio record sessions with clients, particularly trainee transactional analysts, who are seeking to obtain audio recordings suitable for presenting in the Certified Transactional Analyst examination. Listening to audio recordings of sessions is often fruitful in enabling the therapist to notice patterns of language and how they are making their interventions, information which they can use to considerably sharpen up their skills. For example, a frequent mistake of beginning therapists is talking too much, or making long interventions. Listening to audio recordings will help to make such errors apparent. Systematic use of audio recordings in personal reflection and self-supervision, and also in individual and group supervision can result in the therapist considerably sharpening their skills, and also developing the capacity to *reflect in action*, as well as *reflect on action* (Schön, 1983).

One method that can be used for reflection upon audio recordings is *Interpersonal Process Recall* (IPR) (Kagan, 1980). IPR is particularly useful in group supervision. Segments of audio recordings of therapy sessions are played, and every few transactions or so, the recording is stopped (any person in the group can call for stopping the recording) and the practitioner describes what their process was at that point, and what they imagine their client's process was. For example, what was the therapist feeling? What were they thinking? What did they want to say? What do they imagine would have happened had they said that? How did they want the client to react? And so forth. In group situations, members of the group can also offer their formulations of what they suspect was going on for both therapist and client.

An additional method of evaluating the therapist's work is to use detailed transcript analysis. In addition to making up a 'front sheet' (Stewart, 1996) for the client, the therapist makes a transcript of the segment of audio recording to be presented. The therapist annotates the transcript, transaction by transaction, with their thoughts, feelings, hypotheses, and intention of each intervention and labels each transaction, even para-verbal prompts such as the commonly used 'uh huh'. The therapist also includes their thoughts on the client's internal process throughout. Wherever possible, the therapist should include standard TA nomenclature to describe the interventions such as 'confrontation to encourage decontamination' or 'heightener to clarify impasse' or 'empathic transaction'.

'Learning to be a therapist is not about producing perfect pieces of therapeutic work. It is concerned with the struggle of being in relationship with another/others' (Eusden, 2006, personal communication). Using IPR and transcript analysis can be used to support the growth and learning of thoughtful and reflexive practitioners. These methods also assist with the development of the therapist's understanding of the 'microprocesses' of therapeutic work and the refining of his or her therapeutic style.

Transcripts can be used of both effective pieces of therapy and problematic pieces, mistakes or alliance ruptures. In engaging with this, the process of reflection-in-action is enhanced, the therapist deepens their theoretical integration. Sometimes the 'difficult and bad' bits of sessions can hold the nuggets of powerful therapeutic work, if we dare to look. Presenting audio recordings and transcripts can appear daunting and embarrassing. However, it is crucial that therapists develop a capacity to view their work in the spirit of openness and willingness, to critique and praise their work and their interventions.

90

Evaluating interventions and enhancing skills

Potent therapists consistently and regularly seek feedback from their clients regarding the therapeutic relationship, the therapy methods and the way of working of the therapist. Yalom (2001) suggests enquiring into the client's experience of therapy and the therapist, and the quality of relating to each other towards the end of each session. I would also recommend this is done in some way in every single session. This process of shared collaborative enquiry is deeply respectful of the client and promotes an experiential sense of the 'I'm OK – you're OK' life position (Ernst, 1971; Berne, 1972) operating within the therapy. Engaging the client in a collaborative, reflective dialogue about the therapy process not only helps the therapist to fine-tune their interventions and approach, but also creates a climate where the client will be more likely to discuss any difficulties they are experiencing in their therapy. In effect, in promoting collaborative reflection and inviting feedback you are asking the client to give you supervision on your work together – a process entirely congruent with the practice of TA. Berne was one of the first psychiatrists to involve his patients in psychiatric hospitals in case discussions about themselves.

Continuous and systematic reflection and enquiry into your own practice is a good habit to get into, and one which will pay dividends in terms of your effectiveness and also client retention. Although identifying errors and mistakes is important, together with identifying how the error came about and how it can be prevented in future, it is also very important to reflect upon what you did well, and also to identify what you did that *did* work, or that was an effective strategy. All therapists are familiar with the experience of feeling a session with a client went well, or was very productive. Effective therapists are not content to just accept this at face value but deliberately seek to think about *what* was important or useful and *why* it was important or useful (Miller *et al.*, 2008).

Schön (1983) describes the process that experienced practitioners in different fields use to understand and work with complex problems. He used the term *reflection-in-action* to describe this process. 'When someone reflects-in-action . . . he is not dependent on the categories of established theory and technique, but constructs a new theory of the unique case' (Schön, 1983: 68). In the context of TA psychotherapy this involves the practitioner taking each client and reflecting upon his or her presenting issues and engagement in therapy and developing their understanding of the unique interactions of the client's script and so on. As part of this process of ongoing reflection-in-action, the therapist is checking the validity of their theories, formulations and interventions, as well as remaining open to any evidence which suggests that their current theory or approach is too limited, partial or inaccurate. A similar process can be used in evaluating skills and interventions. The systematic enquiry, reflection and evaluation in these processes enhance the practitioner's capacity to develop a meta-perspective in their work. Developing such an open and reflective stance is not easy, and supervision, particularly group supervision, can be used to facilitate these processes.

One way to increase the rigour of one's reflection-in-action is to use the research processes developed in action research. Action research involves a cyclical and iterative process of planning, acting, observing and reflecting (Lewin, 1946). In a TA psychotherapy context, this process means developing a (diagnostic or treatment planning) hypothesis based on careful client observation, making an intervention on the basis of the hypothesis, noticing the client's reaction, critically reflecting upon the action and the outcome, and returning to the beginning of the cycle once more and making a new hypothesis (with continuing observation of the client and one's own process throughout). This process will be familiar to psychotherapists of all traditions, who essentially use this process in an ongoing manner in their sessions with clients. The difference in action research is that the process is more conscious and explicit than it normally is, and involves formulating a clear hypothesis (or hypotheses) and also requires more critical reflection. The process of reflection then determines the next hypothesis and the next intervention.

91

Record keeping in TA therapy

Effective note keeping is an essential skill for therapists. All therapists develop their own method of keeping notes over time, but it is worth periodically reviewing how you keep notes to make sure that the method used is the one which is most helpful, both for refreshing your memory and for treatment planning and tracking a client's progress. It is hard for a therapist to remember a lot of details about any given client, and with a full caseload, this becomes even more difficult.

Session notes are a reminder of the journey and process of the therapy. Notes keep track of the progress of your client, including improvements, deterioration or 'no change'. They are adjuncts to any notes you might have regarding the client's history, your notes on diagnosis (such as the diagnosis checklist in Point 47) and your ongoing individualized treatment plan (see Points 57 and 58). Efficient notes should take no more than a few minutes to write up, and are best written up as soon as possible while the information is still fresh in your mind, ideally immediately after each session.

Various health professionals use the 'SOAP' formula for keeping clinical records (Weed, 1971). SOAP is an acronym for: subjective (report of client); observation (of client); analysis (of subjective report and observation); and plan (treatment plan). This formula is easy to remember and keeps the therapist focused on what is observable. I have adapted this formula, which I present below with an example. I invite you to use this approach, and adapt it to suit your own purposes.

Example: 'Claire'

Session date: 1st September *Session number:* 26
Subjective report of client: Claire reports a fairly good week, with no further arguments with partner or family. Still rather upset

over argument with son two weeks ago. Managing work stress fine. No significant improvement in mood overall.

Observation of client: Despite not feeling much better, did seem more positive, and appeared more energized.

Hypotheses from observation: Suspect she is worried that any gains won't last and is anticipating failure, which would confirm script beliefs.

Observation of therapist: Felt distracted when going over previous argument with son.

Hypotheses from observation: Countertransference to 'helpless and pointless' beliefs and guilt?

Observation of interaction: Generally good. Getting 'straight into the work' in last few sessions rather than 'talking about' for twenty minutes. Get a sense she is trying to please me and is looking for approval.

Hypotheses from interaction: Client feeling safer in the therapy? Client trusting herself more? Result of previous recontracting? Pleasing – part of client pattern of relating to others (look after others first).

Interventions used: Enquiry, empathic responding, decontamination/confrontation ('helplessness'), some deconfusion (grief).

Analysis: Therapy presently mostly deconfusion work and strengthening and supporting previous changes, with invitations to reinforce script.

Progress with case formulation and overall contract: The therapy seems to be progressing fine, although the pace has slowed somewhat over the past few weeks.

Plan/reminders for next session: Check for anticipating failure and associated script beliefs and watch for intensification of attempt to confirm script in therapy.

Themes to monitor: Grief over grandmother's death. Think this will need to be revisited.

92

Promoting mentalization

Mentalizing involves a joint thinking and feeling *about* the feelings, thoughts and mental states of both self and others. As a concept it includes both empathy and open, reflective understanding in relation to both self and others. It involves a stance of curiosity and enquiry. Mentalizing also involves an acceptance that there are multiple influences and explanations behind the behaviour of self and others. It is mostly an implicit and preconscious process and we mentalize regularly without realizing it. Developing the capacity to implicitly mentalize is desirable, although in psychotherapy we also seek to develop the ability to explicitly and consciously mentalize. Poor or absent mentalizing, or breakdown of mentalization, becomes a vicious cycle in mental health problems: 'psychiatric disorders impair mentalizing and impaired mentalizing contributes to psychiatric disorders' (Tobias *et al.*, 2006: 255).

Characteristics of mentalization relating to the thoughts and feelings of others include an attitude of curiosity and genuine interest in others and their thoughts and feelings. It also requires imaginativeness in generating thoughts regarding the emotional and mental states of others. Although mentalizing involves developing ideas about what another person is experiencing, mentalizing is characterized by an absence of concrete attributing. An example of concrete attributing would be 'He did that because he hates me'. In mentalizing we have an acceptance that one cannot entirely know what is going on in the mind of another, and that others may have very different perceptions even of the same event. In relation to understanding one's own mental functioning, mentalizing requires a stance of curiosity about one's own thoughts, thought processes and feelings and includes an acceptance that our view of ourselves can and does change over time. This includes an awareness of how our feelings colour our perceptions. It also includes an acceptance 'that at any one time one may not be aware of all that one feels . . . [this includes] a recognition that one's feelings can be confusing' (Bateman and Fonagy, 2006: 69). Mentalizing includes the quality of mindfulness, and indeed mindfulness develops the ability to mentalize (see Point 93).

Self-awareness is greatly enhanced through mentalizing, as is the ability to problem solve, and the capacity for affective regulation – a capacity which often appears to be limited in many clients presenting for psychotherapy. Mentalizing also enhances relationships and deepens the capacity for intimacy. When we are mentalizing we can influence others and be influenced in a mutually constructive manner. As stated above, psychiatric disorders impair mentalizing, which in turn exacerbates psychiatric disorders. It stands to reason that deliberately promoting mentalization will positively impact upon psychiatric disturbance. Systematically maintaining a mentalizing stance, and seeking to enhance our client's capacities for mentalization, is therefore clearly desirable in psychotherapy.

From a TA perspective, inviting our clients to stay in their Adult ego state, while simultaneously reflecting upon what they are experiencing in their Child and/or Parent ego states, will promote mentalization. Explanation can sometimes help facilitate mentalizing by giving our clients a framework to understand and think about their experiences (or experiences they encounter in interactions with others). Using the theories of TA to consider what is potentially going on for someone, or for ourselves, may encourage mentalizing. However, mentalizing effectively stops when TA theory is used from a position of certainty, rigidity or in defining the person or situation as opposed to a position of possibility or enquiry. For example, the statement 'You're in your Parent!' is a statement that is probably given from a non-mentalizing stance.

It is very possible that one benefit of group therapy is that therapy in groups often promotes mentalization. Certainly, couples therapy generally results in an increase in the capacity of both parties to mentalize in their relationship, both internally and about their partner. It is also possible that increased mentalization is an outcome of TA procedures such as the

Parent Interview (attributed to B. Heiller by C. Sills, relational TA forum 9 June 2006).

Interventions that explore the here-and-now interaction between therapist and client, such as those used in relational approaches, most significantly enhance mentalization. The two-person psychologies promote the mind of both therapist and client being simultaneously 'held' by both, and the interaction between the two is explored. Empathy, active and interactive listening, describing here-and-now experiences and mental states; all features of effective psychotherapy are mechanisms which encourage and model mentalizing. Indeed, many therapeutic methods can be used to promote mentalization by a therapist who is consciously seeking to do so.

93

Cultivating mindfulness

Mindfulness is a concept and practice that has its origins in Buddhism. Essentially it involves a deep awareness of *now*. In practising mindfulness, the individual seeks a total immersion in the present moment, in their *experiencing*, but does so from a position of observing. For example, mindfulness can involve an awareness of the sensory input one is experiencing at any given moment. It can be practised in many situations, and requires no special equipment. Household chores can be approached mindfully, for example in washing the dishes, the water is felt on the hands, the plates are each felt and the different textures are noticed and appreciated. The smell of the detergent is noticed, together with the visual stimulus of the bubbles and the way that the light catches them. Another approach involves consciously directing one's attention to one's breathing. The breathing is not deliberately changed, but rather noticed: noticing the in-breath, and the little pause, and then the out-breath and then the next little pause before breathing in again. In mindfulness, one is not seeking to discover anything, or even *do* anything; one is just being.

As mindfulness practice involves a deep engagement with what is here-and-now, it is theoretically consistent to assume that mindfulness practice will by definition be something one does in one's Adult ego state. Regular mindfulness practice is also very likely to generally strengthen the Adult ego state and be a useful tool for decontamination. The cultivation of an attitude of acceptance implicit in mindfulness is also likely to have a beneficial impact in relation to promoting self-acceptance. In some respects, mindfulness is antithetical to the goal-driven contractual approach to TA, in that in mindfulness, there is no goal.

When we let go of wanting something else to happen in this moment, we are taking a profound step toward being able to encounter what is here now. If we hope to go anywhere and develop ourselves in any way, we can only step from where we are standing. If we don't really know where we are standing – a knowing that comes directly from the cultivation of mindfulness – we may only go in circles, for all our efforts and expectations. So in meditation practice, the best way to get somewhere is to let go of trying to get anywhere at all.

(Kabat-Zinn, 1994: 15–16)

It is my view that practising mindfulness regularly is a deeply beneficial practice and one which enhances TA therapy, both for the therapist and for the client who begins regular mindfulness practice.

Safran and Muran (2003) particularly recommend the use of mindfulness techniques in the training of relational psychotherapists.

Trainees are instructed to observe the contents of their awareness without judgement and without letting themselves get caught up in or identified with any particular content of awareness . . . Trainees are instructed that the goal is not to eliminate thoughts or feelings, but rather to become more fully aware of them as they emerge on a moment-to-moment basis without judging them or pushing them away. Gradually, over time, this type of mindfulness work helps trainees to become more aware of subtle feelings, thoughts and fantasies emerging on the edge of awareness when working with their patients, which can subsequently provide an important source of information about what is occurring in the relationship. One of the most valuable by-products of this kind of mindfulness work is a gradual development of a more tolerant and accepting stance toward a full range of emotional experiences.

(Safran and Muran, 2003: 210)

It would make sense that similar processes also occur within clients who regularly practise mindfulness, including the deepening of self-awareness, and increased ability to observe the self (observing ego). Greater accounting of one's own process, sensory input and interoceptive processes will probably reduce discounting. Noticing one's own internal flow, and flow between ego states, is another potential outcome. The development of evenly suspended attention (Freud, 1912), without judgement and the accompanying increased awareness, also would logically enhance one's degree of autonomy (Berne, 1964).

94

Script development: an ongoing process

Some traditional views of TA consider the process of scripting to be complete by the time a person is in late childhood. Berne's own view on this was that scripting was largely complete by around seven years old and in his last book he defined script as 'An unconscious life plan, made in childhood, reinforced by the parents, justified by subsequent events and culminating in a chosen alternative' (Berne, 1972: 445). Various TA sources indicate the period marking the end of scripting to be somewhere between seven and eleven years old. Woollams and Brown share this view of script as being established in early life, as highlighted in their definition: 'A script is a personal life plan which an individual decides upon at an early age in reaction to her interpretation of both external and internal events' (Woollams and Brown, 1978: 151).

This view of script as a static, ossified phenomenon is not consistent with what we now understand from recent developments in both developmental theory and also from our understanding of adult learning theory. Viewing script as static does not account for the sometimes radical re-scripting that occurs in people who have experienced a severe and overwhelming trauma in adult life, for instance rape or an assault. Various TA authors have questioned the inflexible and fixed view of script and have added in such definitions as: 'A life plan based on decisions made at any developmental stage which inhibit spontaneity and limit flexibility in problem solving and in relating to people' (Erskine, 1980). Erskine's definition does allow for later development, but maintains the position that script is a negative, limiting pattern and is not a view which supports the positive and adaptive aspects of script. Cornell (1988) critiques various theories of script, particularly the implication in much of script theory that the child is a passive recipient of script messages from their parents. Cornell emphasizes the creativity of children in finding influences from outside the family, and reminds transactional analysts of the importance of accounting for these influencing factors in script analysis.

Newton reviews script theory from the perspective of adult learning theory, and considers scripting to be an ongoing process (Newton, 2006). Newton insightfully uses the experiential learning cycle of Kolb (1984) to conceptualize this continuing process of scripting. Taking Kolb's model, Newton proposes that script is developed along similar lines: we experience something, we reflect upon the meaning of the experience, we develop script beliefs as a result of our reflection, and we then experiment with behaviours which either 'confirm' or 'refute' our beliefs. This process begins from our earliest experiences, whereby the infant is making sense of the world and developing a story, a sense of what happens and the reasons why it happens. Over time this story becomes coherent, consistent and is generalized by the infant's interactions with the world. This links to Stern's concept of representations of interactions that are generalized (Stern, 1985). The process continues, as Newton diagrams, in a spiral manner, with each experience paving the way for the next experience cycle. 'New experiences can thus provide updating evidence or can be interpreted through the theory, that is, filtered through the script' (Newton, 2006: 193).

Thus more recent theories regarding script acknowledge the primary role of our early experiences in the formation of the self but also allow room for considering script as an ongoing developmental process. Perhaps more importantly for therapists, these theories provide a means by which we can understand the process of change and development. They also provide a reminder for the therapist of the sometimes cyclical nature of the change process, and how our clients need to 'go round the loop' many, many times, making small, incremental changes to the existing script before their script patterns are significantly changed to the extent that we might consider the person 'autonomous'. They also provide a challenge to concepts such as autonomy, suggesting that rather than becoming completely script-free the individual simply develops a new more appropriate and flexible script.

95

Helping clients identify and build on their strengths

As therapists we look for problems and spend a lot of time working out where and how things have gone wrong for our clients. We are perhaps less likely to help our clients look for their strengths and find out what is going right for them. Within TA, the psychotherapy field of application is focused on healing and change, whereas the counselling field of application is more focused on strengths and resources (see *EATA Training and Examinations Handbook*, 2008, Section five). I believe that TA therapists can learn from this positive approach. As part of our goal to facilitate change, promote healing, engagement with life, and the finding of meaning we can draw upon theories and methods that seek to promote positive engagement and self-actualization.

Martin Seligman, a leading figure in the positive psychology movement, has identified a series of personal character strengths (he refers to them as signature strengths) which include: curiosity, love of learning, critical thinking, creativity, social intelligence, perspective, courage, perseverance, genuineness, kindness, ability to give and receive love, fairness, leadership, self-control, prudence, humility, gratitude, appreciation of beauty, optimism, playfulness and enthusiasm (Seligman, 2002).

Seligman believes that when we identify our signature strengths and use them wisely, positive feelings are generated. It is interesting that his approach does not focus on weaknesses or encourage systematic development of areas where one is weak as areas for personal growth (Seligman, 2002). Instead, the focus is on helping clients identify their personal character strengths and using these strengths in different aspects of their lives. This is not achieved superficially through the therapist pointing out their client's strengths and stroking them, but through facilitating the client's own discovery of their strengths and then applying them consciously. A quick way to identify these strengths is to register with Seligman's website www.authentichappiness.org and complete the Values in Action Institute strengths survey.

Positive psychology also seeks to encourage the experiencing of positive emotions towards our past (satisfaction, contentment, pride), the future (optimism, hope, confidence) and to promote pleasure, engagement and positive emotions about the present. It can sometimes be difficult to see how clients whose lives have been so full of pain and abuse can experience positive emotions about their past, but it is possible for them to reach a place of peace about their past. Furthermore, living a positive, productive and satisfying life will provide something one can look back on with satisfaction, and even pride in how one has overcome adversity.

A full life is considered to be one where the individual experiences a range of positive emotions in relation to their past, present and future, and regularly uses their signature strengths to engage with life, in relationships with others, and in service of 'something larger' (perhaps the community, or a cause such as the environment).

The relevance of this to TA therapy is that these principles can be woven into our humanistic framework and the guiding values of our work. As part of the ongoing diagnostic process in therapy, we can pay attention to noticing our client's strengths and facilitate our client's discovery of their strengths. These strengths may be held in any of their ego states, and may indeed spring from how they adapted and developed in response to pain and adverse conditions in their past (for example, independence can be a great strength which is sometimes a product of a neglectful environment). In this sense, strengths can be a positive adaptation to the constraints of a sub-optimal environment and testament to the ingenuity and sometimes positive and useful nature of aspects of one's own script. We can also use the above principles to help guide our treatment planning, by considering how we can help the client heal their past pains, engage positively with the present, draw upon and apply their strengths, and begin constructing a positive future.

96

Exploring therapist's motivations

What is it that makes someone want to become a psychotherapist? Even Freud, the father of psychotherapy, described it as an 'impossible' profession (Freud, 1937). The process of training is often deeply unsettling and involves sacrificing large amounts of time, energy and money. Practising as a psychotherapist involves sitting with people in the depth of their despair, and leaving ourselves open to feeling all kinds of unpleasant and disturbing emotions, and hearing first-hand stories of profound inhumanity and even torture. Why would someone want to do this? Maroda suggests 'We are there because we want something that goes beyond earning a living and beyond a commitment to social service or intellectual inquiry. We seek to be healed ourselves and we heal our old "afflicted" caretakers as we heal our patients' (Maroda, 2004: 37–8). Clearly becoming a therapist is a deeply personal matter, and one which is influenced by our own life experiences and our script. The effective and ethical practice of psychotherapy requires that therapists repeatedly revisit their reasons for training as and becoming psychotherapists and examine honestly what of their own needs their work is seeking to meet, to reduce the potential for exploitation of clients. The therapist's experience, sensitivities and script can impact their work in many different ways, for example therapists who came from volatile families, or even families where expression of feeling was inhibited, may find it extremely difficult to tolerate and contain their client's anger.

McLeod (1993, 2003) discusses experiences common in the personal history of therapists that contribute to their career choice. He identifies three themes, of which at least one will have been present in the life of the therapist.

1   An experience of being in a caretaking role. This can include the role of 'peacemaker' in the family. Often a way of

relating to others that involves a caring, helping role is a pattern in early life experiences of those who become therapists.

2　A period of intense personal distress or crisis. This generally includes experiences of loss in childhood or adolescence. Many therapists have also experienced episodes of depression. McWilliams (1994) also contends that a significant number of therapists have a depressive character type that predisposes them to working therapeutically. The 'wounded healer' model is a widely accepted archetype for therapists (Barnett, 2007). Extreme crisis in adolescence or early adulthood is also common, and it is possible that either the experience of having been helped or the absence of help has stimulated the desire to work as a therapist, in addition to providing a personal resource for understanding the deep distress and pain of others.

3　Experience of having been an 'outsider', with high levels of isolation or aloneness in childhood or adolescence. This includes experiences of prolonged illness, cultural differences, repeatedly moving home, or being the victim of bullying. McLeod suggests that 'these types of childhood experience can encourage the development in the young person of a rich "inner life", in compensation for the absence of companions and playmates, and a capacity to observe and speculate on the motives and behaviour of others' (McLeod, 1993: 3).

This is supported by Barnett (2007), who states:

> the two main themes that emerged . . . concerned experiences of loss and deprivation, especially in early life, and the failure of carers to meet the normal narcissistic needs of childhood. The resultant painful effects of early loss often lead to difficulties in respect of intimacy, dependency and separation, and where there has been narcissistic injury, to issues around control, selfless giving and a need to be needed. Resulting defences mask an underlying sense of vulnerability.
>
> (Barnett, 2007: 259)

Clearly, personal therapy is a vital resource in the process of becoming a psychotherapist to minimize the potential for these issues to be acted out destructively in the therapists' own work.

> Feelings of inferiority and experiences of humiliation may give rise to a need to feel loved and admired. Evaluation of trainee therapists' ability may feel like an evaluation of the self as a person (Wosket, 1999) and fear of 'failure' will affect his practice and inhibit his client's use of him.
>
> . . . Situations in childhood may have contributed to an inability to tolerate gaps, uncertainties, periods of 'not-knowing', resulting in a therapist's desire to take charge of a session and steer the course of the therapy, rather than allowing adequate space for the client's own feelings and thought processes to emerge.
>
> (Barnett, 2007: 261)

This is particularly relevant for the practice of transactional analysis and other therapeutic approaches that have models for the therapist working directively, or which encourage the therapist into an active, 'knowing' stance. The anxiety 'not knowing' can provoke can be deeply unsettling for therapists who have these underlying issues and can propel the therapist into working ever more actively and in an authoritarian manner to avoid the painful, unconscious experiences. Clearly this is an example of acting destructively based on one's own script, rather than on clinical need.

The ethical and professional practice of transactional analysis psychotherapy requires that we undertake a thorough and lengthy personal therapy, and return to therapy periodically throughout our career to address these unconscious, 'scripty' motivations for our work. Beginning therapists are often unaware of the pervasive influence these forces have upon their motivation, and may react with outrage to requirements that they undertake personal therapy. It is questionable whether these issues will ever be truly resolved, and in some respects, the practice of psychotherapy may reinforce some of them for individual therapists. Our work can be like repeatedly picking a scab off a wound, meaning it will not heal, or will not heal cleanly.

It behoves therapists of all levels of training and experience to be open to awareness of how their experiences and script influence their work, and their choice of work.

97

Self-reflection and appropriate self-disclosure

Self-disclosure is where the therapist reveals something of their own experience in the therapy with the client. Self-disclosure is one of the most controversial and potentially problematic interventions a therapist can use, and yet there is research evidence that appropriate self-disclosure can enhance the therapy. Self-reflection is an essential precursor to effective and ethical self-disclosure. Yalom (2001) divides therapist self-disclosure into three different kinds: disclosure on the mechanisms of therapy; disclosure of the therapist's here-and-now feelings; and disclosure of the therapist's personal life. He advocates full and frank disclosure regarding the processes of therapy in a way that most transactional analysts would identify as being part of a clear contracting phase at the outset of therapy, and as part of the orientation stage to assist clients in learning how to 'do therapy'. This process is ongoing in that the therapist may disclose their reasons for pursuing certain lines of enquiry, or may discuss aspects of their treatment plan and the rationale behind it with their client. Yalom goes on to advise the selective reporting of the therapist's here-and-now feelings in the therapy (linked to client diagnosis, presenting problem and whether it might help the client with exploring some aspect of their relational script), and cautious disclosure about the therapist's personal life.

Maroda (1994, 2003) invites the therapist to remain attuned to their own internal affective state, and to use this awareness and their countertransference as a potent therapeutic tool. I recommend her book for a fuller description of using the therapist's responses to the client as a therapeutic tool.

Initial sessions

At the initial consultation, it is common for therapists to provide some basic information about themselves, their experience

TRANSACTIONAL ANALYSIS: 100 KEY POINTS

and so forth for prospective clients. Although it is good to provide clients with some information, I have heard numerous stories from people who had seen a therapist for the initial consultation and then not returned because they didn't feel heard and felt bombarded with information about the therapist. In many respects, *how* the therapist interacts with the client will be of more use to the client's decision-making process than lots of details about the therapist's background and experience (see Point 18).

Metacommunication

Part of therapy involves the therapist being aware of their own ongoing process, and being curious about the client's process and maintaining awareness of the unfolding and continually shifting interpersonal process happening between them in the room (Widdowson, 2008). In observing these processes, the therapist may use metacommunicative transactions as a means of disclosure about the here-and-now experience of the therapist (see Point 78).

Matching disclosure level to client diagnosis

Greater levels of therapist self-disclosure are often needed with clients who are more profoundly disturbed. The distinction here is significant in that clients who are more disturbed

> . . . have such total, encompassing transferences that they can only learn about their distortions of reality when reality is painted in stark colours in front of them, while [less disturbed clients] have subtle and unconscious trans-ferences that surface only when the therapist is carefully opaque.
>
> (McWilliams, 1994: 75)

Being honest

Being honest with our clients can be extremely difficult. For example, having the courage to admit when we feel stuck can feel dreadfully exposing and deskilling for a therapist. Simply being honest and saying, 'I'm feeling stuck right now, and I am not sure where to take this' can be liberating and can open up a new avenue of exploration. Furthermore, our clients often know at some level when we feel stuck and are not being honest about it. Acting as if we know what is going on when we do not can feel (and is) false and disingenuous.

(Widdowson, 2008: 69)

Responding to direct questions from clients

Sometimes clients ask their therapists very direct questions about the therapist's personal life or life experiences. On occasions, these questions are fine and answering will not be particularly problematic, and answering can make the therapist more real and human to the client. There are other times where the questions are not so clear-cut, and should not be taken at face value. Questions can have a hidden significance, and one which may be out of the client's awareness at the time of asking. As a general principle, the therapist can invite the client to explain the significance of the question, and what the answer would mean to them.

A client recently asked a very direct question regarding my personal experience and whether I had experienced a particular problem they were facing. I asked the client to tell me what it would mean to them if I said yes I had faced the same problem, and what it would mean if I said no, I hadn't. In the end, I decided not to answer my client's question. Refusal to answer a client's questions can also help the client articulate their fantasies about the therapist. This can be a very frustrating experience for clients, and it is important that, when refusing to answer, the therapist empathically acknowledges the client's frustration in response to their refusal. It can also be useful for the therapist to explain something of their rationale in their refusal to answer.

When clients ask direct questions regarding what we are feeling (e.g., 'Are you irritated with me?'), these need to be taken seriously; it is worthwhile for the therapist to take a moment to reflect on whether there may a grain of truth in what the client is saying. The client's transaction is often a response to some transactional stimulus of which we may not be immediately aware . . . One option is for the therapist to express his or her reaction to the question and to invite the client to explain some of the rationale behind the question (e.g., 'I am a little surprised by your question and am wondering what you experienced that led you to ask it'). Again, the therapist needs to be truly receptive to hearing the client's response, which may result in uncomfortable feedback.

(Widdowson, 2008: 69)

Sometimes it is therapeutic to provide our clients with confirmation of their experience (Erskine and Trautmann, 1996) with comments such as 'me too' or 'I would feel the same in that situation'. Such disclosure can be positive, but needs to be thought about carefully before the disclosure is made. The final decision as to whether we should make a disclosure or not should be guided by our answer to the following question: 'To what extent will my disclosure be therapeutic for my client?'

98

The Adult ego state revisited

The Adult ego state has been relatively neglected in the TA literature (Tudor, 2003). There seem to be conflicting thoughts about the nature of the Adult. Compare the following two descriptions of the Adult:

> The Adult functions as a probability-estimating computer. It appears not to be a fully autonomous ego state, but rather functions mostly at the request of one of the other ego states.
>
> (Woollams and Brown, 1978: 15)

> [The Adult is] a pulsating personality, processing and integrating feelings, attitudes, thoughts and behaviours appropriate to the here-and-now . . . at all ages, from conception to death.
>
> (Tudor, 2003: 201)

Which of these descriptions do you prefer? Which seems to most accurately reflect your own subjective sense of your Adult ego state?

Often it seems that the Adult is identified by a process of elimination, by identifying Child and Parent ego states and determining that what is left is Adult. This is an approach that does not adhere to Berne's four methods and criteria for diagnosis of an ego state (Berne, 1961). The Adult ego state can be defined as: the ego state which is present-centred, here-and-now and appropriate to the current situation. This definition can be operationally checked using all of Berne's four methods. In the light of this definition, to define the Adult as a 'probability-estimating computer' is unnecessarily restrictive and highly discounting of the range of here-and-now experiences we engage with. Furthermore, to describe the Adult as not being 'a fully autonomous ego state' also seems grossly inaccurate; if the Adult is appropriate to the current situation and is based in the here-and-now, then by definition, the Adult is *only ever* autonomous.

Erskine (1988) and Tudor (2003) draw on the description Berne gave of Parent and Child ego states as fixated ego states and identify Adult as being the part of our self that is (relatively) free and un-fixated. 'As the neopsychic Adult is in constant process, it may not be fixated either clinically or conceptually' (Tudor, 2003: 222). A number of TA authors posit that Child and, to some extent, Parent ego states are dynamic and changing throughout our lifespan (Blackstone, 1993). Differing views exist on whether these ego states are dynamic or static and fixated. However, the Adult ego state is by definition dynamic, vibrant, adaptive (in the true sense of the word) and malleable. The purpose, goal and signature characteristic of the Adult ego state, according to Tudor (2003), is integration (noun), and the Adult is considered to be continually engaged in integrating (verb). Although this is true, because of implicit memory and the nature and role of our unconscious, it is perhaps impossible to totally integrate all of our experiences into our Adult ego state.

There is a convention in TA that Parent and Child ego states are named in the plural as ego *states* whereas the Adult is named as a single state of the ego. This again seems to be restrictive and not accounting for the complexity and richness of the many processes and states we can engage with appropriately in the here-and-now. Perhaps it is more accurate to talk of Adult ego *states*, than *the* Adult ego state.

With our Adult ego states we compare, interpret, define, discriminate, apply, analyse, critique, differentiate and appraise. Although many of these words appear to be rather dull cognitive processes, they can also refer to Adult functioning in the affective realm. The Adult is also intuiting, creating, relating, feeling, empathic, mentalizing and engaging. We can also use adverbs to describe *how* the Adult works in process, such as the Adult operates imaginatively, maturely, congruently, appropriately, reflectively.

The Adult ego states are also the source of adult sexuality. Sometimes sexuality is erroneously ascribed to the Child ego states. However, this is inaccurate as behavioural, social, historical and phenomenological diagnosis would not support locating an adult sexuality in the Child ego states. The Child ego states include sensuality, which of course has a part to play in sexuality and sexual expression but Adult ego states are the (age-appropriate) source of adult sexuality.

In the light of all of the above, an emphasis on growth is relevant to promoting development of Adult ego states. Although it is clinically useful to use our models of pathology and healing to clear away obstacles that inhibit full growth and use of Adult ego states, this approach is limited in that they simply clear away these obstacles and do not necessarily encourage growth. This can be likened to clearing away weeds in a garden to help the growth of our plants, but to help our plants truly flourish, we need to enrich the soil and increase their optimal growth conditions. The relatively new approach of positive psychology (Seligman, 2002) can provide therapists with theories and tools that can be used to enrich and optimize the growth conditions of the Adult ego states.

99

TA as an existential psychotherapy

As a model of psychotherapy, people have claimed different philosophical allegiances for TA. I agree with Clarkson (1992), who feels TA is part of the humanistic and existential tradition. Berne referenced, and was influenced by, existential authors such as Kierkegaard (Berne, 1966) and indeed in *Principles of Group Treatment* discusses links between transactional analysis and existential therapy (Berne, 1966).

> Insofar as actual living in the world is concerned, transactional analysis shares with existential analysis a high esteem for and a keen interest in, the personal qualities of honesty, integrity, autonomy and authenticity, and their most poignant social manifestations in encounter and intimacy.
>
> (Berne, 1966: 305)

Although TA is a humanistic therapy, Berne retained the concept of *mortido* (Berne, 1969), thus accounting for destructive tendencies and placing TA within an existential framework as an approach to therapy, which is less certain of human goodness and accounts for destructive forces (Deurzen-Smith, 1997).

'Existential psychotherapy is a dynamic approach to therapy which focuses on concerns that are rooted in the individual's existence' (Yalom, 1980: 5). In existential psychotherapy conflict is seen to arise from an individual's confrontation with the 'givens of existence' (Yalom, 1980). The role of the therapist is to enable the client to come to terms with, and adjust to, these givens in their own unique manner. The process of coming to terms with these givens is seen as one which will inevitably produce anxiety. However, this existential anxiety is different from the limiting, fearful anxiety many clients present to therapy with. The goal of therapy is not the removal of existential anxiety, but of facilitating adjustment to it and the anxiety which is the product of an authentic, autonomous life.

The four existential givens as identified by Yalom (1980) are:

- death;
- freedom;
- isolation;
- meaninglessness.

Facing and accepting our mortality is clearly a process that will generate anxiety. Our scripts and magical thinking provide us with a means to avoid death anxiety, or even a blueprint about how we will die, thus creating the illusion of a sense of control over death. Existential approaches to psychotherapy, like TA, emphasize the importance of the client taking responsibility for their life. Existential approaches recognize that the taking of responsibility and claiming one's own freedom can paradoxically induce intense anxiety (Sartre, 1943). It is the realization that we truly are the masters of our own destiny and the weightiness of this realization can induce terrible fear (Kundera, 2000a; 2000b). It is possible that our scripts and their limiting nature help us to avoid this anxiety. TA emphasizes personal responsibility and freedom – an approach which can trigger such anxiety reactions. The therapist is wise to explore this should their client experience unaccountable, free-floating anxiety following therapy sessions which focused on responsibility and freedom. The existential approach considers it is not desirable to seek to resolve this anxiety, but rather is it preferable to help the client live with the anxiety of uncertainty. The given of isolation means that ultimately we must face the world on our own. Again, our scripts can determine and give explanations that help us manage the anxiety of this isolation, but also maintain the isolation by preventing meaningful relating to others. Our scripts are our 'meaning-making mechanisms' and give us reasons for why we and others are the way we are. An existential approach to therapy seeks to uncover the process of meaning making one uses, and how one construes the world, oneself and others. The realization that life, in and of itself, has no inherent meaning is a common source of torment for many of our depressed clients. Meaning cannot be given or generated but rather it is something that each individual has to find for themselves. Perhaps one of the tasks of the psychotherapist is to help our clients find their own meaning and purpose, just as we have done in our work of healing and service to others (even if this was called for in our scripts). The making of meaning is a central feature of most psychotherapy, as is coming to terms with events and experiences which are meaningless and for which we can find no explanation. Perhaps the approach of positive psychology, with its focus on using personal strengths, will be of use in facilitating meaning making.

Being mindful of the four existential givens and their impact on the psyche and discussing these with clients can add great depth and poignancy to the therapy process. Pursuing the existential goal of authenticity is entirely compatible with the TA goal of promoting autonomy. Both require taking a conscious stance in relation to how one is choosing to live, as well as an awareness of how one perceives (Sartre, 1943) and examining one's values (Deurzen-Smith, 2002). Existential conflicts and tensions are not something to be avoided, but something to engage with and to dialogue with our clients about. The existential approach does not turn away from pain, suffering and ugliness, nor does it teach us how to avoid it, but rather it invites us to accept these things as a reality of life.

100

Analysing transactions

In several places throughout this book I invite the reader to engage in analysis of transactions – a practice which inexplicably appears to have gone out of fashion amongst TA therapists. I finish this section on refining technique and the whole book by referring back to this potent yet basic TA method.

A therapist will find that their work, the therapeutic process and relationship, and their way of understanding both their self and their client will be greatly enhanced by the analysis of transactions. Analysis of transactions can be done very effectively through listening to audio recordings of sessions, but can also be done by reflection and process recall. I invite you to either listen to recordings or reflect back and analyse your client's transactional stimuli, and your reciprocal transactional responses. What do these transactions mean? What is your client seeking in their transactions with you? To what extent is your response a needed response, and to what extent is it a repeated response of some previous painful interaction from your client's history? What happens to the client in response to the therapist's response, and what does this mean?

In turn, analyse your own transactional stimuli towards your client – at both the professional and personal level. What are you ostensibly seeking in each transactional stimulus? What is your intention? What is the significance of the transaction for you personally? What are the inner transactions you experience internally but do not voice? What influence do these internal transactions have on your work? What was your client's response to your transactional stimuli? What happened for your client internally in response to your stimuli? What might they have held back from verbally expressing? What does their transactional response tell you about the impact of your stimuli? How does your client's response impact you in return? Go beyond the simple plotting of ego states and the transactional vectors between them to include the internal transactions that each person is experiencing simultaneously to the interpersonal transactions, and adopt a stance of curiosity in relation to them. A great deal of learning about one's self, and one's client can be gained through such a simple method. Account for the potentialities of the relationship. In analysing transcripts, speculate on what *might* have happened had the transactions been different in some way. What trajectory might the work have taken?

What I am proposing is mindfulness in practice, a reflection *in* action (Schön, 1983). Berne (1966) was clear in his position: each transactional analyst should know what they are doing, and why they are doing it, in each moment of the therapy. If what we are doing with a client is exploring the unknown in an open-minded way and just being with the anxiety of uncertainty, or immersing ourselves in the present experience, this process should be intentional.

Above all, I invite you to be tentative. We can never truly be certain and, as I have discussed previously, certainty closes down the process of mentalizing. Finally, remember, transactions, like ego states, are just a fascinating fiction. A metaphor. A story we tell to bring order to our thoughts and experiences. A means of making sense, structure and meaning where there is none. A model for creating new narratives: a new angle on the past, a new experience of the present, and a set of new potentialities for the future.

References

Alexander, F., French, T. F. and Bacon, C. L. (1946) *Psychoanalytic Therapy: Principles and Application.* New York: Ronald Press.

Allen, J. R. and Allen, B. A. (1995) Narrative Theory, Redecision Therapy and Postmodernism. *Transactional Analysis Journal,* 25(4): 327–34.

American Psychiatric Association. (2000) *Diagnostic and Statistical Manual of Mental Disorders* (4th edn, text revision) (DSM-IV-TR). Washington: American Psychiatric Association.

Ayres, A. (2006) The Only Way Out: A Consideration of Suicide. *Transactions Issue,* 4: 4–13.

Barnes, G. (ed.) (1977) *Transactional Analysis after Eric Berne: Teachings and Practice of Three TA Schools.* New York: Harper's College Press.

Barnett, M. (2007) What Brings you Here? An Exploration of the Unconscious Motivations of Those who Choose to Train and Work as Psychotherapists and Counsellors. *Psychodynamic Practice,* 13(3): 257–74.

Barr, J. (1987) Therapeutic Relationship Model: Perspectives on the Core of the Healing Process. *Transactional Analysis Journal,* 17(4): 134–40.

Bary, B. B. and Hufford, F. M. (1990) The Six Advantages to Games and Their Use in Treatment. *Transactional Analysis Journal,* 20(4): 214–20.

Bateman, A. W. and Fonagy, P. (2006) *Mentalization-Based Treatment for Borderline Personality Disorder: A Practical Guide.* Oxford: Oxford University Press.

Beck, A. T. and Beck, J. (1995) *Cognitive Therapy: Basics and Beyond.* New York: Guilford Press.

Beisser, A. (1970) The Paradoxical Theory of Change. In Fagan, J. & Shepherd, I. L. (eds) *Gestalt Therapy Now: Theory, Techniques, Applications.* New York: Harper Colophon. (http://www.gestalt.org/ arnie.htm)

Benjamin, L. S. (2003) *Interpersonal Diagnosis and Treatment of Personality Disorders.* New York: Guilford Press.

Benjamin, L. S. (2006) *Interpersonal Reconstructive Therapy: Promoting Change in Non-Responders.* New York: Guilford Press.

Berne, E. (1961/1986) *Transactional Analysis in Psychotherapy.* London: Souvenir Press. (First published 1961, New York: Grove Press.)

Berne, E. (1964) *Games People Play.* New York: Grove Press.

Berne, E. (1966/1994) *Principles of Group Treatment.* Menlo Park, CA: Shea Books. (Republished 1994.)

Berne, E. (1968) *A Layman's Guide to Psychiatry and Psychoanalysis.* New York: Penguin.

Berne, E. (1970) *Sex in Human Loving.* London: Penguin.

Berne, E. (1971) Away from a Theory of the Impact of Interpersonal Interaction on Non-Verbal Participation. *Transactional Analysis Journal,* 1(1): 6–13.

Berne, E. (1972) *What Do You Say After You Say Hello?* London: Corgi.

Bion, W. R. (1970) *Attention and Interpretation.* London: Tavistock.

Blackstone, P. (1993) The Dynamic Child: Integration of Second Order Structure, Object Relations and Self Psychology. *Transactional Analysis Journal,* 23(4): 216–34.

Boliston-Mardula, J. (2001) Appetite Path Model: Working with Escape Hatch Resolution with Clients who use Drugs and Alcohol. *TA UK,* 61 (Autumn): 9–14.

Bordin, E. S. (1979) The Generalisability of the Psychoanalytical Concept of the Working Alliance. *Psychotherapy: Theory, Research and Practice,* 16(3): 252–60.

Bordin, E. S. (1994) Theory and Research on the Therapeutic Working Alliance. In Horvath, O. and Greenberg, S. (eds) *The Working Alliance: Theory, Research and Practice.* New York: Wiley.

Boyd, H. and Cowles-Boyd, L. (1980) Blocking Tragic Scripts. *Transactional Analysis Journal,* 10(3): 227–9.

Burns, D. (2000) *The Feeling Good Handbook.* New York: Plume.

Clark, B. (1991) Empathic Transactions in the Deconfusion of the Child Ego State. *Transactional Analysis Journal,* 21(2): 92–8.

Clark, F. (1996) The Client's Uniqueness: A Personal Discovery of Therapeutic Relationship. *Transactional Analysis Journal,* 26(4): 312–15.

Clark, F. (2001) Psychotherapy as a Mourning Process. *Transactional Analysis Journal,* 31(3): 156–60.

Clarkson, P (1988) Ego State Dilemmas of Abused Children. *Transactional Analysis Journal,* 18(2): 85–93.

Clarkson, P. (1992) *Transactional Analysis Psychotherapy: An Integrated Approach*. London: Routledge.

Clarkson, P. (2003) *The Therapeutic Relationship*. London: Whurr Publishers.

Cornell, W. (1986) Setting the Therapeutic Stage: The Initial Sessions. *Transactional Analysis Journal*, 16(1): 4–10.

Cornell, W. (1988) Life Script Theory: A Critical Review from a Developmental Perspective. *Transactional Analysis Journal*, 18(4): 270–82.

Cornell, W. (1994) Shame: Binding Affect, Ego State Contamination and Relational Repair. *Transactional Analysis Journal*, 24(2): 139–46.

Cornell, W. and Bonds-White, F. (2001) Therapeutic Relatedness in Transactional Analysis: The Truth of Love or the Love of Truth. *Transactional Analysis Journal*, 31(1): 71–93.

Cornell, W. and Hargaden, H. (2005) *From Transactions to Relations: The Emergence of a Relational Tradition in Transactional Analysis*. Chadlington, Oxfordshire: Haddon Press.

Cornell, W. and Landaiche, N. (2006) Impasse and Intimacy: Applying Berne's Concept of Script Protocol. *Transactional Analysis Journal*, 36(3): 196–213.

Cox, M. (2000) A Dynamic Approach to Treatment Planning. Workshop presentation, Institute of Transactional Analysis Annual Conference, Canterbury, UK.

Crossman, P. (1966) Permission and Protection. *Transactional Analysis Bulletin*, 5(19): 152–4.

Dashiell, S. (1978) The Parent Resolution Process. *Transactional Analysis Journal*, 18(4): 289–94.

Davies, J. M. and Frawley, M. G. (1994) *Treating the Adult Survivor of Childhood Sexual Abuse: A Psychoanalytic Perspective*. New York: HarperCollins.

Deurzen-Smith, E. (1997) *Everyday Mysteries: Existential Dimensions of Psychotherapy*. London: Sage.

Deurzen-Smith, E. (2002) *Existential Counselling and Psychotherapy in Practice*. London: Sage.

Drego, P. (1983) The Cultural Parent. *Transactional Analysis Journal*, 13(4): 224–7.

Drye, R. (2006) The No-Suicide Decision: Then and Now. *The Script*, 36(6): 3–4 (reprinted in *ITA News*, 27: 1–6).

Drye, R., Goulding, R. and Goulding, M. (1973) No Suicide Decisions: Patient Monitoring of Suicidal Risk. *American Journal of Psychiatry*, 130(2): 118–21.

Dusay, J. (1972) Egograms and the Constancy Hypothesis. *Transactional Analysis Journal*, 2(3): 37.

English, F. (1969) Episcript and the 'Hot Potato' Game. *Transactional Analysis Bulletin*, 8: 32.

English, F. (1971) The Substitution Factor: Rackets and Real Feelings. *Transactional Analysis Journal*, 1(4): 225–30.

English, F. (2007) I'm Now a Cognitive Transactional Analyst, Are You? *The Script*, 37(5): 1, 6–7.

Ernst, F. (1971) The OK Corral: The Grid for Get-On-With. *Transactional Analysis Journal*, 1(4): 231–40.

Erskine, R. G. (1980) Script Cure: Behavioral, Intrapsychic and Physiological. *Transactional Analysis Journal*, 10(2): 102–6.

Erskine, R. G. (1988) Ego Structure, Intrapsychic Function and Defense Mechanisms: A Commentary on Berne's Original Theoretical Concepts. *Transactional Analysis Journal*, 18(4): 15–19.

Erskine, R. G. (1993) Inquiry, Attunement and Involvement in the Psychotherapy of Dissociation. *Transactional Analysis Journal*, 23(4): 184–90.

Erskine, R. G. (1994) Shame and Self-Righteousness: Transactional Analysis Perspectives and Clinical Interventions. *Transactional Analysis Journal*, 24(2): 87–102.

Erksine, R. G., Moursund, J. P. and Trautmann, R. L. (1999) *Beyond Empathy: A Therapy of Contact-in-Relationship*. New York: Brunner-Routledge.

Erskine, R. G. and Trautmann, R. L. (1996) Methods of an Integrative Psychotherapy. *Transactional Analysis Journal*, 26(4): 316–28.

Erskine, R. and Zalcman, M. (1979) The Racket System: A Model for Racket Analysis. *Transactional Analysis Journal*, 9(1): 51–9.

European Association of Transactional Analysis. (2008) *The EATA Training and Examination Handbook*. Konstanza, Germany: EATA. (http://www.eatanews.org/handbook.htm)

Fonagy, P., Gergely, G., Jurist, E. and Target, M. (2002) *Affect Regulation Mentalization, and the Development of the Self*. New York: Other Press.

Freud, S. (1912) Recommendations to Physicians Practising Psychoanalysis. In *Complete Psychological Works* (Standard edn), 12. London: Hogarth Press (pp. 109–20).

Freud, S (1937) Analysis Terminable and Interminable. In *Complete Psychological Works* (Standard edn), 23. London: Hogarth Press (pp. 216–53).

Gill, M. M. (1979) The Analysis of the Transference. *Journal of the American Psychoanalytic Association*, 27: 263–88.

Gobes, L. (1985) Abandonment and Engulfment Issues in Relationship Therapy. *Transactional Analysis Journal*, 15(3): 216–19.

Gomez, L. (1997) *An Introduction to Object Relations*. London: Free Association Books.

Goulding, M. M. and Goulding, R. L. (1979) *Changing Lives Through Redecision Therapy*. New York: Grove Press.

Goulding, R. and Goulding, M. (1978) *The Power is in the Patient*. San Francisco: TA Press.

Greenson, R. (1967) *The Technique and Practice of Psychoanalysis.* New York: International Universities Press.

Griffin, Emory A. (2003) *A First Look at Communication Theory.* Boston: McGraw Hill.

Guichard, M. (1987) Writing the Long Case Study. Workshop Presentation, EATA Conference, Chamonix (unpublished).

Guistolise, P. G. (1996) Failures in the Therapeutic Relationship: Inevitable and Necessary? *Transactional Analysis Journal,* 26(4): 284–8.

Hahn, A. (2004) The Borderline Personality Disorder. In Masterson, J. F. & Liebermann, A. R. (eds) *A Therapist's Guide to the Personality Disorders: A Handbook and Workbook.* Phoenix: Zeig Tucker.

Hargaden, H. (2007) Love and Desire in the Therapeutic Relationship: Transformation or Betrayal? *Transactions,* 6: 4–14.

Hargaden, H. and Sills, C. (2002) *Transactional Analysis: A Relational Perspective.* Hove: Brunner-Routledge.

Hargaden, H. and Sills, C. (2003) Who am I for you? The Child Ego State and Transferential Domains. In Sills, C. & Hargaden, H. (eds) *Ego States.* London: Worth Publishing.

Harper, R. and Ellis, A. (1969) *A Guide to Rational Living.* New York: Image Book Company.

Holloway, W. H. (1973) Shut the Escape Hatch. In *The Monograph Series,* Numbers I–X. Ohio: Midwest Institute for Human Understanding Inc.

Holmes, J. (2001) *The Search for the Secure Base: Attachment Theory and Psychotherapy.* Hove: Routledge.

Horvath, A. and Greenberg, L. (1994) *The Working Alliance: Theory, Research and Practice.* NewYork: Wiley.

International Transactional Analysis Association Education Committee. (1969) Minimal Basic Science Curriculum for Clinical Membership in the ITAA. *Transactional Analysis Bulletin,* 8: 108–10.

Jacobs, A. (1994) Theory as Ideology: Reparenting and Thought Reform. *Transactional Analysis Journal,* 24(1): 39–55.

Jacobs, M. (1988) *Psychodynamic Counselling in Action.* London: Sage.

James, J. (1973) The Game Plan. *Transactional Analysis Journal,* 3(4): 14–17.

James, M. (1974) Self-Reparenting: Theory and Process. *Transactional Analysis Journal,* 4(3): 32–9.

James, M. (1981) *Breaking Free: Self Re-Parenting for a New Life.* Reading, MA: Addison-Wesley.

James, M. (2002) *It's Never Too Late to be Happy! Reparenting Yourself for Happiness.* Sanger, CA: Quill Driver Books.

James, M. and Jongeward, D. (1971) *Born to Win: Transactional Analysis With Gestalt Experiments.* Reading, MA: Addison-Wesley.

Johnson, S. (1994) *Character Styles.* London: W.W. Norton.

Kabat-Zinn, J. (2000) *Wherever You Go, There You Are*. London: Piatkus.

Kabat-Zinn, J. (2001) *Full Catastrophe Living: Using the Wisdom of Your Body and Mind to Face Stress, Pain and Illness*. New York: Delta.

Kagan, N. (1980) Influencing Human Interaction – Eighteen Years with IPR. In Hess, A. K. (ed.) *Psychotherapy Supervision: Theory, Research, and Practice*. New York: Wiley (pp. 262–86).

Karpman, S. (1968) Fairy Tales and Script Drama Analysis. *Transactional Analysis Bulletin*, 7(26): 39–43.

Karpman, S. (1971) Options. *Transactional Analysis Journal*, 1(1): 79–87.

Klein, M. (1957) *Envy, Gratitude and Other Works*. London: Hogarth Press and Institute for Psycho-Analysis.

Kohut, H. (1984) *How Does Analysis Cure?* Chicago: University of Chicago Press.

Kolb, D. A. (1984) *Experiential Learning: Experience as the Source of Learning and Development*. Englewood Cliffs, NJ: Prentice-Hall.

Kübler-Ross, E. (1969) *On Death and Dying*. New York: Macmillan.

Kundera, M. (2000a) *The Unbearable Lightness of Being*. New York: Faber and Faber.

Kundera, M. (2000b) *Immortality*. New York: Faber and Faber.

Kupfer, D. and Haimowitz, M. (1971) Therapeutic Interventions Part 1. Rubberbands Now. *Transactional Analysis Journal*, 1(1): 10–16.

Lammers, W. (1992) Using the Therapist's Kinesthetic Responses as a Therapeutic Tool. *Transactional Analysis Journal*, 22(4): 216–21.

Lapworth, P., Sills, C. and Fish, S. (1993) *Transactional Analysis Counselling*. Oxfordshire: Winslow Press.

Leader, D (2008) *The New Black: Mourning, Melancholia and Depression*. London: Hamish Hamilton.

Lee, A. (1997) Process Contracts. In Sills, C. (ed.) *Contracts in Counselling*. London: Sage.

Lee, A. (1998) The Drowning Man (diagram). In Tilney, T. *Dictionary of Transactional Analysis*. London: Wiley Blackwell.

Levin-Landheer, P. (1982) The Cycle of Development. *Transactional Analysis Journal*, 12(2): 129–39.

Lewin, K. (1946) Action Research and Minority Problems. *Journal of Social Issues*, 2(4): 34–46.

Lister-Ford, C. (2007) *Skills in Transactional Analysis Counselling and Psychotherapy*. London: Sage.

Little, R. (2001) Schizoid Processes: Working with the Defenses of the Withdrawn Child Ego State. *Transactional Analysis Journal*, 31(1): 33–43.

Little, R. (2006) Ego State Relational Units and Resistance to Change. *Transactional Analysis Journal*, 36(1): 7–19.

Luborsky, L. (1984) *Principles of Psychoanalytic Psychotherapy: A*

Manual for Supportive-Expressive Treatment. New York: Basic Books.

Lynch, V. (2007) TA and Developmental Dyslexia. Unpublished Manuscript for M.Sc. in TA Psychotherapy, Kegworth. The Berne Institute.

McCormick, P. and Pulleyblank, E. (1985) Stages of Redecision Therapy. In Kadis, L. (ed.) *Redecision Therapy: Expanded Perspectives.* Watsonville, CA: Western Institute for Group and Family Therapy.

McLaughlin, C. (2007) *Suicide-Related Behaviour: Understanding, Caring and Therapeutic Responses.* Oxford: Wiley-Blackwell.

McLean, D. and Nathan, J. (2007) Treatment of Personality Disorder: Limit Setting and the use of Benign Authority. *British Journal of Psychotherapy*, 23(2): 231–47.

McLeod, J. (1993) The Counsellor's Journey. Unpublished paper. Keele University.

McLeod, J. (1998) *An Introduction to Counselling.* Buckingham: Open University Press.

McLeod, J. (2003) *An Introduction to Counselling* (3rd edn). Maidenhead: Open University Press (pp. 489–93).

McNeel, J. (1976) The Parent Interview. *Transactional Analysis Journal*, 6(1): 61–8.

McWilliams, N. (1994) *Psychoanalytic Diagnosis.* New York: Guilford Press.

Mahler, M., Pine, F. and Bergman, A. (2000) *The Psychological Birth of the Human Infant: Symbiosis and Individuation.* New York: Basic Books.

Maroda, K. (1994/2004) *The Power of Countertransference: Innovations in Analytic Technique.* Hillsdale, NJ: Analytic Press.

Maroda, K. (2003) *Seduction, Surrender and Transformation: Emotional Engagement in the Analytic Process.* New York: Routledge.

Masterson, J (1981) *The Narcissistic and Borderline Disorders: An Integrated Developmental Approach.* New York: Brunner/Mazel.

Masterson, J. and Lieberman, A. (2004) *A Therapist's Guide to the Personality Disorders: A Handbook and Workbook.* Phoenix: Zeig, Tucker & Theisen.

Matze, M. G. (1988) Reciprocity in Script Formation: A Revision of the Concept of Symbiosis. *Transactional Analysis Journal*, 18(4): 304–8.

Mellor, K. (1980) Impasses: A Developmental and Structural Understanding. *Transactional Analysis Journal*, 10(3): 213–22.

Mellor, K. and Schiff, E. (1975) Discounting. *Transactional Analysis Journal*, 5(3): 295–302.

Miller, S., Hubble, M. and Duncan, B. (2008) Supershrinks. *Therapy Today*, 19(3): 5–9.

Moiso, C. (1984) The Feeling Loop. In Stern, E. (ed.) *TA: The State of the Art*. Dordrecht: Foris Publications (pp. 69–76).

Moiso, C. (1985) Ego States and Transference. *Transactional Analysis Journal*, 15(3): 194–201.

Morrison, C., Bradley, R. and Westen, D. (2003) The External Validity of Efficacy Trials for Depression and Anxiety: A Naturalistic Study. *Psychology and Psychotherapy: Theory, Research and Practice*, 76: 109–252.

Mothersole, G. (1996) Existential Realities and No-Suicide Contracts. *Transactional Analysis Journal*, 26(2): 151–9.

Müller, U. and Tudor, K. (2001) Transactional Analysis as Brief Therapy. In Tudor, K. (ed.) *Transactional Analysis Approaches to Brief Therapy*. London: Sage (pp. 19–44).

Nathanson, D. (1994) Shame Transactions. *Transactional Analysis Journal*, 24(2): 121–9.

Newton, T. (2006) Script, Psychological Life Plans, and the Learning Cycle. *Transactional Analysis Journal*, 36(3): 186–95.

Norcross, J. C. (ed.) (2002) *Psychotherapy Relationships That Work*. New York: Oxford University Press.

Novellino, M. (1984) Self-Analysis of Countertransference. *Transactional Analysis Journal*, 14(1): 63–7.

Novellino, M. (2003) On Closer Analysis: A Psychodynamic Revision of the Rules of Communication Within the Framework of Transactional Psychoanalysis. In Sills, C. and Hargaden, H. (eds) *Ego States*. London: Worth Publishing (pp. 149–68).

Nuttall, J. (2006) The Existential Phenomenology of Transactional Analysis. *Transactional Analysis Journal*, 36(3): 214–27.

O'Brien, M. and Houston, G. (2007) *Integrative Therapy: A Practitioner's Guide*. London: Sage.

Ogden, T. (1982) *Projective Identification and Psychotherapeutic Technique*. Lanham, MD: Aronson.

Oller Vallejo, J. (1986) Withdrawal: A Basic Positive Adaptation in Addition to Compliance and Rebellion. *Transactional Analysis Journal*, 16(2): 114–19.

Orlinsky, D. E., Grawe, K. and Park, B. K. (1994) Process and Outcome in Psychotherapy. In Bergin, A. E. and Garfield, S. L. (eds) *Handbook of Psychotherapy and Behaviour Change* (4th edn). New York: Wiley (pp. 270–378).

Perls, F. (1969) *Gestalt Therapy Verbatim*. Moab, UT: Real People Press.

Petriglieri, G. (2007) Stuck in a Moment: A Developmental Perspective on Impasses. *Transactional Analysis Journal*, 37(3): 185–94.

Pine, F. (1985) *Developmental Theory and Clinical Process*. New Haven: Yale University Press.

Racker, H. (1968) *Transference and Countertransference*. Madison, CT: International Universities Press.

Rogers, C. (1957) The Necessary and Sufficient Conditions of Therapeutic Personality Change. *Journal of Consulting Psychology*, 21: 95–103.

Rogers, C. (1980) *A Way of Being*. Boston: Houghton-Mifflin.

Roth, A. and Fonagy, P. (1996) *What Works for Whom? A Critical Review of Psychotherapy Research*. New York: Guilford Press.

Rothschild, B. (2000) *The Body Remembers: The Psychophysiology of Trauma and Trauma Treatment*. New York: Norton.

Safran, J. D. and Muran, C. J. (2003) *Negotiating the Therapeutic Alliance: A Relational Treatment Guide*. New York: Guilford Press.

Sanders, D. J. and Wills, F. (2005) *Cognitive Therapy: An Introduction*. London: Sage.

Sartre, J.-P. (1943) *Being and Nothingness: An Essay on Phenomenological Ontology* (Trans. Barnes H., 1956). New York: Philosophical Library.

Schiff, A. and Schiff, J. (1971) Passivity. *Transactional Analysis Journal*, 1(1): 71–8.

Schiff, J., Schiff, A., Mellor, K., Schiff, E., Fishman, J., Wolz, L., Fishman, C. and Momb, D. (1975) *The Cathexis Reader: Transactional Analysis Treatment of Psychosis*. New York: Harper & Row.

Schlegel, L. (1998) What is Transactional Analysis? *Transactional Analysis Journal*, 28(4): 269–87.

Schön, D. A. (1983) *The Reflective Practitioner: How Professionals Think in Action*. London: Temple Smith.

Schore, A. (1999) *Affect Regulation and the Origin of the Self: The Neurobiology of Emotional Development*. New York: Psychology Press.

Seligman, M. (2002) *Authentic Happiness*. London: Nicholas Brealey.

Shadbolt, C. (2004) Homophobia and Gay Affirmative Transactional Analysis. *Transactional Analysis Journal*, 34(2): 113–25.

Shea, M., Widiger, T. and Klein, M. (1992) Comorbidity of Personality Disorders and Depression: Implications for Treatment. *Journal of Clinical and Consulting Psychology*, 60: 857–68.

Shivanath, S. and Hiremath, M. (2003) The Psychodynamics of Race and Culture. In Sills, C. and Hargaden, H. (eds) *Ego States*. London: Worth Publishing (pp. 169–84).

Sills, C. and Hargaden, H. (eds) (2003) *Ego States*. London: Worth Publishing.

Stark, M (2000) *Modes of Therapeutic Action*. Northvale: Jason Aronson.

Steiner, C. (1966) Script and Counterscript. *Transactional Analysis Bulletin*, 5(18): 133–5.

Steiner, C. (1968) Transactional Analysis as a Treatment Philosophy. *Transactional Analysis Bulletin*, 7(27): 63.

Steiner, C. (1971) The Stroke Economy. *Transactional Analysis Journal*, 1(3): 9–15.

Steiner, C. (1974) *Scripts People Live: Transactional Analysis of Life Scripts*. New York: Grove Press.

Steiner, C. (2000) Radical Psychiatry. In Corsini, R. (ed.) *Handbook of Innovative Psychotherapies*. New York: Wiley.

Steiner, C. and Perry, P. (1999) *Achieving Emotional Literacy*. New York: Avon Books.

Stern, D. N. (1985) *The Interpersonal World of the Infant*. New York: Basic Books.

Stern, D. N. (2004) *The Present Moment in Psychotherapy and Everyday Life*. New York: W.W. Norton.

Stewart, I. (1992) *Eric Berne*. London: Sage.

Stewart, I. (1996) *Developing Transactional Analysis Counselling*. London: Sage.

Stewart, I. (2007) *Transactional Analysis Counselling in Action*. London: Sage.

Stewart, I. and Joines, V. (1987) *TA Today: A New Introduction to Transactional Analysis*. Nottingham: Lifespace.

Stummer, G. (2002) An Update on the Use of Contracting. *Transactional Analysis Journal*, 32(2): 121–3.

Summers, G. and Tudor, K. (2000) Cocreative Transactional Analysis. *Transactional Analysis Journal*, 30(1): 23–40.

Swede, S. (1977) *How To Cure: How Eric Berne Practiced Transactional Analysis*. Berkeley, CA: Southey Swede.

Terlato, V. (2001) The Analysis of Defense Mechanisms in the Transactional Analysis Setting. *Transactional Analysis Journal*, 31(2): 103–13.

Thomson, G. (1983) Fear, Anger, and Sadness. *Transactional Analysis Journal*, 13(1): 20–4.

Tobias, G., Haslam-Hopwood, G., Allen, J. G., Stein, A. and Bleiberg, E. (2006) Enhancing Mentalizing Through Psychoeducation. In Allen, J. G. and Fonagy, P. (eds) *Handbook of Mentalization-Based Treatment*. Chichester: John Wiley and Sons.

Tryon, G. S. and Winograd, G. (2001) Goal Consensus and Collaboration. *Psychotherapy*, 38(4): 385–9.

Tudor, K. (1995) What Do You Say About Saying Goodbye? Ending Psychotherapy. *Transactional Analysis Journal*, 25(3): 228–33.

Tudor, K. (2003) The Neopsyche: The Integrating Adult Ego State. In Sills, C. and Hargaden, H. (eds) *Ego States*. London: Worth Publishing (pp. 201–31).

Tudor, K. (2009) Understanding empathy. *Transactional Analysis Journal*, (in press).

Tudor, K. and Hobbes, R. (2007) Transactional Analysis. In Dryden, W. (ed.) *Dryden's Handbook of Individual Therapy*. London: Sage.

Tudor, K. and Widdowson, M. (2001) Integrating Views of TA Brief Therapy. In Tudor, K. (ed.) *Transactional Analysis Approaches to Brief Therapy*. London: Sage (pp. 114–35).

Tudor, K. and Widdowson, M. (2008) From Client Process to Therapeutic Relating: A Critique of the Process Model and Personality Adaptations. *Transactional Analysis Journal*, 38(3): 218–32.

Ware, P. (1983) Personality Adaptations (Doors to Therapy). *Transactional Analysis Journal*, 13(1): 11–19.

Weed, L. L. (1971) *Medical Records, Medical Education and Patient Care* (5th edn). Cleveland: The Press of Western Reserve University.

Westen, D., Novotny, C. and Thompson-Brenner, H. (2004) The Empirical Status of Empirically Supported Psychotherapies: Assumptions, Findings and Reporting in Controlled Clinical Trials. *Psychological Bulletin*, 130(4): 631–63.

Widdowson, M. (2005) Developmental Aetiology of Borderline Personality Disorder. *Transactions: The Journal of the Institute of Transactional Analysis*, 2: 20–8.

Widdowson, M. (2008) Metacommunicative Transactions. *Transactional Analysis Journal*, 38(1): 58–71.

Widdowson, M. and Ayres, A. (2006) Journaling Methods for Psychotherapy Trainees. *ITA News*, 23: 13–14.

Winnicott, D. W. (1946) Hate in the Countertransference. In Winnicott, D. W. (1958) *Through Paediatrics to Psychoanalyis*. London: Tavistock Publications (republished 1987, London: Hogarth Press).

Winnicott, D. W (1960) The Theory of the Parent–Child Relationship. *International Journal of Psychoanalysis*, 41: 585–95.

Winnicott, D. W. (1965) *Maturational Processes and the Facilitating Environment*. London: Hogarth Press.

Winnicott, D. W. (1971) *Playing and Reality*. London: Tavistock Publications.

Woods, K. (1996) Projective Identification and Game Analysis. *Transactional Analysis Journal*, 26(3): 228–31.

Woods, K. (2000) The Defensive Function of the Game Scenario. *Transactional Analysis Journal*, 30(1): 94–7.

Woollams, S. and Brown, M. (1978) *Transactional Analysis*. Dexter: Huron Valley Institute.

Wosket, V. (1999) *The Therapeutic Use of Self: Counselling Practice, Research and Supervision*. Hove: Routledge.

Yalom, I. (1980) *Existential Psychotherapy*. New York: Basic Books.

Yalom, I. (2001) *The Gift of Therapy: An Open Letter to a New Generation of Therapists and Their Patients*. New York: Harper Collins.

Young, J., Klosko, J. and Weishaar, M. (2003) *Schema Therapy: A Practitioner's Guide*. New York: Guilford Press.

Author Index